MORAL NEXUS

ETHICS OF CHRISTIAN IDENTITY AND COMMUNITY

Twenty-fifth Anniversary Edition

JAMES B. NELSON

Westminster John Knox Press
Louisville, Kentucky

Grateful acknowledgment is made to Harcourt Brace & Company for permission to reprint an excerpt from "Choruses from 'The Rock'" in *Collected Poems* 1909–1962 by T. S. Eliot, copyright 1936 by Harcourt Brace & Company, copyright © 1964, 1963 by T. S. Eliot.

Book design by Jennifer K. Cox
Cover design by Kim Wohlenhaus

First edition

Published by Westminster John Knox Press
Louisville, Kentucky

This book is printed on acid-free paper that meets the American National Standards Institute Z39.48 standard. ∞

PRINTED IN THE UNITED STATES OF AMERICA

96 97 98 99 00 01 02 03 04 05—10 9 8 7 6 5 4 3 2 1

Library of Congress Cataloging-in-Publication Data

Nelson, James B.
  Moral nexus : ethics of Christian identity and community / James B. Nelson — 1st ed.
     p.   cm.
  "Twenty-fifth anniversary edition"—Contents.
  Includes bibliographical references and index.
  ISBN 0–664–25678–3
  1. Christian ethics. I. Title.
BJ1251.N38   1996
241—dc20   96-22894

MORAL NEXUS

For Kristin Elizabeth Nelson

Contents

Introduction to the
Twenty-fifth Anniversary Edition

When over a good dinner Davis Perkins, president and publisher of the Presbyterian Publishing Corporation, and Stephanie Egnotovich, managing editor of Westminster John Knox Press, suggested that *Moral Nexus* be reissued twenty-five years after its initial publication, I had two immediate responses. First, I was pleased and grateful. I felt that the book could still make a contribution to the current discussion in Christian ethics, especially with the fresh interest in moral agency that had blossomed in the past two decades.

My second reaction was that, while the book's general argument was still significant and the supporting data still largely relevant, a revision in its language was imperative. *Moral Nexus*, written during a sabbatical leave in Oxford in 1969–1970, was a shortened and updated revision of my doctoral dissertation for Yale University, done ten years earlier. Though by the late 1960s the second great wave of the feminist movement in North America was under way, I had yet to become conscious of the significance and absolute necessity of gender-inclusive language. Not long after that writing, I began to learn.

On the suggestion of the book's reissue, it was immediately apparent to me that simply adding a new introduction with an explanatory note and apology about the masculinized language just would not do. The text itself would need changing. For one thing, it would be patently unfair and offensive now to ask readers to wade through all the "mankinds" and "God-he's" when (since the author was still alive and now somewhat wiser) it could be otherwise.

Further, however, the gender-exclusive language of the original text unwittingly violated the book's central thesis: the personal/universal identity, moral ethos, and community that are made possible by the personal/universal God. Sexist hierarchies, expressed by and buttressed by exclusive language, are simply incompatible with any notion of universal inclusiveness. And, by the same token, they are also inimical to authentic personhood and personal community.

So as a matter of justice and for consistency with the central argument, I have made the language and illustrations gender-inclusive in this reissued volume. But I have not attempted to update the source materials. Because of other commitments and desires, I had neither the time nor the energy. That was one reason. In addition, however, I truly believe that the book's central thesis still stands, and the basic insights of those theological ethicists and social scientists cited herein are still persuasive.

Nevertheless, a "how my mind has changed" commentary is in order. Were I to undertake a thorough rewrite of *Moral Nexus* today, I would stand by the original thesis. It still makes persuasive sense to me. In articulating and defending it, however, I would do several things differently.

I would say more about the "Is-Ought" question in dealing with the social science material so that the connections between the phenomenology of moral experience and normative ethics might be clearer. Further (and quite obviously, given the passage of time), I would update the sociological and psychological research. While the fundamental theories concerning socialization, reference groups, roles, and identity in chapters 4 and 5 have stood the test of time, new data from recent years could make those concepts even richer. The material on the American society in chapter 8 is somewhat dated, of course; nevertheless, the general picture I presented there still holds—and in an even more pronounced way than I had envisioned twenty-five years ago. Written today, the sketch of the churches in chapter 9 would need to account for the rapid rise of conservative and fundamentalist groups and for the further attrition in numbers and influence of the so-called mainline denominations. But these religious developments of the past quarter century, like those in society at large, have not called the book's argument into question. Rather, they provide even more striking illustration of the two perils in Christian community that I examine: identity foreclosure (in the "Christian Right") and identity diffusion (in the "mainline").

Were I to write the book today, the influence of liberation theologies and ethics would be evident. Increasingly, they have made me aware of my own social location—economically, racially, sexually. Indeed, one of the critical (sometimes painful) gifts from liberationists has been their unmasking, in a host of ways, of my unconscious ideologies. While I do not believe that the argument for the personal and the universal dimensions of community, morality, and moral identity would change in principle, my presentation of that argument would be affected by greater consciousness of my own social relativities.

In particular, feminist insights have greatly affected me in these intervening years. For example, in moral development psychology Carol Gilligan has made me (and many others) aware of the unconscious gender biases present in Lawrence Kohlberg's research and theories.[1] Her important critique would surely affect my reference to Kohlberg's material in chapter 4. But Gilligan's relationalist corrective to her colleague's individualistic rationalism would simply add generous data to the argument I present here.

The theological ethicists on whom I relied in *Moral Nexus* are all males (white, middle-class, professional ones, at that). Yet they were delineating a contextual-relational perspective that was, ethically speaking, somewhat countercultural a quarter century ago. At that time most Christian ethicists were largely grounded in rationalistic and individualistic assumptions. In contrast, the insights of those on whom I relied had a much more social view of selfhood, a relational understanding of ethics, and a deep sense of the foundational importance of community. Their perspectives would now be enriched by the approaches of many feminist ethicists. I think of Beverly Wildung Harrison, Carter Heyward, and Carol S. Robb, for example.[2] And the directions of influence go both ways; each of these feminists shows considerable indebtedness to this book's principal mentor, H. Richard Niebuhr.

I have long had the conviction that the components of ethical reflection are essentially five in number: ethical method, theological assumptions, norms, moral agency, and interpretation of the facts. *Moral Nexus* deals with all five of these. It delineates a contextual-relational method. That method is grounded in a theology of divine activity. It argues for a moral ethos informed by norms, particularly the principal norms of the personal and the universal; more specific norms, it holds, are best interpreted in a prima facie manner—as nonabsolute presumptions. The book gives major attention to moral agency, contending that the identity of the moral agent—whether group or individual—is of incalculable importance in ethics and moral action. Finally, the factual data about our social existence as persons and communities are interpreted through these foregoing perspectives. However, even while I attempt to speak to all the dimensions of ethics, *Moral Nexus* is not in any sense an attempt to lay out a comprehensive Christian ethic. Its aim is much more modest: a focus on moral agency that might show how the church is essential as context of the moral life.

At the time *Moral Nexus* was written, the focus of the ethical debate was heavily on method and norms. In fact, to some it appeared that the issue was method versus norms, for the "situation ethics" debate was then raging. In his influential essay "Context vs. Principles: A Misplaced Debate in Christian Ethics," James M. Gustafson argued that both were necessary.[3] But what was largely ignored twenty-five years ago was moral agency, and doubtless for several reasons. Under the impact of neo-Reformation theology, Christian ethicists, especially Protestants, were wary of emphasizing virtue and character, fearing that sanctificationism and justification by works would raise their dangerous heads once again.

Further, the philosophical ethics that then informed most Christian (particularly Protestant) ethics simply considered moral agency issues secondary. William K. Frankena's influential introduction to philosophical ethics argued that the fundamental tasks of ethics were to justify moral terms and to clarify the differences between appeals to duty and appeals to consequences.[4] Frankena and most other philosophers of the time saw virtues as merely supplemental to the real determinants of right or good actions. The agent's virtues were only motivational components to ethical principles and other norms, which were considered more basic. The neglect of moral agency at that time is evident, for example, in the fact that the first edition of the *Encyclopedia of Bioethics* had no entry on virtue or character, a fact noted by Stanley Hauerwas in his fulsome article on this subject in the recent second edition.[5]

Now in the past quarter century a welcome interest in moral agency has arisen. The most evident manifestation is the current emphasis on *character ethics*. Character is typically defined as the relatively persisting combination of qualities that distinguish one person from another and describe the usual manner of a self's relation to the world. Character ethics, in turn, focuses on the search for normative language to guide individuals and communities in the functions of character formation.[6]

Character ethics with its focus on the moral agent thus emphasizes *being* more than *doing*. While normative ethics emphasizes the question, What should we *do?*, agency ethics is principally concerned with asking, What should we *be?* What are the images of the good person and the good society, and how can these be formed? Advocates of character ethics argue that while normative ethics tends toward universalizing abstractions, their own focus moves toward particularity and concreteness. While normative ethics tries to formulate principles and rules, character ethics deals more with telling stories and reflecting on them.

It has been a salutary movement. Normative ethics had been excessively rationalistic. Still heavily entangled with the legacy of the Enlightenment, normative ethics shared that philosophy's concern for using reason to establish human autonomy over against the imprisoning forces of institutions and traditions. When the Enlightenment did speak of character, it referred to the qualities of "one who was able to abstract herself or himself from historical, affective, or other nonrational influences on moral choice."[7] Such rationalism persisted into twentieth-century philosophical and theological ethics, and the emphasis on the rational clearly discouraged ethical reflection about the social, affective, and particular features of character.

About the time that *Moral Nexus* was written, however, Anglo-American philosophy had just begun to focus increasingly on issues related to the concerns of this book. Thus, attention to the perspectives of agents, the nature of desires and feelings, and the ways these interacted with thought, the language of motivations—all these concerns resurrected classical ethical interests in the formation of character. In turn, as theological character ethics later developed, it too attempted to avoid the Enlightenment's divorce of the rational and universal from the affective and particular. Thus there has been renewed and welcome attention to feelings, imagination, and memory, and hence also to image, metaphor, and narrative in ethical reflection.

One form of character ethics deserves special mention: *narrative ethics*. Such ethics builds on the assumption that we as humans are a narrative species and each of us is "narratively formed." As young children we learn to talk in order to give some account of our experiences. We are simply fated to develop explanatory accounts—stories—of how the world works and what our lives and actions mean. Such accounts remind the ethicist of the unavoidable relativism of our standpoints, for there is no Archimedean platform on which a narrator can stand free of bias or particularity, seeing "truth" in its purity. Thus, narrators and their audiences must test the sources of their accounts, compare their versions, and search for common stories that will bind them together in meaningful moral discourse.[8]

For *Christian* narrative ethics that common story is "the Christian story," the story that Christians tell about God. Both authentic selfhood and authentic action are defined by the correspondence of the self's story to that narrative, though it, too, has many versions and interpretations. And because the Christian story is a communal story, life in the church becomes a central concern for ethics.[9]

Those who emphasize the primacy of reason and principles in ethics frequently charge that the concreteness of narrative and other character ethics makes a universalizable public discourse impossible. In response, however, character ethics contends that narratives are the inescapable medium of moral discourse. Religious narratives make the virtues and affections of the good life accessible to persons. Hence, we are necessarily concerned with the formation of persons within those communities that express visions of the good in specific images and stories.[10]

Were I to rewrite this volume today, I would try to make clear—and to expand beyond the current discussion—the important connections of narrative ethics to the church as moral community. While in recent years exponents of character ethics have begun to reclaim the church as context for the Christian moral life, they have done so largely with attention to the *conscious* functions of the community. Still left largely unexplored are the *unconscious* ways that communities nurture and form the moral identities of people by the very nature of those communities themselves and the moral ethos they embody. These latter things are the major concern of *Moral Nexus*.

The emphasis on the conscious and intentional moral functions of the church is important, to be sure. For example, writing about character in *The Westminster Dictionary of Christian Ethics*, Richard Bondi says, "The community in which this continual formation takes place is important in at least two ways. It provides the historical and cultural setting for the appropriation of stories and their moral vocabulary . . . and insofar as the community self-consciously claims such tasks, it will charge certain members with the proclamation, teaching, and evocation of normative stories and with responsibilities in assisting its members with their attempts at character formation."[11] In the same volume Ronald Preston's treatment of the formation of conscience similarly emphasizes the conscious influences that the church can have—in prayer, sacraments, Bible study, instruction in the church's tradition, and moral counsel.[12] Nevertheless, as important as these influences are, the role of the community's unconscious influence remains largely unnamed and unexplored. Even James Fowler's faith development studies, which have drawn extensively on the developmental psychology of Piaget and Erikson (sources important to this book) and have given us a phenomenologically rich model of religious formation, have not fully connected individual psychology with the significant communal contexts of moral and spiritual identity.[13] Thus, one way that *Moral Nexus* might still contribute to the ethical discussion is through an exploration of those critical "unconscious influences" on the Christian moral life, to use Horace Bushnell's good term of a century ago.

Further, in that exploration in the following pages, I lift up the principles of the personal and the universal. I underscore that fact here, for one of the important challenges today is that we clearly grasp the *integrity* of the ethical task. Ethics is all of one piece. Each of its several dimensions—method, theology, agency, norms, and data interpretation—involves and presupposes the others. Thus, for example, we need to speak of the integration of agency ethics and normative ethics. Speaking of persons and communities as moral agents (the concern of character ethics) is important. But also essential is seeing the deep connections of agency issues with normative ethics. The principles that should guide action are, after all, the same principles that should describe agency and its formation—thus, moral *nexus*—the connection.

It is evident to the reader, I suspect, that in the foregoing paragraphs I have been doing several things. I have given my reasons for revising the language of the original book without augmenting or changing the source material. I have attempted to locate *Moral Nexus* within the framework of current ethical discussion, suggesting that its central thesis is still important. And I have hinted at some of the ways I would enlarge the argument were I writing it today. One last issue needs comment. Have I been too hopeful, even idealistic, about the church?

Twenty-five years ago several reviewers said as much. They might be prompted to say that even more strongly today, wondering aloud whether churches in this society have enough discipline, enough vision, enough imagination, enough texture to function as contexts and shapers of the moral life for Christian people. It is a valid question and obviously a basic one. Perhaps, as some have suggested, the best we can hope for is that the churches continue somehow to articulate the basic Christian symbols and to tell the story. But that they embody that story in the very fabric of their community life is too much to ask.

To that I have but two responses. First, Whoever said it would be easy? Second, a disembodied story is never persuasive, never real. If anything, my theological perspective has become increasingly incarnationalist over the years. The "Body of Christ" without human embodiment is of little hope to me. But, to change the familiar words a bit, who can hope for what he or she has not seen? Despite all the distortions, the inadequacies, the diffusions, the foreclosures—yes, the faithlessness—of our churches, I have seen and experienced enough to know that the hope is not in vain. And when I observe persons whose moral wisdom and courage make me stand in awe, I also learn that their resources are invariably rooted in communities that have embodied and hence have shaped something of the personal-universal life. More than that I cannot say.

The acknowledgments section in the first edition expressed my deep appreciation to three Yale University mentors and friends— the late H. Richard Niebuhr, James M. Gustafson, and James E. Dittes—who stimulated my interest in the problem of this book and guided my work there in an earlier form of its argument years ago. I am still deeply grateful to them. And now I want to mention especially James Gustafson, currently at Emory University and still involved in his highly distinguished career as a teacher and scholar of Christian ethics. I owe him a word of special thanks for drawing recent attention to this book at an annual meeting of the Society of Christian Ethics and thus stimulating renewed interest in it. My work with Davis Perkins and Stephanie Egnotovich of Westminster John Knox Press continues to be a source of enormous pleasure, for which I am truly grateful. Their support, guidance, and friendship through the processes of several books have been marvelous gifts.

My original dedication of the book was to my spouse Wilys Claire and to our children, Stephen and Mary. Twenty-five years later, they embody in even more remarkable and sustaining ways for me the meanings I have attempted to convey in these pages. For this new edition it is a delight to make the dedication to our wonderful granddaughter Kristin Elizabeth, daughter of Stephen and Denise.

Part 1

PERSPECTIVES
FROM CHRISTIAN ETHICS

1

Becoming More Conscious of Some "Unconscious Influences"

The Question

In his sermon "Unconscious Influence," written a century ago, Horace Bushnell had this to say: "Thus it is that [people] are ever touching unconsciously the springs of motion in each other; thus it is that one [person] without thought or intention or even consciousness of the fact is ever leading some other after him [or her].
. . . We overrun the boundaries of our personality—we flow together."[1] Bushnell then describes the two types of influence on persons: that which is active and voluntary (teaching, argument, persuasion, threats, offers, promises) and "that which flows out from us, unawares to ourselves."[2] The importance of Christian efforts in various kinds of voluntary moral influence, he argues, is immense, and we fervently hope that our activity will become far more vigorous and effective than it now is. Then he adds, "But there needs to be produced at the same time, and partly for this object, a more thorough appreciation of the relative importance of that kind of influence or beneficence which is insensibly exerted. The tremendous weight and efficacy of this compared with the other, and the sacred responsibility laid upon us in regard to this, are felt in no such degree or proportion as they should be; and the consequent loss we suffer . . . is incalculable. The more stress too needs to be laid on this subject of insensible influence, because it is insensible; because it is out of mind and, when we seek to trace it, beyond a full discovery."[3]

It is true that Horace Bushnell's name is not exactly common currency in today's ferment about the church and the Christian moral life. But to our loss we have unduly neglected his perceptive

urging that we become more conscious of the forms of unconscious influence in the Christian community. Indeed, community
is both the goal and the medium of human existence. And the
church's moral significance lies not only in its conscious moral instruction, persuasion, and corporate action—important though
these be—but also in the less visible ways in which personal identity is shaped and reshaped, motivations to action are nurtured,
and moral styles are appropriated.

This question, then, is our focus: What are the interrelationships—the moral nexus—of the Christian's moral identity, the
pattern and style of his or her ethics, and the nature of the church
in which the Christian participates? Attention to this question is
by no means new to the modern age. The Bible and the writings
of certain of the early church fathers are pregnant with relevant
insights. The same concern could be traced through any of the
formative figures in Christian theology, though clearly it is not evident in all of them. Yet today the question of selfhood, moral
style, and the self's formative groups is being raised with some urgency from a variety of both secular and theological perspectives.

Dozens of books by social philosophers and social scientists,
particularly within the last two decades, point to the problem of
identity in a mass society. They sound the contrapuntal themes of
liberation and confusion. Traditional society ascribed an identity
to the individual that nurtured personal security but also the
provincialism and injustices of the fixed status. Today's mobile society affords new freedom in identity choices, but also confusion,
alienation, and the temptation to new forms of provincialism as
"escapes from freedom." Lying behind the varied descriptions of
depersonalization in a technological society, the normlessness and
"anomie" of many lives, and the erosion of meaningful identification with one's work, is a recurring theme. The theme is this: the
profound dislocations that the individual currently experiences in
society are intimately linked with the dislocations of the small
groups that have traditionally furnished the social matrix for selfhood.[4] We are just beginning to appreciate that the personality's
structure, the person's motivations and incentives—which earlier
rationalists assumed were inherent in the individual—are intimately dependent upon the person's meaningful involvement in
groups and communities.

There is an interesting parallel between much in contemporary social analysis and much in current theology. The social analysts are virtually unanimous in pointing to the quest for identity in modern society, though few of them give "equal time" to the quest for community. Likewise among the theologians we find a strong chorus of voices calling for a new Christian humanism in response to God's humanizing work in the world, though few of them speak in detail of the ways in which Christian community is inextricably bound up with such humanization. No inclusive answer to these concerns is attempted in this book—if an inclusive answer, indeed, be possible. Yet this more modest attempt seems both possible and timely: that from an orientation in Christian ethics we pursue an interdisciplinary conversation that might shed additional light upon the interdependence of moral community, moral selfhood, and moral style.

A Task for Christian Ethics

Christian ethics, like moral philosophy, always engages three central and persistent questions: "the good, the moral self, and the criteria for judgment and action."[5] It is true, as James M. Gustafson maintains, that in some ethical writings more emphasis is placed upon one of these questions than upon the others, but the others are usually present either explicitly or implicitly.

Our problem seems to involve particularly two of the three questions: the moral self and the criteria for judgment and action. Then we appear to add an additional concern: moral community. In a very real sense, however, this is not a fourth element, but rather a reflection of the first, "the good." Not that the church is an absolute good for the Christian—an ecclesiastical idolatry that always leads to gross moral distortions. God is the good, and the church is not God. Yet we cannot speak of God in divine aseity but only in relation to creation, in community with God's creatures. Thus the element of community is inseparable from the notion of the good. If the church is called to exist not for itself but for God's universal-personal community, then in this limited but important sense the Christian moral community also becomes part of the threefold ethical question.

There is some virtue, nevertheless, in giving relatively more emphasis to the notion of moral selfhood in our inquiry. For one thing, the moral self has been unduly neglected in recent Christian ethics. For another, we can better see the importance and interrelationships of all three questions by using one of them as a particular focus for the other two. In recent years European Christian ethicists have given somewhat more attention to the question of the good, whereas their American counterparts have tended to focus upon the criteria for judgment and action. Although this generalization has many exceptions, it does appear that European ethics has focused upon the moral implications of God's authority and action, whereas in America the norm-context debate has occupied center stage. In any event, the question of the moral self has been a secondary concern on both sides of the Atlantic, particularly among Protestant theologians.

There are clear signs, however, of newly awakening interest in moral selfhood. We are beginning to realize the extent to which our decisions are "pre-ethical," significantly shaped and conditioned prior to our rational reflection about them. Because of this, Christian ethics cannot afford to focus solely upon the conscious and the rational.[6] This emerging realization has been stimulated by the work of psychologists and sociologists, and the view that ethics is not concerned with psychological and sociological elements of the pre-ethical is a regrettable limitation of its task.

Actually the pre-ethical elements are not simply "pre-" in a temporal sense. Consider how the nature and the structure of the groups to which we give our loyalties condition our conscious ethical reflection continuously. Henry David Aiken writes, "From an ethical point of view, the life of the ordinary person—that is, the conventional political [person], educator, churchgoer, family [person], art lover, good citizen, and good [person]—is largely (if never entirely) a matter of what the philosopher F. H. Bradley called 'my station and its duties.' The code of such a person consists of obligations incurred by the institutional relationships and practices in which his [or her] life involves him [or her]. He [or she] does not elect to have a father and a mother, be an American or the member of a particular race. Such ties are simply *there*, and in discovering them he [or she] also finds . . . ethical identity."[7]

It is important to recognize how much of the moral life, especially in its daily routines, is intimately involved with the obligations and expectations we perceive by virtue of the institutional and group roles in which we find ourselves. That I did not, for example, elect my parents is both an obvious and a profound fact. What is not so obvious, however, is the process by which I have defined what it means to be a son. I have decided the meaning of my sonship through innumerable decisions, large and small, affirmed and modified over a period of time, and made within a network of the other roles and relationships in which I stand. Thus do elements of freedom and choice enter into the "givens" of our moral situations.

In the moral problem of finding identity as a son or daughter we can see how the three central questions of ethics interlock. "Honor your father and your mother" is a moral injunction. It describes a desirable relationship between child and parents. But reflection about that relationship involves us at once in questions of the good, the moral self, and the criteria for judgment and action. The good is involved when I ask, What authority does this moral claim have upon me? Is this God's command? How is God's intention for my parents and me related to the divine activity in Jesus Christ? How is my allegiance to my parents conditioned by my ultimate allegiance to God's realm? The criteria for judgment and action, likewise, are involved. Are there several norms (from the Bible, from natural law, moral norms derived from theological affirmations, etc.) by which I can measure the meaning of parental honor? Or is love the single criterion needed to decide what filial relation is most appropriate in any given situation?

Yet our understanding of this command—"Honor your father and your mother"—is incomplete until we raise particular questions about our own moral identities. In my own case I must also ask what it means to me that I am a son to these parents in this particular society. And how is my role as son related to my other roles? How is my filial role conditioned by the fact that I am not only my father's son but also the father of my own children, not only my mother's son but also husband to my wife? What has my sonship to do with my roles in citizenship and occupation? What is the relationship of my churchly identification to my sonship and the relationship of all these roles to my sonship within the family of God? In such ways as these our attention to moral selfhood raises significant questions about the relationship of identity to moral judgment and action.

Attention to the moral self also forces us into a healthy

concreteness concerning moral motivation. It may not be a primary task of Christian ethics to motivate and exhort us to action. It *is* part of our task, however, to analyze that which *does* motivate us. Inquiry into the specific relationships in which we live and through which we experience our motivation, and understanding the operational reality of the wider society, thus become important. This does not mean that moral motivation can be understood exclusively or even primarily through inquiry into the moral self. Each of the three great ethical questions is involved in its own way. It does mean, however, that our understanding of motivation is unduly truncated whenever we bypass the self and its relations.

In questions of motivation, the nature of the good is obviously involved.[8] What we as Christians believe about God does indeed give shape and style to our moral action. The intensity of our trust in God, the passion with which we believe, as well as what we believe, will always be significant in our motivation. When we fail to act, our failure may be linked to despair over our potential effectiveness, though it also may be occasioned by the weakness of our conviction about the good that we consciously affirm. Thus, while I believe that God wills me to be peacemaker, my motivation to act may be undercut by the belief that after all, I am a powerless person in a society where the important decisions are made by the power elites. Or, disturbed by the thought that certain peacemaking acts might threaten my personal comfort and security, I can simply give my own welfare higher moral priority than God's claim upon me as a peacemaker. Analysis of the relation between, on the one hand, belief in God and certain convictions about God and humanity, and, on the other hand, moral motivation, clearly is an important part of the ethicist's work.

Yet the problem of motivation is not exhausted at this level alone. Left here, our ethics would be excessively rationalistic, for, while they are necessarily part of every relationship with God, beliefs do not constitute the whole of that relationship. Nor is the question of motivation probed sufficiently if we look only at the criteria for judgment and action. This is even more obvious. The analysis of norms, principles, and rules of action is an important part of Christian ethics. But descriptions of relationships have distinctly limited power in creating the relationships themselves. For example, God's claim upon me to be a peacemaker necessarily involves my analyzing the meaning of peace and those actions that might contribute to its realization.

Nevertheless, however refined my analysis of these may be, it is quite possible that I will not be moved to act. Indeed, the very focus upon decisional criteria and action guidelines presupposes certain things about motivation—for example, that it is possible as well as desirable to overcome the relational distance that separates groups involved in destructive conflict. But how is this distance overcome? To probe this question, we must move beyond the criteria for moral judgment. We must ask questions about the good—God's enabling activity on our behalf. We must also inquire into the nature and situation of the moral actor.

When we turn to moral selfhood as a focus for understanding motivation, additional and important questions come into view. If it is indeed true that God is the ultimate source of our moral motivation, how does God work through the flesh-and-blood personal and social relationships in which we are enmeshed? If the self is a social self, then the communities and societies in and through which we find our clues to self-identification and worldview will enter the picture. Thus, if I would be a peacemaker in the midst of racial turmoil, then those communal relationships which motivate me to do the work of racial justice are significant. Important also are the manner in which I perceive my own racial identification, the social sources of this identity, and the part it plays in my moral motivation.

New questions likewise appear if we look at moral patterns through a perspective on the self. There is a danger, to be sure, that we can concentrate so intently upon the moral self that we end up with an overly simplified ethics of disposition. In this case we would assume that the Christian can apprehend what is required in any concrete situation without benefit of pattern of moral guidance. All that is needed (depending upon the particular emphasis) is faith plus facts, or love plus facts, or pure intentions plus knowledge of the situation. The main task of Christian ethics then would be the study of the faithful, loving, or virtuous self. But such a limited focus is inadequate.

Inadequate also is a singular concentration upon the criteria for moral judgment—norms, principles, rules, ideals, laws, ends, and the like. Those who limit their ethical attention to such criteria are still faced with a question: How is the distance between the ultimate good and the concrete situation to be bridged? This question cannot be answered without attention to the person who is doing the deciding and acting. Every moral decision is more complex than the rational application of principles to a situation. A decision always brings into question, even if not consciously, the person's identity. In important ways we will always *do* what we *are*. It could be said that we use principles in decision making, but *we* make the decisions, the principles do not. In a sense, of course, that is true, though misleading. For if principles are to be effective, they are always somehow incorporated into the self's own structure. Realizing this, it becomes more difficult to see how ethics can talk meaningfully about one without talking also about the other.

For one thing, in the process of internalization, norms are always shaped, modified, and interpreted. To understand this process we must look at the community contexts within which such "moral socialization" takes place. Each community has a moral ethos or style of life. That ethos is not limited to the moral pattern it *consciously* affirms or teaches. Also involved is the structure of the community: the patterns of authority and power, the ways in which the group and the individual interact, the style of interpersonal relations, and how the group itself interacts with other groups in society. When there is harmony between the consciously taught moral pattern and other elements in the community's ethos, one kind of internalization will take place. When there is noticeable conflict, we might expect a different process of internalization. A congregation might articulate an ethic of universal love and at the same time practice racial discrimination. Or a church might talk about an ethic of forgiveness, while a judgmental attitude of moral scrupulosity actually prevails among its members. The medium as well as the message is germane to the task of ethics.

Another link between moral pattern and moral selfhood is found in the nature of identity. Identity is never a once-for-all achievement. It is reaffirmed or modified in every significant decision the person makes. The question, What shall I do? involves not only, How shall I apply my moral pattern to this particular situation? but also (and often less consciously), Who am I in this situation? The moral self is nurtured in community. But we live in a pluralistic society, and we are nurtured, shaped, influenced, and pressured by a whole range of groups, large and small. An ethical approach that ignores such connections will treat moral conflicts primarily as conflicts of principles and values. They are surely that, but not only that. They are also conflicts within the self—contests among our internalized social loyalties.

All of this does not imply that the moral self is the only key to Christian ethical thinking. It is no exaggeration, however, to suggest that insofar as Christian ethics neglects this dimension of its task it runs the danger of abstraction from the daily world in which we make our decisions and live out our lives. Indeed, it becomes abstracted from those very processes through which we become what we are.

Ethics and the Social Sciences

Several distinguishable methodological orientations are currently used in Christian ethics. At least three general types stand out.[9] The first uses methods congenial to those of philosophy. Some Christian ethicists working in this framework concentrate upon ontology, inquiring into the moral significance of the nature of God; others more indebted to linguistic analysis work at clarifying Christian moral language. A second, perhaps more common, orientation treats Christian ethics as a branch of systematic theology. Thus one begins with doctrinal affirmations and from these derives appropriate moral norms that subsequently can be applied to specific problems. Valuable ethical insights come from both of these orientations.

A third and somewhat different approach, however, seems more fruitful. Here the beginning point is more empirical and analytical. The focus is directed more toward the nature of the moral life, and Christian ethics then becomes a "critical reflection on the moral actions of the Christian community and its members."[10] When we approach ethics in this manner we quite naturally turn to the social sciences for assistance. Indeed, it is well-nigh impossible to draw sharp lines between "ethical data" and the data of the social sciences if our aim is an adequate understanding of moral action.

Consider for example Gerhard Lenski's reflection on Max Weber's work: "Weber was largely unconcerned with these rather

obvious, deliberate, and calculated efforts to influence secular institutions in which most religious groups occasionally indulge.
Rather, he was concerned with the fact that all religious groups are
continuously shaping and molding the personalities of their adherents who then, as private individuals, staff the economic, political, educational, and other institutional systems of society. This
he felt to be the far more influential process by which religious
groups influence secular life."[11] When this kind of work is being
done in the social sciences, Christian ethics pays a high price in ig-
noring it. The process should be, in fact, a two-way street. Ethics
and the social sciences need each other, for, as Gibson Winter observes, each tends toward preoccupation with abstract models
without such dialogue. "Each discipline is impoverished by insu-
lation from the inquiries and findings of the other."[12]

Christian ethics, then, is best understood as a discipline interdependent with both theology and "worldly wisdom," and in regard to the latter the social sciences play a key role.[13] Ethics is not
merely a deduction from theological doctrine, as if a sufficient inquiry into the nature of God, Christology, justification, or sanctification would tell us what we ought to do. Neither is Christian
ethics simply a branch of the social sciences, as if sufficient inquiry
into the social psychologist's understanding of selfhood would result in a delineation of the Christian moral self. Rather, the Christian ethicist pursues the critical understanding of the moral life in
interdependence with both disciplines. The ethicist is aware of the
problems of methodological ambiguity in this posture, but even
more fears the insularity that comes with resisting the insights of
nontheological disciplines.

Where in the profusion of social science materials shall we turn
for that which is pertinent? While the work in several fields would
contribute valuable insights, social psychology and sociology seem
most germane, and with some admitted arbitrariness I shall limit
the present conversation with ethics to these fields. These social
sciences themselves are clearly interdependent. The spotlight of
social psychology is upon "the response of individuals to their interpersonal and more extended social environment," and that of
sociology upon "the social environments in which individuals are
located."[14] Yet within these two fields we must be selective. Thus
I shall emphasize those materials that most directly illuminate
the social dimensions of selfhood and the group influences upon

the person, on the one hand, and the contexts of our society and of the contemporary church, on the other.

Not only the materials but also the mind-set regnant in these particular social sciences is important to us.[15] There is "a sociological consciousness" determined to unmask levels of reality that are not obvious on the surface of things. A certain not-necessarily-respectable attitude is necessary for probing behind the taken-for-granted postures of respectable society. There is openness to the possibility that ideas, values, and identities are relative to specific social locations. Such a mind-set can be of considerable significance for a Christian ethics that attempts to probe the rich complexity of moral action.

We must use these social science materials with attention to their implicit values. Gone are the days when the majority of social scientists would claim to deal only in fact, leaving to the ethicists the problem of values.[16] Indeed, the very recognition of the impossibility of a value-free social science has opened the door to a new level of dialogue with ethics.

Ethicists have suggested more than one way in which we can pay attention to the values in social science materials. One way is to distinguish among those ("the quantifiers") who attempt to maintain thorough objectivity, those who admit that their own values enter into their interpretations particularly in the poetic metaphors by which they make sense of human behavior, and those who attempt not only to interpret behavior but also to prescribe remedies for human ills.[17] By attending to the manner in which scientists see values in their own work, we can (even when we disagree with their own self-estimates) better assess their values in the light of our own.

A second approach, equally important, is to assess the framework of meaning about human beings and society that is implicit in each social science perspective, determining whether or not such a hypothesis is compatible with our own assumptions about human existence. Thus we pay attention to the different assumptions made by behaviorists, functionalists, and voluntarists, noting that approach not only has an implicit social philosophy but also will tend to assume different things about such value-laden concepts as freedom, justice, alienation, responsibility, and the like.[18]

The problem of moral identity, moral community, and moral

style in the Christian life will lead us into social science materials that embody differing value assumptions. Attentiveness to the above concerns will be necessary, and the two time-honored tests of the philosopher will apply to this task: consistency and adequacy. Are the social science data under consideration consistent, "hanging together" in a meaningful interpretation with congruous internal elements? But also, is the material adequate? Adequacy for our purposes means not only a competent grasp of relevant factual data but also the power to illuminate our human experience. Since Christian ethics is always done from a faith commitment, we shall and must judge adequacy in illuminating human experience in terms of our Christian assumptions about human nature and society under the God of Jesus Christ.

Tillich's "theological circle" is thus applicable to the Christian ethical task. Though we work in a discipline that is not simply a deductive branch of systematic theology, we also work as those who are committed and not detached. From our middle ground between doctrine and social analysis, we attempt to understand moral behavior, making explicit our own faith assumptions and yet allowing the insights of the social scientists to modify and expand as well as illuminate the very stuff of ethics with which we work. There is, indeed, "a common grace" that can operate in ordinary human relationships and in secular discourse about them. This, after all, is the reality that makes the ethical conversation with non-theological disciplines possible and imperative.

2

Clues from
Relational Christian Ethics

Moral Selfhood, Community,
and Ethical Method

What are contemporary Christian ethicists saying about the moral self in relation to the community of faith? To see where we are in current ethical reflection on the subject is the task of this chapter. To establish the directions in which we need to move is the intention of the next. In a brief survey no conceivable justice can be done to the variety of sources in Christian ethics which bring some illumination to bear upon the questions before us. Thus, in being selective I shall emphasize the "relational" approach, which is, I believe, most illuminating of this particular subject as well as being most instructive in general Christian ethical reflection.[1] (The adjective "contextual" is also used by some who are committed to this approach; while perhaps less adequate than "relational," it is preferable to the rather confusing term "situational.") Several characteristics of this stance are of importance to us.

First, the posture of moral reflection is more analytical than prescriptive.[2] The principal task of Christian ethics is not to prescribe but to understand and describe. Since we are concerned about the manner in which we make moral decisions and about the way in which our persons and values are formed, we are concerned about all those networks of relationships in which we exist. Moral life is responsive life. It is life lived in response to other beings under God. Thus, because relationships (not ideals or norms) are the

Some of the concerns of this chapter and chapter 3 were explored in my article "The Moral Significance of the Church in Contemporary Protestant Contextual Ethics," in *Journal of Ecumenical Studies*, vol. IV, no. 1 (1967). An abbreviated form of the same article appeared in *Theology Digest*, vol. XVII, no. 1 (Spring, 1969).

primary "stuff" of ethics, we must inquire into the meaning of a person's moral communities, particularly the meaning of the church to the Christian.

Further, Christian ethics is primarily indicative and only secondarily imperative. This does not mean that we are free from moral demands. It does mean, as Paul Lehmann says, that "the ethical demands acquire meaning and authority from the specific ethical relationships which precede and shape these demands."[3] The basic shaping relationship is, of course, that with God. God is worldly, speaking not only to the world through the church but at least as frequently to the church through the world. Of this we are rightly reminded by much recent theology. However, clues for recognizing God's activity and criteria for judging the faithfulness of our responses will not be forthcoming if we neglect the church as the locus for Christian ethical reflection.

A third characteristic of the relational stance is its understanding and use of moral norms. Using the word at this point in a very general sense to include principles, laws, rules, maxims, and so on, we may say that norms are absolutely necessary but that they are not necessarily absolute. They are descriptive more than prescriptive, describing those kinds of relationships which in a Christian perspective are desirable. They are illuminating devices that help us to clarify and understand situations, assisting us in our moral judgments. We do not respond primarily to norms, but norms when internalized color the manner in which we respond to other persons, groups, powers, and things.[4] Since such internalization takes place through social interaction, a relational Christian ethics must take seriously the role of the church as well as other moral communities in the Christian's life. Indeed, it is as we take the social ethos seriously, the ethos through which internalization occurs, that we are led to pay attention not only to the dramatic and unusual examples of moral dilemmas but also to the more routine and everyday decisions through which our moral lives take basic shape.

A fourth characteristic, underlying the third, is a relational value theory. H. Richard Niebuhr, in his decisive statement on this matter,[5] has shown us that the common split in value theory between the objectivists (values exist independently of the person who is doing the valuing) and the subjectivists (values exist only within the person who is making value judgments) can be resolved if we recognize the truth to which each of these positions points.

If we see value as relational, we will deny that it is an objective kind of reality, yet we can also affirm that it is objective in the sense that value is independent of the desires of persons. We can affirm with the subjectivists that values are always related to our personal existence, yet deny the subjectivist claim that our desires therefore constitute that which is valuable. "Value is the good-for-ness of being for being in their reciprocity, their animosity, and their mutual aid. Value cannot be defined or intuited in itself, for it has no existence in itself; and nothing is valuable in itself, but everything has value, positive or negative, in its relations. Thus value is not a relation but arises in the relations of being to being."[6]

Several important implications for the problem of moral selfhood and community arise out of this approach. One is that we must affirm the ethical necessity of empirical knowledge of human relationships not simply in order to apply those values which we have learned elsewhere but in order to understand values in the first place. We are driven immediately to investigate the relations in which we exist, including how our ties to the Christian community affect those with other persons, groups, and institutions. Moral decisions, after all, are always specific. They are not, fundamentally, choices among values; rather, they are choices in the "how" and "why" of our relations with others.

Relational value theory also suggests that every value system is inherently "religious" (in a broad but important sense of that word). In making decisions, I must (whether consciously or not) affirm some center of value in relation to which goodness and rightness can be judged, something that is valuable in and of itself. It is highly questionable whether anyone can live by any thoroughgoing ethical relativism, a relativism that refuses to assign intrinsic worth to any center of value. Surely there can be many relative value systems.[7] Yet, with Luther, Niebuhr reminds us that whatever our hearts ultimately cling to and rely upon, that in actual practice is our god. In fact, we do not live only as moral monotheists, having one absolute and universal center of value. We also function as moral polytheists, now making this decision in the light of this unquestioned good, then making the next decision with reference to another loyalty accepted as intrinsically worthful. At times we may be moral henotheists, having one focused center of value, but one that is partial, exclusive, and limited—a god of the tribe who is not the universe's God. If our Christian ethics is self-critical, it is important that we recognize and criticize the ways in which our moral decisions are frequently polytheistic or henotheistic. But if our self-critical ethics is Christian, we will affirm relative loyalties and value centers only in the wider context of faith in the God who alone is worthy of absolute loyalty and who judges and converts all our relative evaluations.

The religiosity of value systems leads us to the question of moral motivation. We are concerned, both in the study of ethics and in the living of life, not only about the truth of our values but also about how they become operational. Rational knowledge of value is not sufficient in and of itself to move us to act.[8] Our loyalties, perhaps functioning as a form of practical reason, are usually more potent and persuasive than our abstract reasons. Alexander Miller sees this in the manner in which parents teach their children responsibility: "If the loyalty is real, the obligation is powerful; if there is no loyalty, there is no meaningful obligation."[9] Indeed, there is no faithless ethics.[10]

The Communal Nature
of Christian Ethics

We can recognize the essentially communal character of Christian ethics in a variety of ways. First, relational value theory suggests not only the religiosity but also the sociality of all value systems. Our centers of value, whether we acknowledge their relativity or affirm their ultimacy, have social embodiments of one sort or another. When we decide that a certain financial investment is good for our family's welfare, a concrete group enfleshes that value center. When I commit myself to some political activity, there is a civil society meaningfully present in my awareness and my decision. We live with multiple loyalties, and our loyalties are social. Specific decisions, then, usually involve such underlying questions as these: Which group reflects the more compelling loyalty in this instance and why? Who is included in the group that reflects my ultimate allegiance? How do the various groups to which I "belong" enter into this decision?

The Christian confesses finding God, more truly being found by God, most decisively through the community of Christian faith. God meets us not primarily in our withdrawal, nor in our introspection, nor in our rational reflection, though each of these may enter in. God meets us most fundamentally in community founded upon living loyalty.[11] We can affirm the church as necessary object of loyalty and center of value while at the same time insisting that it is only relative. Ecclesiastical idolatries, past and present, are convincing evidence of the church's relativity. Yet as fleshly creatures we are never without the need for fleshly vehicles of our loyalties, even of that Loyalty who will not be confined to any partial community.

The communal nature of Christian ethics can be seen in several other ways. The very style of biblical faith is profoundly social, communal, and historical. A New Testament scholar writes, "The structure of biblical ethics deals with God's action in creating the conditions and possibilities for human community and with human action to fulfill those conditions and possibilities through an appropriate response. In this structure we can find a basic unity in biblical ethics, even though individual writers vary greatly."[12] Community, then, is God's goal for human existence. God's "political work," in Paul Lehmann's words, is "to make and keep human life human in the world."[13]

Community, however, is not only the *telos* of life but also the *medium* through which God is now at work. While the forms of human relatedness are realms of sin, they can also be those vehicles through which God's intentional activity is expressed. Through the various forms of community in the world, human creative activities are nurtured. Through the patterns of community custom and ethos, persons are sustained in their meanings for, and interaction with, one another. Communities perform restraining activities, maintaining order that makes common life possible. James Gustafson rightly maintains, "God creates, sustains, restrains and makes possible better qualities of life through the existence of [persons] in all three aspects of community."[14]

There is another persuasive ethical reason for us to affirm the Christian community as an appropriate point of departure for ethical reflection: it can clarify the manner in which the will of God is translated into the practical situation. Lehmann observes that some contemporary ethics that begin with biblical norms or anthropology have "not satisfactorily explained how to live constructively in the gap between the will of God, theologically understood, and the concrete human situation, pragmatically understood."[15] The gap becomes more bridgeable when we begin with the *koinonia*, for not only there does God decisively reveal the divine activity and purpose to Christians but also it is this very concrete fellowship that is already living in the ethically ambiguous situation. "To start to think about ethics from this point gives to Christian ethics a clarity and relevance otherwise unattainable."[16]

Christian ethics is communal, then, in several ways. We affirm community as both the goal and the medium of human existence under God. The Christian community is charged with the particular task of witnessing to God's work in releasing the world from bondage and drawing all into the divinely intended universal community.[17]

The Human Self:
Religious and Social

Every value system is inherently religious because human beings are.[18] From the prophets denouncing Baal, to Paul standing in the Areopagus, the Bible pictures the basic human question not as God-versus-no-god but rather as true-God-versus-false-gods. Just as with the communality of Christian ethics, so also the self's religiosity is expressed in a variety of ways. Emphases in current Christian ethics on the three theological virtues illustrate this. H. Richard Niebuhr sees *faith* (with the emphasis upon trust, confidence, and loyalty) as basic to human life, arguing that the great ethical question is always the question of faith: In what do we trust?[19] Likewise, Gordon Kaufman writes, "One's deepest convictions—those which provide the criteria for all [of one's] higher level judgments and decisions—are rooted in a kind of unquestioned faith, not in logical demonstration. This faith . . . orients all thought and action."[20]

Hope is another way of expressing human religiosity. James Sellers uses the categories of "promise" and "fulfillment" as his ethical stance, claiming that hope is not an option. All persons and not simply those who are self-consciously "religious" are motivated and guided by the way in which they seek their promised wholeness. The real issue is what kind of hope or wholeness we pursue.[21]

Daniel Day Williams affirms essentially the same of *love*. We are born to love. The real question is not whether to love but rather what and how to love, for our basic craving is to belong, our fundamental anxiety that of non-belonging, not counting. "When we ask what really constitutes being for [persons], the answer is that it is belonging, or communion, which constitutes its heart."[22] The Bible is a history of the love of God moving amidst the human loves, while "the great ethical question is how the human loves serve God."[23]

If the self is religious, it is also social and dialogical. In dealing with this theme, contemporary ethicists show their indebtedness not only to the recovery of biblical anthropology stimulated by Martin Buber[24] but also to the symbolic interactionists in American social psychology and philosophy.[25] What kinds of insights about this dialogic self emerge?

First, we know what it means to be "a self" only in relation with other selves.[26] The interpersonal dialogue is the very matrix in which the self emerges. Lacking instincts, as John MacMurray says, the infant "is, in fact, 'adapted,' to speak paradoxically, to being unadapted, 'adapted' to a complete dependence upon an adult human being. [The infant] is made to be cared for. [The baby] is born into a love relationship which is inherently personal."[27] While it is often assumed that speech is crucial in distinguishing human beings from animals, this is true only in a broad sense of the word. After all, individuals without hearing or speech are still human. It is more broadly *communication* that is crucial for humanization, and the human infant's sole adaptation to the world is the impulse to communication. The self, then, does not find its dialogue originating within. Niebuhr has rightly criticized the idealists who see the dialogue taking place between the "higher" and the "lower" dimensions of the individual—between reason and emotion or between soul and body.[28] The dialogue takes place more fundamentally between the self and the other, a relation that is experienced internally. This understanding becomes a powerful image for the ethicist, as Niebuhr himself demonstrates: "What is implicit in the idea of responsibility is the image of [person]-as-answerer, [person] engaged in dialogue, [person] acting in response to action upon him [or her]."[29]

The dialogue between the self and the other involves the whole range of human communications: ideas, emotions, attitudes, memories, hopes. We internalize the significant memories and hopes of those communities to which we are bound by love and loyalty. This is as true of the church as it is of other groups, of course, and these internalized convictions "may subtly shade and color the way in which Christians think and live rather than be a set of prescriptive propositions applicable to life."[30]

Thus, the self is in dialogue with the past as well as the present. "We are in history as the fish is in water," and we cannot understand ourselves apart from our histories.[31] It is "internal history" that is of fundamental importance for the self. External history is objective, quantitative, and the self's relation to it is that of an impartial observer. Internal history, the history of practical reason rather than pure reason, is personal and subjective. It gives shape to the person's activity and meaning to her or his action. To an important extent we create ourselves by our decisions. We create each other, in the sense that decisions and actions of others affect us. And we are created by our history. "We are what we are because of the unnumbered decisions of the entire human past which are stored up in the vast reservoirs not only of individual memory but in social structures and institutions, customs and habits, mores and ideologies, artifacts and written records."[32]

Yet the question now arises, why does some history become particularly important and internal to the self while the rest remains external? Inner history is always a matter of faith. We affirm some portions of our experienced history as peculiarly significant for us. "[The self] as a practical, living being never exists without a god or gods; some things there are to which [it] must cling as the sources and goals of [its] activity, the centers of value."[33] But just as our history itself is social, so also the faith choice that enables parts of our history to become internalized is social. The pledges of loyalty I make to my god or my gods are allegiances made in the company of others. Whether the others are present physically or in my mind, "a cloud of witnesses" surrounds me with encouragement, symbols, and memories supporting my pledge of faith. This appears to be true whether the god in question happens to be my nation, my social class, my occupation, my family, or the God of Jesus Christ.

Each of us lives in a plurality of societies, and that plurality of societies lives in each of us. In the dialogue within myself I may meet the internalized images of several of my societies as I ponder a particular decision. I may encounter an internalized image of my family, of my occupational group, and of my church while I am deciding my attitude toward a certain political issue. This plurality may lead to practical polytheism, as Niebuhr suggests with characteristic insight: "A [person] has one internal history so far as he [or she] is devoted to one value. For the most part persons and communities do not have a single internal history because their faiths are various and the events of life cannot be related to one continuing and abiding good. They have 'too many selves to know the one,' too many histories, too many gods. . . . Without a single faith there is no real unity of the self or of a community, therefore no unified inner history but only a multiplicity of memories and destinies."[34]

Adjudication among the self's societies now becomes an important ethical issue. Is there one society whose judgment is final? Insofar as the individual does have such a society, "it has god, a being on which it is absolutely dependent for its value and one whose judgment it cannot deny without denying itself."[35] Furthermore, it appears that when one has such "a court of last resort," there are consequences for the unity of the self: "At the least, the unity of the self and the other go hand in hand and it is impossible to ascribe priority to the former."[36] The authorship of judgments in this inner dialogue is a "joint authorship." For example, "when the other in the mind is the image of Jesus Christ and the dialectical reflection leads to a command or a judgment, it is possible to affirm either that the self, as a Christian, has judged or that Christ within has judged, but in truth the authorship of the command or judgment belongs to the society of the self and Jesus Christ."[37]

One further question: What induces the self to accept these laws or judgments arising out of this joint authorship? It appears that the consequence of transgressing or evading such a judgment is the self-exclusion from the society represented by the other. This fear of exclusion (or, put positively, the desire to maintain and extend the relationship) seems to apply both to the internal society of self and other and also to the external, visible group.

In this discussion of the dialogic nature of the moral self I have followed H. Richard Niebuhr's argument quite closely. More than any other contemporary relational ethicist he has illuminated certain dimensions of this issue, and his insights raise precisely the kinds of issues that Christian ethics must now press into further conversation with the social sciences.

Before leaving the subject of the dialogic self, we may briefly raise a final question: Where does the visible, empirical church fit into the Christian's inner dialogue? Most Christians would confess that the "internal society" of themselves and God is necessarily related to, though not identical with, an external, embodied society—the church. Though the God of Jesus Christ is not revealed exclusively in the church and much less is the divine activity confined to the church, Christians have experienced their decisive meeting with God through the mediation of *this* historic community. This appears true even of such lonely, agonized spiritual wrestlers as Kierkegaard and Simone Weil.[38] Based upon this conviction—that Christian community and the Christian relation to God are necessarily intertwined—Lehmann formulates the ethical question in this manner: "What am I, as a believer in Jesus Christ and as a member of his church, to do? The answer is, 'I am to do what I am.'"[39] Thus, the self's crucial society and consequently the self's identity are integral to the ethical question.

The Moral Self, Conscience, and Freedom

Two related questions are raised by implication in the foregoing discussion. When we speak of the moral self, are we simply speaking of "conscience," or is conscience but one element of more inclusive reality of moral selfhood? And when we place such emphasis upon the relational self in continuity with its communities and its history, in what sense can we speak meaningfully of moral freedom?

First, what is conscience? Joseph Fletcher observes that our most common definitions have been intuition (an innate, built-in faculty), inspiration from God (guidance from the Holy Spirit or an immediate sensitivity to God), introjection (the internalized value system of one's culture or group), and the reason making moral judgments (as Thomas Aquinas defined it). Though he is somewhat partial to Thomas Aquinas's notion, Fletcher adds a fifth definition, insisting that conscience must be understood as a verb rather than a noun: "There *is* no conscience; 'conscience' is merely a word for our attempts to make decisions creatively, constructively, fittingly."[40]

There is wisdom in J. S. Mill's principle that people are generally right in what they affirm and wrong in what they deny,[41] particularly when it comes to the matter of conscience. It seems much more adequate to speak of several interrelated dimensions of the human experience of conscience, dimensions that include those aspects listed above.[42] These elements might be summarized in terms of the familiar "ethical triad"—God, neighbor, and self— the three terms in Jesus' summary of the commandments.

First, "God." The conscience points to the self's ultimate loyalty or center of value. This is the fundamental authority of and to the conscience, but it is always mediate as well as immediate. Thus when we speak of the guidance of the Spirit or of sensitivity to divine activity in the world, we are always speaking of a relationship to God that involves our companions in faith. Such is both the fate and the joy of being a social self. The community gathered by this faith, the community that articulates, symbolizes, and points to its history of faith, is always part of, and in tension with, the self's experience of its God.

The "neighbor" as a second dimension points to the whole realm of relations in which we live. Our diverse communities and societies all give structure to the moral obligations that we feel. We perceive expectations that others have of us because of our place in the social network. Some of our relations with others come by virtue of our choices, others have been chosen for us, and all give moral structure to our lives because they confront us with responsibilities, duties, possibilities, and new choices.

The "self" is part of the conscience in the sense that the self is not simply the sum of its varied relations, histories, and communities. Beyond these we experience a movement toward integrity, toward wholeness, toward consistency. I respond to others, but it is *I* who respond, and this self-transcending capacity to evaluate the self's own relations and personal structure, this never-finished and dynamic thrust toward being a centered self, is also part of the experience of conscience.

In each of these three dimensions, to be sure, there are beliefs and ideas, socially mediated but individually appropriated and interpreted, that affect the conscience. Our beliefs about our loyalties and about our world always color our judgments and actions. The Christian's beliefs about God, about human nature, about sin and salvation, about the destiny of history, about the created universe—all of these are part of the experience of God, self, and neighbor, and hence part of the conscience.

Paul Lehmann's suggestive interpretation rightly emphasizes

the *koinonia* as the context for a theonomous conscience. If the conscience is bound to external law, then it has been abandoned to heteronomy, whereas if it is viewed as a "built-in" human device for discerning the good and the right, then it is violated by autonomy. "The *theonomous* conscience is the conscience immediately sensitive to the freedom of God to do in the always changing human situation what [God's] humanizing aims and purposes require. . . . It is from and within the Christian *koinonia* that conscience acquires ethical reality and the power to shape behavior through obedient freedom."[43]

The value of Lehmann's description lies particularly in his emphasis upon the *koinonia* as the context of conscience. Nevertheless, he has been rightly criticized at several points. His sharp bifurcation between context and rules tends to cloud the recognition that the church as social body is made up of patterns of meanings and has an ethos filled with moral norms. He tends to ignore the other nonchurch contexts of relations in which Christians find themselves. In his emphasis upon the Christian's "immediate sensitivity" to what God is doing, he slights the social dimensions of selfhood and community (which mediate both sensitivity and insensitivity), and he does not deal realistically with the continuing sin of the *koinonia's* members.[44]

We need a thoroughly social understanding of conscience. Niebuhr expresses this: "The experience of conscience is not *like* being judged by another person; it is indeed being judged by another, though the other is not immediately or symbolically and physically present to sense-experiencing [persons]. Conscience is a function of my existence as a social being, always aware of the approvals and disapprovals of my action by my [human companions]."[45] This social view does not mean that we are simply prisoners of the approvals and disapprovals of our various communities. Nor does it discount the role of the basic beliefs and transcending loyalties of our human groups. It does, however, insist that "when we judge our actions, approve and disapprove of ourselves, value and disvalue our evaluations, the situation is the same social situation in which we transcend ourselves by knowing ourselves as knowers."[46]

There is little to be gained, then, by drawing a distinction between such terms as "conscience," "moral self," and "moral identity." Because "conscience" has been used in such disparate ways in ethics and theology, I have chosen to minimize its use. Further, the concepts of selfhood and identity furnish more direct links with the data of the social sciences that are important to us. If we think of conscience with its several interrelated and social dimensions, then it is obvious that we are pointing not only to one particular element or faculty but to the entire moral self in all its richness and complexity.

Having emphasized these social dimensions of conscience and self, are we not pushed toward a social determinism that denies a person's genuine moral freedom? Indeed there are those who so fear social determinism that they see social relations as merely incidental to human selfhood.[47] While a social, dialogic view of the self certainly involves *predetermination*, this is not contrary to freedom. Kaufman puts the issue well: "On the one hand, freedom involves predetermination: by *decision* we mean precisely a movement in the present moment through which the future course of events will be determined. If such predetermination were not possible, the concept of decision would be meaningless and [we] would have no freedom. . . . On the other hand, predetermination involves freedom. To 'determine' (cf. 'terminate') means to set limits; to predetermine is to set limits prior to the event. . . . But such power significantly to bind the future is precisely what is meant by freedom."[48]

Thus when we speak of free behavior we are not speaking of behavior that has no relational and historic antecedents. Such utterly spontaneous behavior would be meaningless. We are both free and unfree, and our histories contain deliberate, purposive action as well as powers and forces that we do not will. Our decisions are liberated as well as channeled by the network of relations, past and present, in which we are immersed. For example, the constructive function of tradition in a community is not to put the mind in a mold but to stretch it by sketching alternatives and giving partial independence from present pressures. It can give what G. K. Chesterton called membership in "the democracy of the dead"— that refusal to submit to "the small and arrogant oligarchy of those who simply happen to be walking about."[49]

Here, then, are some elements of contemporary relational ethics that bear importantly on the problem before us. These conceptions of ethics and values, community and the self also open up questions that must be pressed further.

3

The Church
and the Moral Self:
Avenues for Inquiry

The Church and the Shaping of the Self

The church can be a significant shaping community for its members—or it may not be. Later we shall explore with the social scientists some elements that bear upon this process, but first we must look at this issue from the viewpoint of relational Christian ethics.

One aspect of personal formation is the meanings that the self internalizes. All the significant communities of our lives contribute meanings to us, though the language by which we describe them can vary. James Gustafson makes some helpful distinctions with his terms "perspective and posture," "disposition," and "intention."[1] By perspective and posture he indicates "the more fundamental points of orientation that are governed by convictions that one has about crucial matters." "Dispositions refer to the self's attitudes, its somewhat stable readiness to speak and to act in particular ways." And by intention he suggests "a basic direction of activity, an articulation of what that direction is and ought to be, a purposive orientation for one's life."[2] Thus, a Christian's perspective and posture may be informed by one's confidence in the goodness of God, one's disposition may be hopeful about life, and one's intention may be directed toward the neighbor's good. All communities, it would appear, give shape to the lives of their seriously involved members through perspectives, dispositions, and intentions, though, to be sure, the content of such community input will vary from group to group.

A related way of viewing the self's moral formation is to see the double-sided relation between one's faith and one's identity or integrity. H. Richard Niebuhr raises the question, How shall we interpret the radical action by which we are cast into the particularities of our existence? We can ignore this radical action or see it as a hostile force, but such are responses of distrust. Yet it is possible, at least partially and occasionally, to come into a trusting relationship with the ultimate power which allows us to affirm "God is acting in all actions upon you. So respond to all actions upon you as to respond to [God's] action."[3] The objective side of such a relationship is the problem of discerning one unified intention, action, and context in all the actions upon me. The subjective side is the problem of my own unity, my own integrity, in short, my identity.

Other ethicists use different ways to speak of the self's shape or form. Particularly striking is Dietrich Bonhoeffer's understanding of "conformation."[4] Bonhoeffer is suspicious of any notion of moral formation that would suggest our human effort to imitate Christ or "to become like Jesus." "On the contrary, formation comes only by being drawn in into the form of Jesus Christ. It comes only as formation in [Christ's] likeness, as conformation with the unique form of [the one] who was made [human], was crucified, and rose again."[5] As Christ shapes us, we are conformed to the Incarnate as real persons; as we are formed into the likeness of the Crucified, we die daily to sin, accepting suffering as a way of enabling us to surrender to God's judgment; and as we are conformed to the Risen One we are new persons, in life even in the midst of death, even though our newness is a secret hidden from the world.

The above three theologians are particularly suggestive, for each of them links his understanding of the shape and form of the moral self, on one hand, with the church, on the other. How do they see this connection? Look at each again. If the Christian life is the life of response to God's activity in the concrete situations of the world, then, according to Gustafson, that response must come through one's perspectives, dispositions, and intentions. These meanings must be internalized if they are to be effective. While Christ is the "collective representation" of the church's abiding meanings, there must also be human structures that give these meanings stability and form. The Bible is the foremost of these, though also important are doctrine, polity, liturgy, and this community's history. All these give content and stability to the

central events in the church's memory, and in communication and
social interaction (such as in preaching, the liturgy, educational instruction, and group meetings) some of these meanings take root
within the member. Through the very human qualities of the
church as a natural and political community, a community of language, interpretation, memory, belief, and action, such internalization is made possible.[6]

Niebuhr's social view of the self likewise finds its corollary in
his recognition that the church is not an accidental but an essential part of the gospel. Though its purposes are variously described, no better definition can be found than "the increase of
love of God and neighbor."[7] The Christian is "the member of a
new community, of a people chosen for service in bearing witness
to the One beyond all the many, elected to live by and to mediate
to others confidence in the principle of being itself and loyalty to
its cause."[8] Organized Christianity, however, is frequently distorted by a church-centered henotheism. When this happens, God
is subtly made a captive of the church, and the church seeks
its unity, holiness, and universality not in faithfulness to God but
as ends to be sought for the church's own sake. Niebuhr's acute
awareness of the distortions of church life is all the more telling,
for he sees that such ecclesiastical idolatry carries an inevitable result for the individual participant: a henotheistic distortion in the
member's religious identity.

For Bonhoeffer, the formation of Christ in the life of an individual is inconceivable apart from the Christian community. The small
band of those in whom Christ has taken form are the church. "The
New Testament states that case profoundly and clearly when it calls
the church the Body of Christ. The body is the form. So the church
is not a religious community of worshipers of Christ but is Christ
. . . who has taken form among [us]. The church is nothing but a
section of humanity in which Christ has really taken form."[9]

Thus, each of these three theologians sees the question of the
self's moral shape and the question of the church as indissolubly
connected. While Bonhoeffer's approach to ethics contrasts in
some important ways with that of Niebuhr and Gustafson, all
three have given attention to the sociological as well as the theological dimensions of the church. And it is no accident that those
ethicists who have developed intimate familiarity with the thought

of social philosophers and social scientists should be most suggestive when it comes to the question of moral formation.

Nevertheless, there are ways in which the dialogue with the social sciences can be expanded to enrich our ethical understanding.
In spite of the relative youth of these human sciences, they have
broken important ground in exploring the ways in which various
types of groups influence their members' identities and attitudes.
Later we will put a variety of questions to them. How are beliefs
internalized, and how does identity function in behavior? What is
the role of the group in the transformation as well as in the formation of the self? What does a strong member-shaping group
look like? What has loyalty to the group to do with loyalty to the
group's cause? Such questions as these are both explicit and implicit in the ethical perspectives we have seen thus far.

The Church
and Moral Motivation

Closely related is the church's significance for its members'
motivation. It is a common and altogether accurate observation in
most Christian ethics that the motivation toward the neighbor's
good stems from our gratitude to God "for our creation, preser-
vation, and all the blessings of this life; but above all, for thine in-
estimable love in the redemption of the world by our Lord Jesus
Christ"—as the Prayer of General Thanksgiving puts it. Indeed,
as Luther so frequently affirmed, our justification in Jesus Christ
constitutes the end of moralistic striving and salvation piety.
Rather, it marks the beginning of a more disinterested and outgoing concern for the neighbor.

However, a serious shortcoming in most Protestant Christian
ethics has been its tendency to speak of God's gratitude-eliciting
work in ways that imply that the church is quite incidental to the
process. Gratitude, in this individualistic view, stems only from
the relationship between God and the self. Motivated by this experience, the person then is committed to the neighbor and the
community. In contrast, a relational theology and ethics must re-
capture, but in a new and broad way, the Roman Catholic and Reformation Protestant claim *extra ecclesiam nulla salus*—outside the
church there is no salvation.

Several moral theologians point the way in which this affirmation may be made meaningfully yet without the imperialistic presumptions that have marred it so frequently in the past. Their claim is not that only through the *Christian* community is the saving relationship experienced. Rather, the broad truth of the claim, as Alexander Miller recognizes, is really this: "Against all individualism and unchurchly mysticism in religion, [this means] that redemption is incorporation, that [we are] nearer to God when [we are] nearer to [our] human [companions]."[10] Only through incorporating us into actual and imperfect community can God's work be accomplished, for the self's bondage is not to a false idea that can be driven out by a superior idea, but rather its bondage lies in its organization around a false center involving concrete loyalties, drives, and lusts. And if the self is a genuinely social being, this reorganization can take place only in a social framework.

Furthermore, the emphasis must be upon meaningful communal involvement rather than formal church membership. It is quite possible to argue, as Gordon Kaufman rightly does, that individuals who are not formal church members can meaningfully be considered Christians and, at the same time, to argue that "individual Christian existence . . . must always be understood as possible only within the matrix of communal Christian existence and history."[11] The point is that God's redeeming work—whether among Christians or among other persons—is a *communal* work, and our gratitude to God is for *human* (not just Christian) creation and re-creation in and through community. Even so, we are grateful as *Christians*, and the continuing life and work of this particular community has made a Christian relationship to God historically available to us in a way that certain other types of relationship are not.

Two other theologians give helpful clues on the communal nature of motivation. As we have seen, Daniel Day Williams affirms that the fundamental human craving is that of belonging, of finding one's membership with others in the community of being. We not only desire to belong, we also crave the security the sense of belongingness can give. But "no group can give all the security we crave. No human community can be as completely fulfilling as we wish, and moreover there are the threats to its existence both from within and from without. Whatever threatens my group threatens me."[12] Thus our will to belong can become our will to preserve "our way" against all others, the passion of self-deification. This powerful thrust toward belongingness can turn into destructive, brutal cruelty, and that which can so pervert it is the anxiety of not-belonging.

Here we see both the positive and the negative aspects of motivation. We are created for inclusive communion. Yet we fear the risks of being human in the great community and choose to be "human" on our own terms, terms that are more immediately satisfying, comfortable, self-protective, and in consequence self-destructive and destructive of others. But our core motivation is clearly belonging and our core anxiety is not-belonging, terms that convey a larger freight of meaning than "acceptance" and "rejection."

Similar affirmations are present in Joseph Haroutunian's examination of the social nature of willing, a concept intimately linked to motivation. "[People] do not will the right or the good outside of their social and common life. They neither know their freedom nor exercise it except as they make decisions for or against actions demanded by the common life and its institutions. A [parent], a student, a business[person], a soldier, a church [member], a citizen, are confronted with their particular moralities and duties. They will as [parent], student, church [member], citizen."[13] If there is no *person* whose existence is logically prior to communion, there is no *will* prior to communion. Even when we violate communion, we are dependent upon it for our very existence. Communion and freedom in willing are, by the grace of God, present only among our human companions.

Thus, just as the self is relational and communal, so also are our motivations and our willing. Just as the Christian is moved by gratitude to God for divine goodness and activity, so also that movement of gratitude is experienced in and through community. Although such experience can and does take place in the many forms of human community, the church has a particular and decisive importance among the Christian's communities of motivation, for here we recognize, symbolize, and celebrate that communion which is the essence of our humanity. In the church we learn to name the name of God who is the source of our gratitude, the Holy One who does not meet us apart from community. In the church we experience also the brokenness and partiality of community and find that our quest for universal communion is a hope as much as a reality, though it could not be hope without also participating in present reality.

The church as a locus of gratitude and loyalty is thus a relative locus. There is an inescapable tension here. Loyalty to the flag of the church must at all times be judged by its fruits: whether or not it participates in and enhances "loyalty to the flag of the universe" and the universe's God. When that tension is lost, idolatry is assured. Yet if the existing, concrete Christian community is not seen as a fitting locus of relative loyalty and object of relative gratitude, we do not understand the nature and dynamics of our motivation.

This communal interpretation does not exhaust the complex question of moral motivation. Yet if "motives and motivation in the broad sense means why [people] behave as they do,"[14] a Christian relational perspective affirms that people behave as they do because they are created by God through and for community. Furthermore, such faith affirmations do not preclude our turning to the social sciences for further insights. Indeed, precisely because God uses our social humanity and expressions of human community as a primary vehicle of divine activity, the human sciences can assist us.

Fundamental to our understanding of moral motivation is the self's will to belong. Is this an accurate understanding of the self? Williams frankly confesses, "We have no absolute precision or dogmatic finality here. But the 'will to belong' does point to what we observe in human motives, cravings, sacrifices, satisfactions, and perversities."[15] Certainly, the social sciences now can aid us as we check our own observations of human motives against what others observe in their disciplined attempts to understand human action. In addition to this central query, a host of more specific questions arise. What is the nature of the group that most strongly motivates its members? Is this power something in the quality of relationships between the person and the group? Or something in the structure of the group itself? Or the group's transcending loyalty? How does a person's position or role affect her or his motivation to work for group goals?

Further, we can seek understanding of the group's wider social and historical contexts. Indeed, it may be no accident that in earlier generations a more individualistic and deductive Christian ethics could appear adequate even though it showed little awareness of the social basis of our motivations. When the "natural" communities of life had stronger bonds and greater resiliency, we were less aware of their motivating power and we could take them for granted. This is true also of the church. Now, however, changes in society and in the churches spur us to grapple with the social context of motivation more seriously, and this effort is part of the Christian ethical task.

The Church and Moral Patterns

The church is a shaper of moral agents and a vehicle of moral motivation. The Christian community is also internally related to the style and content of its members' moral patterns. The church not only transmits or witnesses to a style of ethics, but also its very existence as a community gives contour and configuration to its ethics. How can we understand this?

First, we must simply notice that there is "something there." There are styles of life, however difficult to describe, that characterize the various Christian communities. The Bible's use of the family analogy for the faith community reminds us that, like a family, the church has an ancestry, family lore, heirlooms, traditions, expectations—all of which carry and give structure to its ethos.[16] The content of the church's ethos is characterized by the way it attempts to express its loyalty to the God of Jesus Christ. The ethos develops certain patterns of response or "moral habits." Because these patterns exist, members are not left with a sheer occasionalism in their moral responses. Christians do not enter the decisional situation "naked"; they are clothed in the garments of a historical community that has faced similar situations before. The garments are not always well designed. The wearer may find them ill-cut and ill-fitting in the new situation. Yet within the structures of the common life there are possibilities of continuing renewal and correction. The church's moral ethos, then, is a curious and dynamic compound of ignorance and wisdom, loyalty to God, and allegiance to the tribal gods. In any event, it is "something there."

There is another and related way in which the church as community enters into the moral pattern. The communal existence itself is indispensable to the interpretation of God's activity. Paul Lehmann maintains that the revelation of God's humanizing work must be our norm of moral judgment. Yet, crucial in Lehmann's understanding, this humanization is known through the *koinonia* not as a rational principle taught and learned but as a content-filled relationship. Though the empirical church in its moral ambiguity violates the very ethical reality that is its foundation, nevertheless it points to the fact that within the church there is the *koinonia, "the ecclesiola in ecclesia,"* which is a "laboratory of the living word," a "bridgehead of maturity." "In the *koinonia* a continuing experiment is going on in the concrete reality and possibility of [our] interrelatedness and openness for [humanity]."[17]

Alexander Miller's "faith plus facts" formula is similar. In the concrete decisional situation there must be a pragmatic calculation of what is best. But this calculation has a faith dimension that both tutors the Christian to estimate the facts with greater disinterestedness and also involves "a very precise understanding of what is good for [people], determined by the revelation of God in Christ."[18] What is good for people is God's will to create a human community out of separated individuals and broken communities. But such understanding of God's will depends upon our participation in that community where this kind of divine action is at work and is consciously celebrated.

H. Richard Niebuhr's account of responsibility also predicates communal involvement. In responding to action upon us, we always respond to *interpreted* action. The context of interpretation in its several dimensions then becomes crucial. In its social context there must be an image of the ultimate society, in its temporal context an eschatological myth, and in its understanding of the self's contingency an image of both the unity and the goodness of the ultimate power. For the Christian, the images by which these contexts of action are interpreted are somehow connected centrally with the key (though not singular) symbolic form of Jesus Christ.[19]

But Jesus Christ as the key paradigm for interpreting action is not known by speculative inquiry; Christ is known in decision and commitment. Kierkegaard was right in this, says Niebuhr, but wrong both in his individualism and his nonhistorical understanding of the present moment. In actuality, it is not "I" who meets Christ, but "we" at every point. We do not know Christ apart from our companions in the faith. The moment of decision is always a social-historical moment, filled with the memory and presence of others who have preceded us in the faith community.[20]

Like Niebuhr, James Gustafson uses the categories of creating, ordering, sustaining, and redeeming to describe God's work. Now, however, it is clear not only that the church is necessary to the Christian's interpretation of divine activity, but also that it is through community relationships (both within and outside the church) that God's work especially takes place. "Precisely the natural community, the political community, the community of language, interpretation and understanding, the community of belief and action, is the Church, God's people. The human processes of its common life are means of God's ordering, sustaining, and redeeming . . . people."[21] And against any misguided Christian particularism, we can insist with Gustafson that God is at work in the whole vast range of human communities. God is of course known outside the church. But we must also say that a *Christian* ethics of response to divine activity is impossible apart from a person's involvement in that particular community to which God has been revealed in Jesus Christ.

Thus, life in Christian community is indispensable for the Christian's interpretation and experience of the God who acts in all times and in all places. Each of the four previously cited ethicists in his own way affirms this. In spite of this agreement there are rather important ethical differences between Lehmann and Miller, on the one hand, and Niebuhr and Gustafson, on the other. The former tend toward a singular interpretation of God's activity ("humanizing"), whereas the latter use a manifold interpretation ("creating, sustaining, ordering-restraining, redeeming"). The former question the legitimacy of moral principles in Christian ethics; the latter affirm their necessity. In these and other ways they differ.

Yet of particular interest to us is the difference disclosed by this question: Is God's work in and through community known through institutional as well as through interpersonal relationships? Here there is a dividing of the ways. It is Gustafson and Niebuhr who most strongly affirm the institutional also as a vehicle of divine action. This significant affirmation needs further ethical probing, for although the institution question has occupied theological discussions of the nature of the church and ethical discussions of God's worldly activity, little attention has yet been given to the question of institutional structure in moral community and moral selfhood. To this we shall return.

In addition to the internalization of an ethos and the communal context for understanding God's activity, relational ethics suggests a third manner of interdependence of church participation and the Christian's moral pattern. This is the empathetic understanding of the neighbor's needs. It is an important element in moral knowledge. Christian relationalists characteristically emphasize the uniqueness of the neighbor to whom love is due, whether that neighbor be a single person or a corporate group. Further, it is commonly recognized that, since what the neighbor *needs* and what the neighbor *desires* are not necessarily the same, we must have a norm by which authentic human needs can be measured. While it is assumed that sensitivity to persons and their needs is indispensable, it is odd that this element is relatively unexplored in the current ethical literature.

The question of sensitivity to others can be raised either as a quality of the moral self or as one of the necessary kinds of moral knowledge. It is both. What moral theologians usually call "knowledge of the situation" or "knowledge of the facts" of course involves this sensitivity. Yet ethicists commonly speak of this knowledge simply as the person's awareness of the particular factors present in the situation and some reasonable assessment of the consequences of potential decisions. But what of the ability to *identify with* others and of the moral knowledge that issues from this identification? And what of the range of those with whom one can identify? It is quite possible, for example, that one might be able to identify quite effectively with radical young people but not with conservative old folk, or with middle-class blacks but not lower-class whites. Further, what of the awareness of and insight into one's own feelings and those of others, the ability to know what these feelings are and to describe them with some accuracy? Assessing the "morally educated" person, philosopher John Wilson points to these two important dimensions among others. He notes that the first (the ability to identify with) is not necessarily or logically implied by the second (insight into feelings), though psychologically it might be that a person cannot develop in such a way as to have much feeling-insight without also having the capacity for identification.[22]

These qualities of empathy and sensitivity, identification and insight, thus point us to another dimension of moral knowledge that is intimately linked with the moral community. For how are such qualities developed except through certain kinds of relationships? And has the church any special role or unique capacity in the development of these abilities?

The connection between the church and the moral pattern raises one last question: What is the relation between Christian ethics and non-Christian ethics? Can an ethics so closely involved with the Christian community have a viable link with those outside the church? Historically, various answers have emerged. Some ethics assume a common rational moral nature in humanity, an assumption present in natural law and, to an extent, in "middle axiom" theories. As it is usually stated, however, this argument raises some serious questions.

Another approach emphasizes the universality of God's activity as the crucial moral datum. Lehmann thus asserts that a *koinonia* ethics affirms that what is ethically common to all persons must be understood "not as a proof of a common rational moral nature but as a sign that the humanizing action of God includes all [people]."[23] A similar though slightly different approach is found in Miller. The cooperative agreement among people that transcends their religious and social communities, he says, has a basis deeper than mutual consent to rational law. Our revulsion against cruelty and our praise of compassion "are part of our human constitution, reinforced by our recognition that the human community is impoverished by the one and enriched by the other."[24] What traditionally has been attributed to natural law "can be accounted for by the recognition of the necessities of human society on the one hand, and on the other by an innate compassion (sometimes hard put to find rational justification) which may wage an uneasy and uncertain war against our latent egoism, yet is powerful enough to put its impress upon our common mind, upon tradition and upon our institutions."[25]

Miller's insight, though helpful, needs correction at one point. Given the social nature of human selfhood, that which is innate in the human constitution is not certain developed *qualities* (such as compassion) but rather certain undeveloped *capacities* that may be aroused and nurtured through interpersonal relationships. In actuality, a person's capacity for compassion and ability to recognize what is helpful for the growth of human community are indissolubly linked with that person's present and previous communal experiences.

Similarly, James Sellers is right in recognizing that the idea of "commonness" among human beings can no longer be located in a given theology or philosophy. He locates the Christian's commonness with other people at the point of action. We can at least fight for justice together even if we do not share confessional unity.[26] But Sellers does not go deep enough. Why do we find ourselves arm in arm with Buddhist monastics in the struggle for peace or with secular humanists in the fight for racial justice? When we go behind the action to the roots of that action, I believe we are driven back to the experiences of community. It is those communal experiences that have similarly nurtured the capacity for outgoing concern and for identifying with the afflicted, even though the nurturing communities themselves may not have flown the same confessional flags.

The Christian community, then, is not the only one that generates mores—all communities do. It is not the only community under God's sovereignty—all are. It is not the only community that nurtures those bonds which facilitate the realization of universal community—many do, and, admittedly, the church does its own share to fracture that very community. Yet its history, language, symbols, and meanings again and again break the church open to a more universal commonwealth. When this happens, Christian persons are again broken open to their larger citizenship and identification, for indeed the "bonds" that tie all people together are none other than living relationships. Laws, traditions, customs, and ethos are indispensable tools of the binding process, but without enfleshment they remain lifeless and abstract. Such affirmations as these also suggest conversational contacts with the social sciences. To that conversation we now turn.

Part 2
PERSPECTIVES
FROM SOCIAL PSYCHOLOGY

4

Socialization, Moral Development, and Reference Groups

Because God uses ordinary human processes, groups, and persons as vehicles of the divine activity, the dialogue with "the human sciences" that we now begin is important. The dialogue has been going on already, however. Those Christian ethicists upon whom we drew in part 1 are those whose thought has already incorporated the fruits of their own discourse with the social sciences. Thus we are not doing a new thing here but rather extending the interdisciplinary conversation along certain particular and needed lines.

Primary Socialization

Socialization is usually defined as that process by which the individual, from the very earliest stages of life, incorporates into her or his personality certain group-defined ways of thinking, acting, and feeling. It is the process whereby culture is transmitted. Our concern for the social dimensions of selfhood should not suggest that the self is determined *only* by social influences. There are biological and psychogenic influences as well. There is, further, an irreducible "I" who is not simply the sum total of social influences and biological heredity. Nevertheless, it is difficult to overemphasize the importance of social influences in turning an infant into a human being. The authenticated cases of drastically undersocialized children are sadly dramatic evidence of this.[1] Socialization and humanization are inseparable.

In terms of its social matrix, how does the self develop? Let us begin with a look at the reflexive or interactional self whose understanding George Herbert Mead pioneered.[2] The child comes

to self-consciousness by the development of the capacity to become an object to itself. In interaction with the mother and later
with others of the family group, the child develops the ability to
assume temporarily the role of the other, to imagine the other's
response, and to adopt the attitudes toward the self that others appear to be taking. The development of gestures (especially language) is both an essential part of this interactional process and a
testimony to the profoundly reflexive character of the self.

The game, according to Mead, illustrates the pervasive role-
taking experience. An organized game such as baseball demands
of the player the imaginative ability to take the roles of all other
players. "[The player] must have the responses of each position involved in his [or her] own position. [The player] must know what
everyone else is going to do in order to carry out his [or her] own
play."[3] The community, like the game, has an organized and re-
ciprocal character. But as the community takes shape for the child,
a process of generalization also occurs. Now, unlike that game in
which particular roles are anticipated, the child anticipates the attitudes of the group as a whole and internalizes this "generalized
other." This movement—from the self as the organization of particular attitudes toward itself to the fuller development that includes also the incorporation of the generalized other or the social group as a whole—constitutes a second stage of growth.

Thus far, the individual sounds extraordinarily passive, like a
mirror simply reflecting others' attitudes. However, there is the
"I" as well as the "me." "The 'I' is the response of the organism to
the attitudes of others; the 'me' is the organized set of attitudes of
others which one . . . assumes. The attitudes of the others constitute the organized 'me' and then one reacts toward that as an 'I'."[4]
There is, then, an unpredictability and uniqueness about the "I"
which can never be reduced simply to conditioned expectations.
Here is Mead's interactionism: the self is always more than a mirror of its social environment, and yet the self cannot be a self, nor
can it act, without depending upon its relations with others.

Several implications for ethics emerge from Mead's thought.
For one thing we can see some ways in which moral development
is intimately related to our social environment. The environment
is not simply the soil in which the "seed of personality" develops;
it is part of the seed itself. As another social psychologist observes,
"A permissive social environment shapes and produces one sort of

personality, an authoritarian one produces another. Permission is not the removal of social influence so that the 'natural' personality can have a chance to develop; it merely replaces one kind of social influence for another."[5]

Nevertheless, the self is never simply a chameleon, changing its color automatically with every change in the social environment. The self develops a structure including a moral structure that may well bring it into conflict with various social influences and group norms. This is part of our freedom. The other dimension of our freedom is the "I."

Some scholars have questioned whether Mead actually preserved the freedom of the "I," for if society provides the substance of the self, then freedom is reduced merely to conformity to those options which society makes available.[6] While some of Mead's conclusions about the "I" tend to be undermined by certain behavioristic assumptions, we can affirm the same dialectic between the "I" and the "me" from a nonbehavioristic orientation. There is, indeed, an "intentional self" (in Gibson Winter's terms), but both the intentional self and its moral freedom are socially developed. We are contending that "the process of self-interaction puts the human being over against [the] world instead of merely in it, requires [the person] to meet and handle [the] world through a defining process instead of merely responding to it, and forces [the individual] to construct . . . action instead of merely releasing it."[7] Actually, Mead's conception helps to correct some of those assumptions presently common in social science, assumptions that tend to see human action simply as a product of social forces playing upon or through the person.

There is a tension between form and dynamic in the self. The self does have a shape, a form; hence, it is appropriate to speak of formation (and, in particular, moral formation). But the self is also and always process. Not simply a medium through which external factors produce certain results, the self is always involved in the process of interpreting and responding in the light of its interpretations.

This leads us to a somewhat different interpretation of socialization from that frequently heard. Usually socialization is understood as the incorporation of group-defined ways of thinking, acting, and feeling—an emphasis upon structure or form. But at least as important is the cultivation of the ability to take the roles of others effectively. The self is developed not only through the internalization of norms, values, and perspectives but also through the cultivation of this capacity of reciprocity. This suggests that the self does not see values solely as "things" existing independently of persons and other beings. Rather, the self in its dynamic role-taking and interpretive process gradually develops a *relational* understanding of norms and values.

Society, like the self, has dynamic process as well as form. Although society is a structure of relations, it is also a varied and ongoing process wherein persons are continually engaged in joint actions, actions that themselves have histories and careers (and hence structure) but that remain action (and hence dynamic). This tension between form and dynamic bears upon our understanding of social roles, to be examined later. At this point one thing must be noted. While roles do exist as structures in society, their importance is not in the determination of action but rather in the manner in which they enter into the process of interpretation and definition through which persons form their joint actions. Thus we avoid the individualistic assumption that social roles are quite external to the individual and do not affect the person's behavior significantly. We also avoid the deterministic assumption that social interaction is interaction between social *roles;* it is, in fact, interaction between and among *persons.*

What, then, holds society together? It is not values as objective entities. Rather, it is certain kinds of *relationships* that have patterns and structures, but that are always in process, being interpreted and reinterpreted, defined and redefined. That Mead's perspective has significant ties with relational value theory is by now quite evident.

Primary socialization has to do not only with the cognitive capacities of the interactional self but also with its *affective* dimensions. The child, we have seen, internalizes values and perspectives and develops the capacity for role-taking. But the child also takes into itself certain deep affective attitudes that color all its more specific perspectives. Basic to these underlying attitudes is the self's feeling of trust or mistrust of the self, of others, and of the environment. Erik Erikson illuminates this element of socialization, insisting that if parents are to mediate such trust effectively, their own lives must be involved in a communal framework or lifestyle of trust.[8]

Observe how Erikson affirms this in certain stages of the self's development. During the first stage of the child's life, the most important development for healthy personality is "the firm establishment of enduring patterns for the balance of basic trust over basic mistrust."[9] This in turn depends not simply upon absolute *quantities* of love demonstrations from parents, but more importantly upon the *quality* of the relationship. This quality, in turn, depends not only upon sensitivity to the infant's needs but also upon "a firm sense of personal trustworthiness within the trusted framework of their community's life style."[10]

Autonomy is developed during the second stage of early childhood, "a sense of self-control without loss of self-esteem."[11] Building upon the basic trust developed earlier, the child's autonomy is nurtured through the parents' sense of individual dignity. Autonomy is basic to the self's capacities for love, cooperation, and self-expression. Furthermore, the possibility of the child's autonomy is directly dependent upon the parents' wider social relationships. "This . . . necessitates a relationship of parent to parent, of parent to employer, of parent to government which reaffirms the parent's essential dignity regardless of . . . social position. It is important to dwell on this point because much of the shame and doubt, much of the indignity and uncertainty which is aroused in children is an expression of the parents' frustrations in marriage, in work, and in citizenship."[12]

In the third stage, roughly between ages four and five, initiative is the key development. The primary social relationship is still with the parents, though the child is now achieving a growing sense of differentiation. If the parents themselves have a sense of personal self-worth, the child is less likely to experience later the moralism characterized by vindictiveness and suppression of others. Likewise, the child may avoid the most serious danger of over-compensated moralism in which one feels that personal worth somehow depends upon what one has done or intends to do rather than upon oneself as a person. Again, the parental sense of personal self-worth is something that must continually be supported and reinforced by the surrounding community if this is to be conveyed convincingly to the child.

One later stage of development—adolescence—deserves comment. In adolescence, "the integration now taking place in the form of ego identity is more than the sum of the childhood identifications. . . . [It is] the accrued confidence that one's ability to maintain inner sameness and continuity (one's ego in the psychological sense) is matched by the sameness and continuity of one's meaning for others."[13] Failure to achieve a sufficient sense of self-identity means not only that the person is exposed to his or her own childhood conflicts, but now, in addition, has a sense of diffusion. The person lacks a reasonably clear sense of who he or she really is. Such diffusion then hinders genuine interpersonal intimacy, and it is only in interpersonal intimacy that a sense of integrity is acquired. Integrity is the person's broad self-acceptance as a person, including all the social relationships this implies. Lacking it, one is subject to despair and to a distrust of other individuals and institutions. With an adequate sense of integrity, however, one accepts one's own life and relationships as meaningful and significant even while recognizing their relativity.

Thus, socialization is not only a cognitive process; it is also and importantly an affective process involving the acquisition of deep underlying feelings about oneself and others. These feelings are conveyed to the developing self by those with whom one has intimate relationships, and yet these formative relationships are always conditioned by those that the "significant others" have in the wider social environment.[14]

Secondary Socialization

While socialization is crucial in the formative years of childhood, it is also a lifelong process. "Socialization is not merely a childhood experience: as adults we are all being continually resocialized, that is, reaffirmed in our normative commitment by the alters [others] in our total role network."[15] As the adult participates in a rapidly changing society and moves into different geographical and social locations, he or she learns new values, transforms old ones, and learns to take into the self the roles of different others. Yet the secondary socializations that take place in the later biography of the individual always build upon (even when they modify and transform it) the massive reality of the child's world of primary socialization.[16]

Society's division of labor necessitates secondary socialization. A child must learn what it is to be a student, an adult must learn what it means to be a parent and a worker. Much of this does not require the intense emotional identification with significant others characteristic of the child's primary socialization. To this extent secondary socialization may be more cognitive than affective. The engineering student simply does not need the strong emotional bond with the professor that a child needs with the parent. On the other hand, the affective element is subject to great variation in secondary socialization. The person aspiring to be an accomplished musician or a professional revolutionary must become immersed in the field more emotionally and identify affectively with maestros and revolutionaries to a degree not necessary for the engineer.[17] Secondary socialization may, in extreme cases, take the form of resocialization in which there are conscious attempts to alter drastically the worldview acquired in previous socializations. Mental hospitals, prisons, and concentration camps may provide instances of this.[18]

The "sociology of knowledge" is relevant to this whole matter of socialization. Its basic claim is that ideas as well as persons are socially located and conditioned. "It rejects the pretense that thought occurs in isolation from the social context within which particular [persons] think about particular things."[19] Thus in primary socialization the child does not apprehend the parents simply as specific individuals, much less see them as socially relative in what they mediate. Rather, the parents are "mediators of reality *tout court;* the child internalizes the world of [the] parents as *the* world, and not as the world appertaining to a specific institutional context."[20] This original world experienced by the child is "home." It appears natural and inevitable. Thus, secondary socializations must somehow build upon this taken-for-granted reality of the person's "mother tongue."[21]

The sociology of knowledge, with few exceptions, has concentrated upon the interactions between social structure and the world of ideas. Little attention has been paid to the self's *internalization* of such socially located ideas.[22] Nevertheless, the sociology of knowledge vividly reminds us that in both primary and secondary socialization the individual is apprehending ideas and feelings that themselves are socially located and that have particular histories. Thus children from middle-class homes are socialized differently from those of working-class homes. There are differences in the ways values are held, the other sex viewed, the political system perceived.[23] Quite clearly, the child's developing ideas and feelings are closely related to the groups in which the parents are enmeshed.

Patterns of
Moral Development

While research on the patterns of moral development has been carried out more frequently by developmental psychologists than by social psychologists, we can appropriately turn to this evidence as importantly bearing upon moral socialization. Jean Piaget's work, stemming from his observations of Genevan nursery school children over a generation ago, has provided a lasting framework for subsequent research and reflection in this area.[24] Piaget's great contribution is his observation of several "stages." The manner in which he and subsequent psychologists have used this term warrants a comment.[25] A stage is a broad period of development. While it has certain distinct characteristics, any one stage is not necessarily exclusively present in a person at any given time. Stages frequently overlap in the person's development; they may run parallel in different moral situations. They vary in duration but may well survive into adulthood, becoming lasting ways or patterns of moral behavior.

Piaget noted that childrens' *understanding of rules* appears to progress through several stages. In the earliest period the child has no conception of rules at all. By the time of preadolescence a generalized "code of jurisprudence" is understood and accepted in the child's society. The significant point is this: the child's changing understanding of rules is inextricably connected with changes in the ability to enter into certain kinds of relationships.

Even more importantly, there are significant stages in the matters of *rule following* and *the nature of moral authority*. In the first stage, "the egocentric," the child understands rules as interesting examples but not as obligatory realities. The only sanctions are short-run anticipations of pleasure or pain. The second stage, however, is markedly different. In this, "the transcendental or heteronomous stage," the child sees rules as sacred and untouchable. They are completely objective things in the environment to be accepted and respected because they are commands from authoritative persons. Moreover, the child begins to internalize these rules so that they become real and binding even when the parent or other adult authority figure is absent. Yet the child's conception of morality is still patterned after the unequal relationship with the adult. Unable to appreciate the real significance of moral rules, the child is able only to respond with conformity. While the law's letter is understood, its spirit is not grasped. This mode Piaget also calls "the morality of restraint."

The third and final stage comes with "the morality of cooperation." With greater abilities in social reciprocity and increasing capacities for give-and-take with the peer group, the child becomes aware of the relational nature of moral rules. Now the rules appear not so much as external things in the environment, things imposed from above, but as ways of solving social problems to be altered by mutual consent when it is for the good of the group. Now the child is aware of the uniqueness of different situations that may call for flexibility in rule application. The rules continue to be internalized, but now they are internalized by a child who is much more aware of his or her social existence.

The contrast between the second and third stages is so marked that Piaget calls them "the two moralities." The morality of restraint is heteronomous and authoritarian, imposed upon the child by the adult world. It is a morality of rules that seem to have objective and permanent value quite apart from the individuals involved with them. The morality of cooperation, on the other hand, is democratic, egalitarian, and based upon cooperation and mutual respect. Its rules typically arise out of the relationships of peers.

Within this third stage Piaget notes two substages. The first is "reciprocity." Because social existence is now much more consciously part of the youth's life, an ethic of mutual respect can develop. Nevertheless, this ethic is still quite legal in its expression. Its practical egalitarianism is marked by a certain rigidity: everyone must be treated in the same way. As the young person continues to mature, however, reciprocity gives way to "equity." This new relationship does not insist upon equality of treatment or conformity to a social consensus. Now the unique factors in differing situations are given much more consideration. Particular needs, claims, and motives of others now receive attention. Reciprocity is now informed by what Piaget calls altruism or social love. "[The] rigid and inflexible concept of equality is replaced by a pliable and flexible concern for people . . . in a word [the] morality is no longer conformist, it is creative."[26]

Again, each of these changes in attitudes toward moral rules and their authority is bound up with changes in the child's relationships to other people. There are rules in each stage. They continue to impose obligations. Yet both the reasons for which the child accepts these obligations and the manner in they are understood change.

Piaget's main conclusions have been confirmed by subsequent research in moral development,[27] and they contain several suggestive implications for our present inquiry. Although the first implication appears obvious, it warrants emphasis: the whole person and not simply one faculty or one part of the self is involved in this moral development. Because Piaget was concerned primarily with the cognitive dimensions, some have assumed that moral development is primarily an intellectual affair. Others, influenced more heavily by Erik Erikson, stress the affective and emotional processes. But the developing child is not only an individual who learns to define her or his own experience (as Piaget emphasizes). Nor is the child just a unique organism striving to establish a distinct style of life in affective experience (Erikson's emphasis). The child is both—one person in whom the cognitive and the emotional are closely intertwined.[28] Indeed, Piaget's own treatment of cognitive development hinges upon the child's ability to grasp the notion that others in a particular situation may have different viewpoints. The child must take the role of the other. And, though Piaget did not emphasize it, this very role-taking ability depends upon some kind of affective relationship (not necessarily positive) with the other person. Merely a cognitive recognition that the other has a different viewpoint will not move the person to experience the other's role internally.[29]

Second, the levels of moral development are not rigidly demarcated in the individual's experience. They frequently overlap. A child does not dramatically and suddenly move from one stage to the next. The movement will likely be much more irregular—going back and forth between two stages even while showing a noticeable development. In adults as well as children more than one stage is likely to be present in the moral experience at any given time. Nevertheless, there can be a relative fixation in a certain moral stage. For instance, though a person has experienced some development beyond the authoritarian-heteronomous stage, this stage yet may persist as dominant. Throughout adulthood this person characteristically may be morally rigid and authoritarian.

That each of these stages may persist into adulthood can be seen in such a routine matter as automobile driving.[30] At the egocentric level one might drive with rank disregard for others, the major concern being one's own pleasure and the strongest limitation on driving behavior the threat of personal pain or injury. At the second level, one might drive carefully out of fear of the law and the consequences of its infraction. Punishment and reward are dominant sanctions at this heteronomous level. In the stage of reciprocity the driver might express concern both for others and for his or her own reputation; social praise and blame are dominant. Finally, one might drive not depending upon the external law nor the force of public opinion as primary constraints, but principally depending upon one's own inner sanctions in which one finds freedom to respond to novel situations as well as to the routine.

In addition, the different types of moral thinking frequently converge within the same person in a given decision. "It may well be that agreement rather than conflict between modes is the more typical situation. Thus, most of us refrain from stealing from a shop because it is harmful to the shopkeeper and to society; and also because we would go to prison if we were caught; and also because authority is against it; and also because we just feel it wouldn't be right."[31] Thus, when we move to a higher stage of moral development, we do not necessarily leave the lower completely behind. This coexistence of the various stages appears to be not only in agreement with current research evidence but also in accord with our everyday experience. We may be quite unaware of the explanation for the varying types of moral thought patterns within ourselves, but we know they are present. Indeed, "as one grows morally, there is no irreparable jettisoning of earlier 'moralities.' These survive and co-exist with the new."[32]

Third, the work on moral stages suggests certain things about the interaction between the person and the group. Lawrence Kohlberg's cross-cultural study showed not only a similarity in the stages of moral development through which male children and adolescents in different societies grow, but also a similarity in the content of the morality toward which such growth takes place. "Moral development in terms of these stages is a progressive movement toward basing moral judgment on concepts of justice."[33] That affirmation, which we will explore later, raises once again the question whether such cross-cultural commonalities in moral judgments indicate an innate, given moral structure in all persons or whether they might also indicate significant similarities in the formative communal relationships in different cultures.

In any event, it seems that the ability of the person to develop through various stages of moral growth is an interactive phenomenon. Neither the givenness of the person nor the givenness of the social environment can be assumed as simply determinative. However, because the social side of this two-sided coin is our major concern, we turn to the kinds of relationship patterns in which the self is both nourished and sustained.

Socialization and the Quality of Relationships

The question of relationship patterns and group structure has long intrigued the social scientists. Charles Horton Cooley pioneered with his analysis of the primary group: "By primary groups I mean those characterized by intimate face-to-face association and cooperation. They are primary in several senses, but chiefly in that they are fundamental in forming the social nature and ideals of the individual."[34] These are the groups that involve the sort of sympathy and mutual identification best described by a "we" feeling. In contrast, relations in the secondary group (though Cooley himself did not use that term) are impersonal, formal, rational, and contractual. Persons participate with less than their whole range of interests, feelings, and commitments.

While Cooley assumed that primary relationships could exist only in a face-to-face group, others later modified this assumption. Ellsworth Earls pointed out that face-to-face relationships, although often facilitating the growth of the primary relationship, are "more accident than essence." The primary relationship may be minimal within some nuclear families. On the other hand, "even in large and scattered groups—particularly those we call 'social movements'—the struggle for liberty, freedom, justice, or any great cause may call into existence the very experiences and relations which we are able to find in the primary group."[35] A stranger might quickly be recognized as a "soul brother."

There is general agreement upon three basic characteristics of the primary relationship.[36] First, there is an identity of ends: the sharing of a basic common concern or interest including the welfare of other members. The relationship, then, is never regarded simply as a means to another end, but rather is valued in and for itself. Second, the relationship is personal. It is a nontransferable, person-centered relationship with specific individuals. Third, the primary relationship is inclusive. One is valued for one's total personality, not simply for a segment or function of one's life. There is an inclusiveness in the responsibility that persons feel for each other and an inclusiveness in the range of communication and influence, covering seemingly trivial matters as well as important ones.

We ought not to assume that primary relations are necessarily morally superior to secondary relations. The rural village and the suburban friendship group alike may be defensive and provincial. Moreover, in many situations the impersonal relationship is extremely valuable. Much of the work of a complex society would grind to a halt if we were to insist upon primary relationships with all whom we encounter. Certain situations actually require impersonality if fairness and equality of treatment are to be preserved, as is the case in many legal procedures. Our particular attention to the primary relationship is based not upon an assumption of its moral superiority but rather upon our interest in the relationships and groups that most decisively contribute to the self's moral shaping.

The primary relationship is of crucial significance both to socialization generally and to moral socialization in particular. Here norms of behavior are first internalized and the capacity to interpret the expectations of others is first developed. After childhood, it is still in primary relationships that norms and interpretations of expectations are either reinforced or changed. The directions of influence vary. We might join a particular political party because it seems to embody attitudes congenial to those in which we have been nurtured. Or we might get politically involved because of social contacts and friendship patterns and then later find ourselves agreeing with certain views initially at variance with our own.

A second way in which the primary relationship affects the person's attitudes and values is through its impact upon the sense of self-identity, a subject we shall explore more fully in chapter 5.

While some social scientists emphasize the critically formative childhood years, abundant evidence indicates that one's sense of identity is continuously affected by one's primary relations throughout life in supportive, modifying, and transforming ways. In his classic study of young adult gang life, William F. Whyte furnishes an illustration. Long John found his identity in the Norton Street gang as "Doc's pal." When Doc left the Nortons for Spongi's gang, Long John lost this identification and became subject to derision by both gangs. His self-confidence suffered, and his bowling, once a prized skill, deteriorated. Not until Doc saw to it that Long John was once more identified as "Doc's pal" by both the Nortons and the Spongis were Long John's difficulties alleviated.[37]

Third, every primary relationship guides behavior through the establishment of patterned relationships and relatively stable ways of dealing with other persons. A family develops a certain style of life and certain habit patterns. Family members know what to expect from one another in recurring types of situations. Just as important, they each know how the others respond to those outside the family, and these patterned responses in turn affect each family member. Something similar is true of some church congregations, neighborhood groups, and work groups. These patterned relationships provide stability of interaction and a sense of continuity. Giving the member a sense of security, the group can either inhibit novel responses to new situations or it can equip its members for a creative freedom.

A fourth function of the primary group is that of reinterpreting goals and rules, adapting them to the special circumstances and capacities of individual group members. Elton Mayo's well-known study of the Western Electric Hawthorne Works makes the point. The factory management set production standards that did not take into account the small, primary working group. The small group in "the Bank Wiring Room" had no direct access to management officials, but it could and did control the production of its individual members in order to protect the slower worker and exercise some control over its own situation. Mayo concluded, "In every department that continues to operate, the workers have—whether aware of it or not—formed themselves into a group with appropriate customs, duties, routines, even rituals; and management succeeds (or fails) in proportion as it is accepted without reservation by the group as authority and leader."[38] This reinterpretation and adjustment of larger group goals and rules by the smaller primary group is not limited to the industrial scene. It is a common phenomenon of group life and a common function of every moral community.

Fifth, and similarly, the primary group mediates the individual's belonging to a larger society. Indeed, "most [persons] are members of the larger society by virtue of identifications which are mediated through the human beings with whom they have personal relations. Many are bound into the larger society only by primary group identifications. Only a small proportion possessing special training or particular kinds of personalities are capable of giving a preponderant share of their attention and concern to the symbols of the larger world."[39] One study of the Wehrmacht after World War II concluded that even when German victory had become doubtful, an individual soldier, though pessimistic about the war's outcome, could still have strong fighting motivation. That motivation apparently came not so much from the soldier's political convictions as from the steady satisfaction of his primary personality needs in his squad and platoon.[40] A different research team studying the American soldier came to similar conclusions. The behavioral influence of the small group was paramount. Here the individual felt security and belonging; here was pressure toward "masculinity"; here were those who would look out for him in a tough situation; here was a code of loyalty, deeply internalized.[41] Though comparable research has yet to be done on the Vietnam war, evidence suggests a similar phenomenon, made all the more striking by the widespread doubts concerning the war's justification.

In short, the primary relationship is crucial to the socialization process throughout life. Here we develop ways of interpreting others' expectations, we internalize and reinterpret our norms, we achieve and modify our self-images. Within the primary relationship our behavior achieves some consistency through patterned responses. Here our unique needs and circumstances are considered by the group, and through this relationship we relate to the larger societies of our lives.

Yet the primary relationship is an "ideal type," as is the secondary group. Neither actually exists in purity. The most personal groups need structure, and the most formalized, rationalized groups crumble without the cohesion of some inner primary relationships. However, groups do differ in terms of the type of relationship that is dominant within them. Further, we should be aware of the interpenetration of primary and secondary groups. A particular family in our society may still be strongly primary in its inner relationships; it may still be, in Cooley's phrase, "the nursery of human nature." The nuclear family, however, is never an independent society. It is a small and highly differentiated subsystem of a larger society wherein parents are not only parents but are persons with other social roles necessary to their functioning as socializers of their children. Parents are selective in the transmission of culture to their children, and what they transmit will be deeply conditioned by those groups (many of which are secondary groups) to which they in some way belong. Further, parents introduce their children to more inclusive membership groups—to neighborhoods, wider kinship circles, schools, churches, and the like.[42]

The plurality of socializing groups suggests our using an additional concept familiar to the social sciences: the reference group. The individual, after all, is not socialized by a single group such as the family, nor is the person socialized by "culture" in some diffuse sense. Rather, one is socialized by a plurality of groups to which one is related in varying ways and which likewise are related to the broader social structure in varying ways.[43]

The Meaning and Efficacy
of Reference Groups

For many years, social psychologists have spoken of "frames of reference" as those perceptual contexts supplied by our previous experience, contexts through which we see and interpret new situations. Seldom if ever do we perceive persons, objects, or situations "raw." But such frames of reference are not disembodied clusters of ideas. We are social selves, and our weightiest attitudes and principal experiences of self-understanding are clearly linked with those groups with which we most strongly identify. These recognitions lie behind the development of reference-group theory in American social psychology within the past several decades.[44]

In addition, the sheer fact of our complex, pluralistic society has given rise to the use of the reference-group concept. We are mobile people, and we live with multiple social loyalties. Not infrequently the perspectives and norms of our different groups fail to mesh smoothly in our decision making. Why certain groups become particularly important to us in certain types of decisions, what happens when our group-anchored attitudes clash—such questions as these (important for ethics as well as for social psychology)—can be illuminated by reference-group theory.

Many groups are formed in order to achieve certain specific goals. When the group has taken shape, however, new motives and goals arise that contribute to its maintenance. The very fact of belonging to the group may provide its member with a sense of being somebody, of having a place in the scheme of things. A prestigious position within the group enhances this feeling. Loyalties and responsibilities to specific members of the group take their place alongside the member's concern for the group's initial cause. All these aspects may enhance the group's reference effect, and the group-related attitudes may increasingly become part of the member's self-concept.[45]

Though lacking regular interaction with a specific group, one may well define oneself as part of it because of agreement with its aims, attitudes, and behavior patterns, and perhaps also because of the aspiration to be recognized someday as a member. This too can be a reference group for the individual, though there is general agreement that "it is the groups of which one is [already] a member that most often and most prominently affect one's behavior."[46]

Further, reference groups have two major functions: the normative function and the comparison function. In its normative function, the group sets and enforces norms upon its members. It is in the position to do this when it has the power to reward or to punish. In its comparison function, the group serves as a standard that the member uses for self-evaluation and for the evaluation of others. Usually both functions will be served by the same group, especially when it is a membership group.[47]

What characterizes those groups which seem to have the strongest reference effect?[48] First, the group's definition of membership is relatively clear rather than vague. In social psychological experiments Roman Catholic college students typically have reflected the official norms of their church more closely than have

Protestant and Jewish students, especially when given subtle but vivid reminders of their religious belonging. They simply have appeared to have greater clarity about both the norms of their church and the meaning of membership in it.[49]

The norms of a strong reference group, in the second place, are likely to be broad in scope, applying to a wide range of human attitudes and activities. The group, further, is likely to encourage considerable intensity of personal involvement. We might expect those churches whose definition of religious concern encompasses a wide range of human activity to have more reference effect for their members than churches whose religious norms are narrowly defined, if the intensity of involvement is relatively equal in the types of groups.

A third significant factor is the duration of the expected membership in the group. The longer one expects to belong, the greater reference effect the group will have. The junior executive anticipating frequent job transfers will less likely be influenced by the "local expectations" of the church in Garden City than will the person of lifelong membership there. Nevertheless, the transient young executive may be just as influenced by the more universal membership expectations that the Garden City church shares with the Bayview church from which that person transferred last year.

Fourth, the size of the group is important, both its "absolute size" (the number of members) and its "completeness" (the ratio of its actual to its potential membership participation). In absolute size, effective groups are usually small enough to afford significant personal interaction. Accordingly, the church whose thousand members have little personal interaction beyond their fleeting contacts at the weekly worship services will have less reference effect than another church of a thousand, most of whose members are lively participants in small mission groups. As to relative completeness, we might expect the church of a thousand members, three hundred of whom are actively involved in the congregation's life, to be weaker in effect than the church of three hundred and fifty members, three hundred of whom are active.

In the fifth place, the more cohesive the group, the greater its reference effect. Cohesion itself may result from factors such as the degree to which the group's norms are internalized, the nature of the organizational structure, and the way in which the group interacts with others in its social environment. Thus, a "cohesive" church would be one whose members have significantly internalized its belief system, whose organizational structure clearly encourages faithful behavior on the part of members, and whose corporate style of life is sufficiently distinctive so that it is distinguishable from other groups in the community.

A sixth characteristic of the effective reference group is that it will expect a fairly high degree of conformity to its norms. The congregation that gives clear signs of expecting its members to act in certain ways will have a stronger reference effect than the one that assumes that most members will not take too seriously its behavioral expectations. But a group need not be coercive to be effective. "The representative fact of conformity is the conformity of members whose very sense of self-identity, sense of pride, sense of security, sense of achievement are derived, in no small degree, from the fact of belongingness in a group with a definite status and role within it. This being the case, in their eyes conformity to the group norms is not perceived as an act of coercion imposed from the outside. It is their group, their norm."[50]

Seventh, the effective reference group tends to have a high degree of visibility or observability. Behavior patterns within the group are readily open to observation by others. Thus, the church member whose varied daily behaviors are observed by other members may well find the church a stronger influence than would the person whose daily routine is quite removed from others in the local congregation.

One last property, difficult to describe with precision, is the attractiveness of the group to the individual. While the acceptance one feels is usually important in the group's attractiveness, individuals vary in their needs for certain types of group acceptance. James E. Dittes's work suggests that the lower the person's self-esteem, the greater the need for group acceptance and hence the greater influence the accepting group will have.[51] Other research also suggests that feeling strongly accepted can give a member freedom to deviate from the group's consensus when it appears that such deviation will be for the group's own good.[52] Thus it appears that churches characterized by warmth and acceptance will have greater reference-group power. In one way this applies to members of lower self-esteem. In another sense it suggests that the member whose acceptance security in the congregation is high will have the freedom to speak "the prophetic word."

We live with many social loyalties and memberships. In some situations, obviously, we will feel discord among them. What is the evidence concerning reference group *conflict?* The research, although still limited, suggests several directions.

For one thing, "the substantively pertinent group" is not invariably the reference group on a particular issue.[53] Common sense might assume that the labor union will always furnish the frame of reference for a member's economic outlook because, after all, this is that individual's major economic reference group. Quite possibly, however, that person's church might furnish a more powerful frame of reference on certain economic issues; it is equally possible that the union might provide the interpretive framework for some "religious" issues.

Further, social psychologists agree that some groups are segmentally rather than totally relevant to an individual's values. "To a considerable extent individuals may invest different groups with relevance for different values."[54] Thus, one researcher found subjects dominantly influenced by their occupational groups in regard to standards of success but influenced by other groups, usually close friends, in the evaluation of ethical standards and moral behavior.[55]

Importantly, groups with a high degree of primary relationships tend to have a more powerful reference effect than do secondary groups in conflict situations. One study of several community disasters (tornadoes, refinery explosions, etc.) discloses that most individuals thought and acted first in terms of their families and close friends, whereas a minority, especially those in positions of responsibility, put the wider community first.[56] Reinforcement of attitudes through continued interaction in close relationships is of signal importance. Theodore Newcomb's celebrated Bennington College studies demonstrate the power of intense interaction to nurture attitude changes and of continued interaction with like minds to sustain changed attitudes.[57]

In brief, most current research strongly points to the importance of prolonged and intensive primary-group interaction if a group's reference effect is to be strong, pertinent, and inclusive for its member. This, of course, should apply to churches as well as to other human groups. But greater clarity on groups and attitude conflicts may come as we look in the next chapter at social interaction from another vantage point—role theory.

5

Roles and Identity

Roles and Their Acquisition

The conception of society as a stage with individuals taking roles in the social drama—a familiar literary idea for hundreds of years—in recent years has found new currency in social psychology.[1] Nevertheless, role theory has yet to be applied with seriousness in ethics, even though moral decisions certainly are affected by our roles and many experiences of moral conflict are also role conflicts.[2]

Like reference-group theory, role theory is a fairly recent outgrowth of earlier work on socialization. Whereas the former focuses upon the group's influence on its member or aspirant to membership, role theory looks at the person's behavior by inquiring into the positions he or she occupies in various groups and social structures. Its basic proposition is that "human behavior is in part a function of the positions that an individual occupies and the expectations held for incumbents of these positions."[3] The links between roles and reference groups may be quite obvious. Only by membership in groups do we have roles, and thus our roles take place within groups that frequently are reference groups for us. Moreover, while society has definitions of the various common roles, the details of interpretation and performance of roles will be affected by our reference groups.[4]

The advantages of role theory are several. We can see the ways in which persons relate to their roles and the ways in which those roles relate to their broader social involvements. Role theory can also draw our attention to the manner in which personalities are related to the structure of their environments. "By playing roles, the individual participates in a social world. By internalizing these roles, the same world becomes subjectively real to [the person]."[5] Furthermore, role theory can enrich our understanding of attitudes and attitude change. While we choose some of our roles because of certain prior attitudes, it is also true that changes in roles bring consequent changes in attitudes.[6]

Definitions of role vary among social psychologists. Some define roles as *normative* cultural patterns: what a person in a particular social position ought to do. According to others, it is the individual's *interpretation* of the position. A third possibility is role as the *actual behavior* of persons occupying certain social positions. A suitable and sufficiently comprehensive definition for our purposes might be this: a role is a set of expectations and evaluative standards applied to a person occupying a particular social position, together with her or his own interpretation of those expectations and standards. Note that this includes both the normative dimension (because Betty is a doctor, she *ought* to put patient welfare ahead of financial gain) and the predictive (because Fred is a father of small boys, he *will* be interested in my story). Moreover, expectations may include notions of the self as well as the self's actions. ("Yes, I agree that clergy these days ought to make more home calls, but more important than that I think they ought to be more spiritual.")

Lest a discussion of role theory make those concerned about Christian ethics nervous because of suspected deterministic implications, let us be clear about several things. First, there is seldom a pure consensus on role expectations. Nevertheless, the presence of disagreement (for example, in a congregation about the minister's role) ought not to blind us to the fact that without some basic agreement no role performance would be possible, and a state of social anomie would exist.[7] Neither does role theory necessarily imply that the individual is only the sum of his or her roles, nor does it suggest that role expectations eliminate individual creativity in role enactment. There are instances, of course, when a role appears to be all-absorbing: in certain politicians, clergy, and entertainment stars there seems to be little to the person beyond the role. More commonly, however, our involvement in roles varies greatly, from casual enactment to high intensity.[8]

Roles and personalities are mutually interactive. A "strong performance" may change the nature of the role (as Franklin D.

Roosevelt changed the nature of the presidency). Likewise, important roles do not leave the personality unaffected.[9] In short, it is clear that role behavior is never fully automatic. It is always personal, even when it is not original. Finally, role theory cannot account for all behavior. It has the more legitimately modest yet important function of drawing our attention to the ways that our behaviors and personalities (including our moralities and our moral selves) are influenced by the positions we hold in social groups and structures.

Much I have said earlier about socialization applies also to the person's acquisition of roles. Roles are learned through both intentional instruction and informal learning. A woman learns the role of a lawyer by going to law school. Also important, however, are her observations of lawyers at work, her perceptions of the expectations of the bar, and her interpretations of what people expect of lawyers in both their professional roles and in their community lives.

The choice of roles, further, is often a combination of personal decisions and capacities and of social needs. Social systems have personnel requirements, and there is a considerable interpenetration between the organization of individual personalities and that of the social system. But this interpenetration works not simply in encouraging certain personality types to accept particular roles. It is also, according to Talcott Parsons, "part of the process of shaping different types of personality which are differentially adapted to different types of role."[10]

Robert K. Merton has shown how the role of the career person in the large bureaucracy has an undeniable influence upon that individual's personality. Bureaucrats are expected to (and largely do) adapt their thoughts, feelings, and actions to the prospect of extended careers in the organization. Many develop a style of life that allows them to function with the greatest possible ease and the least strain in their work. This ethos seems to affect more, however, than just "the occupation part" of these persons, for they find it increasingly difficult to divorce themselves from it during their off-hours; it becomes part of their personalities.[11] Some social psychologists call this "role salience": "the more salient a role the greater will be [the] 'investment' in it and its components, the more will [these persons] tend to organize [their] 'view of things' around it, the more will [they] strive to augment its clarity, the more will [they] tend to resist change in it once cognitively organized and, hence, the more will it tend to dominate [their] behavior."[12]

Role Conflicts and Their Resolution

Most of us, most of the time, seem to manage our various roles without undue conflict.[13] Many of our roles are included in the norms commonly shared by one group. Though we may have several different family roles (spouse, parent, child), we usually can shift fairly smoothly from one to the other because the family shares certain norms that govern its members' behavior in various situations. Further, some roles seldom overlap. They are called forth in different groups and at different times. And we may keep certain roles apart by putting them into logic-tight compartments, seeing them in different frames of reference.

Nevertheless, we all experience role conflicts some of the time, and as society grows more complex the opportunities for role conflict increase. Role conflict is simply a person's perception of incompatible behavioral expectations. Such conflicts (while variously categorized by different social psychologists) appear to be of three basic types.[14] First, *inter-role conflicts* are experienced between or among two or more of the roles that a person occupies. The military chaplain is both an ordained minister and a military officer, and some chaplains are keenly aware of various conflicts between these two roles.[15] Second, in "intra-role conflicts" a person experiences conflicting expectations from different persons or groups about *one* particular role. School superintendents can be caught in a cross fire of conflicting expectations on a particular issue; students, parents, teachers, and the school board may each have different expectations, and there may be factions within these groups. Third, there may be "personality-role conflicts" in which we simply object to the expectations we perceive. A minister may see her role in quite a different light from the expectations she interprets from her parishioners and denominational officials. In addition to role conflicts, of course, there are simply situations of role ambiguity in which a person perceives no clear consensus about expectations and has no clear idea of the role itself.

According to current evidence, there are several major ways in which we handle our role conflicts. First, we can give *centrality to one of the roles.* Indeed, this may be the most important method of conflict resolution for a great many people. Analyzing the conflicts between military chaplains' roles as officers and as ordained ministers, one researcher found that in the majority of cases the role of officer provided the chaplain's major focus. The role that provides the primary identification for the individual will take first place in the hierarchy of role obligations the person perceives and responds to.[16] Other researchers have arrived at similar conclusions: "There seems to be a *major role* to which one must commit [oneself] in order to determine [the] action at choice points, despite contrary expectations attaching to other roles [one] may simultaneously occupy."[17]

We may handle role conflict also by *compartmentalizing* our roles. We choose to avoid the conflict by deciding that the roles do not really overlap after all—each of them is valid in its own place. And we often find allies by assuming that almost everyone else also perceives the two roles in quite different frames of reference: "After all, everyone knows that religion and politics, like oil and water, don't mix."

Third, we may try to *compromise* in the attempt to conform, at least in part, to the differing expectations. Just how this compromise is shaped will depend upon our views of the legitimacy of the varying expectations and the possibility of negative sanctions, as well as our own personal orientations. The school superintendent is expected by the teachers to work for their maximal salary increase and by the school board to keep increases to the minimum. In the face of these expectations, the superintendent may decide to be a reconciler or an agent of compromise. The point is, however, that this person is not simply deciding on a course of action but also is claiming a role identity.[18]

Finally, *escape* is a way of dealing with role conflict. The shop steward, unable any longer to stand the pressures from both above and below, may choose to go back to the assembly line. The rural physician with family life deteriorating because of long hours away from home may move to the city for more regular hours in a clinic practice. Escape from role conflict has many other forms besides occupational and geographical change: food or sleep, drugs or alcohol, physical or mental illness, even suicide.[19]

Although there are others, these appear to be the main patterns of role-conflict resolution, and the "major role" hypothesis seems to have the greatest support among the social psychologists.[20] Yet the fact that I may identify most fully with one of my roles does not exclude other modes of conflict reduction. I may interpret my roles as parent, church member, and citizen in terms of my role as business executive. In this very process, however, I may also compartmentalize the other roles, thus for example defining my parent role narrowly so that it does not conflict with my role in the corporation.

A possible objection arises. When we speak of a person's major role as that in which the individual is most intensively involved, are we not simply pointing to her or his personality? After all, do not persons of particular personality types choose certain kinds of roles in which to express themselves? While role choices are undoubtedly influenced by personality, persuasive evidence still suggests that personalities, attitudes, and behaviors are also influenced by significant roles. Thus, research indicates that industrial workers elevated to positions of shop steward undergo significant changes in attitudes toward management and their companion workers, and when they later return to their original work roles (for reasons not directly connected with attitudinal changes) they move back toward their original attitudes.[21] Perhaps both the change in reference groups and the need for self-consistency are at work in this phenomenon. Such a change in roles does involve a change in reference groups. Since at the same time it involves a change in work functions, it is quite plausible that the person's need for self-consistency is being expressed through having attitudes internally consistent with one's work patterns.[22]

Further, it would be an error to look simply at individual personality without considering the group in which we find our major roles. Such a group has a great deal to do with the role's attractiveness, for when the sense of cohesiveness is strong and our sense of belonging great, our motivation to engage in the role intensely is correspondingly strong. Group members stimulate each other as they visibly demonstrate their own motivation to take their roles in "proper" ways. Frequently there is a spiraling effect: the person gets caught up in the group's expectations, and "what happens under these circumstances is that what the individual *wants* to do and what he [or she] perceives as *demanded* by [the] role come to be identical."[23]

Another connection between the major role idea and reference-group theory is this: our roles in more *inclusive* groups tend to provide the dominant frame of reference for us.[24] In the lifestyle of my social class I find clues to a wide range of situations. But the more inclusive group may not be numerically the largest. Often it is not. I may define what it means to be "a good American" by reference to the behavior and attitudes of my social class. Not that I never encounter other social classes that might enlarge my frame of reference, but my primary groups and my daily communication are concentrated within my own. Hence, a shared frame of reference easily leads to the illusion of universality: other groups are, or at least *should* be, as "we" are.

The basic proposition of role theory—that our attitudes and actions are influenced by the expectations we perceive through our various social positions—is sound. Social interaction is not the only influence on human behavior, and role theory is not an adequate interpretation of all social interaction. Nevertheless, it draws our attention to certain factors important to Christian ethics, factors that we might otherwise overlook.

Identity and
Its Acquisition

Albert Einstein once said, "If my theory is successful, the Germans will claim that I am a German and the Swiss will say I am a Swiss. But if it were to fail, the Swiss would say I was a German and the Germans would say I was a Jew."[25] The social dimensions of our identities are clearly important. Further, the importance of identity in human behavior (and hence to the study of ethics) is great. We take our personal identities so much for granted that we do not realize the extent to which our lives are structured by the conceptions we form of ourselves. Those things we do voluntarily, in some cases even involuntarily, depend on the assumptions we make about the kind of persons we are and about the way we fit into the scheme of things in our worlds.[26] Indeed, personal identification is fundamental to organized social life. In meeting strangers, without knowing *who* they are (including what their important roles are and how they interpret them), we lack clues for meaningful conversation.

While there are a variety of definitions of identity in social psychology, one that reflects rather general agreement might be this:

identity is the appropriation of and commitment to a particular self-conception or series of self-conceptions. The implications of this are several. First, our emphasis will be upon identity's *social* dimensions, the "con-" in self-conception.[27] We need not assume that identity describes the totality of the person. Identity emphasizes (in Mead's terms) the "me," the person's structured self-awareness. Remember, however, that there is an active, dynamic "I" or ego always present as well. A person *is* an "I" or an ego. The person *has* a "me," a self, an identity.[28] Bearing this distinction in mind, we can say that "identity is socially bestowed, socially sustained and socially transformed."[29]

Further, identity as self-conception is not simply cognitive ideas about oneself. Along with how we perceive ourselves there is also the important *value* dimension—how we value ourselves in relation to others. In addition, both *continuity* and *change* are present. One psychologist can rightly describe identity as "a subjective sense of an invigorating sameness and continuity."[30] Just as truly, another writes: "Once formed it is not immutable throughout life. . . . Throughout life, as the individual acquires new social ties, new roles, and changed status, because of . . . accomplishments or . . . age, the self system does change and must change if [the person] is to behave consistently in terms of . . . altered relationships and responsibilities."[31]

The acquisition of identity is always a *social* phenomenon. We need identity tags to distinguish ourselves from other individuals, and we need those other persons in order to distinguish ourselves. "It is implicit that a contribution to George being George is the fact that John is John."[32]

Communication is of immense significance, as we have seen. "The use of language is the most important mechanism of interpersonal conduct and the major source of knowledge of ourselves."[33] Such language involves not only the verbal communication of ideas but also the nonverbal sharing of feelings and meanings. As I communicate with another I become more real to myself as well as to the other, and the capacity of this communication to give form and structure to my subjectivity lasts far beyond the actual face-to-face situation. Truly, we must talk about ourselves until we know ourselves.[34] Furthermore, communication is a *group* phenomenon. If a group is to act in concert it must have a common terminology, for "the direction of activity depends upon the particular ways that objects are classified."[35] When we name and classify persons and things we arouse expectations that have to do with our relationships with each other in both memory and anticipation. It is, then, through communication in groups that we have the principal source of self-knowledge.

Beyond this emphasis on communication (an accent shared with socialization concepts), current identity theory emphasizes several additional elements in the self's formation process. One is *selectivity in the "generalized other."* Mead saw the person responding rather indiscriminately to a generalized other that was a communal composite of evaluations of the self. Now we realize, however, that persons are more selective. We tend to value the self-images we already possess and hence respond to those who either reinforce and confirm that self-image or offer us one even more favorable. This very selectivity in our choice of significant others is a mark of freedom. Our reference groups and roles provide limitations in our identities, but not determinations.[36]

Further, recent work has emphasized *the historical dimensions of our identities,* an important emphasis not clearly recognized earlier. Anselm Strauss rightly notes: "Identities imply not merely personal histories but also social histories. . . . Individuals hold membership in groups that themselves are products of a past. If you wish to understand persons—their development and their relations with significant others—you must be prepared to view them as embedded in historical context."[37] This is true not only for one with a vivid awareness of Irish ancestors, it is also true for one trying anxiously to reject a rural background in the quest for urban sophistication.

We need *identity confirmation.* Because our identities are acquired in social interaction, they must be sustained in social interaction. The congregation's presence at a wedding or a baptism testifies to this. In these events new identities are being recognized, and the community is being called upon to sustain these persons "from this day forward" in such identities. Language is important in identity confirmation as well as in its acquisition. Names, labels, uniforms, titles, ranks—we have a variety of confirming symbols that remind us who we are.

Beyond that, communities develop "symbolic universes," articulated bodies of tradition by which the community interprets that which is particularly real for it.[38] The family has its own lore, its heirlooms, its private language and jokes. The church has its scripture, its particular doctrinal interpretations, its sacramental symbols, its peculiar localized traditions. Such symbol systems are "universes" in the sense that they tend to present their versions of reality as inevitable and encompassing, if not necessarily exclusive. "There may be other ways to be a family member, but this is *our* way."

We receive identity confirmation from "insignificant others," too. While we need the explicit, emotion-laden identity confirmations our significant others bestow upon us, even everyday "contacts" and casual acquaintances will confirm or modify our sense of who we are.[39] The successful white male executive's deferential treatment from his barber and from the commuter-train conductor reinforces his sense of identity. In comparison, persons marginalized for racial, ethnic, or sexual reasons may invest much more importance in their significant (and positive) others; nevertheless the condescension they receive from casual acquaintances or total strangers has an impact upon their identities, particularly if such experiences are numerous.

The importance of ongoing identity confirmation reminds us of the unfinished quality of selfhood. True, as more psychoanalytically oriented theorists emphasize, there are certain stages in a person's developmental sequence that are more crucial than others. Nevertheless Erik Erikson can say, "While the end of adolescence . . . is the stage of an overt crisis, identity formation neither begins nor ends with adolescence: it is a lifelong development largely unconscious to the individual and to . . . society."[40] Identity, then, "is never gained nor maintained once and for all. Like a 'good conscience,' it is constantly lost and regained."[41]

Identity and
the Moral Life

While there is no simple agreement among the psychologists of identity regarding its moral implications, several persistent themes in this literature are suggestive. First there is *the person's quest for consistency*. Erikson maintains that, although the development of a focused ego identity is crucial in the adolescent stage, such striving continues throughout adult life. In adolescence we see most dramatically the perils in the person's search for consistency. Adolescents are threatened by "identity diffusion"—strong doubts about who they really are. In order to keep themselves together, they may temporarily overidentify with cliques and crowds, stereotyped heroes and enemies, almost to the point of seeming to lose their own identity. The intolerance, so frequently evident in adolescence, may be a necessary defense against this identity diffusion: "It is difficult to be tolerant if deep down you are not quite sure that you are a man or woman, that you will ever grow together again and be attractive, that you will be able to master your drives, that you really know who you are."[42]

But the threat of identity diffusion is painful, and the adolescent is tempted to escape this confusion through "identity foreclosure." Foreclosure is premature integration. It is the hasty espousal of inadequate self-conceptions—hasty because the young person is fleeing the anxieties of diffusion, inadequate because such foreclosed self-conceptions are truncated and premature, inadequate to the mature adult identity. Indeed, foreclosure in personal identity is often analogous to totalitarianism in society.[43]

Successful avoidance of prolonged identity diffusion or foreclosure usually depends upon an "identity moratorium," according to Erikson. This is a time for experimentation. Basic decisions about one's identity are temporarily postponed so that various identities may be tested. While exceptional individuals may establish their own moratoria, most of us require some kind of community sanctioned moratorium to handle the threats of diffusion and foreclosure successfully.[44]

Although the achievement of identity integration is the particular task of adolescence, the experience of diffusion and foreclosure its particular perils, and identity moratoria its particular need, these are by no means limited to young people. In all human beings there is a constant striving for ego identity, even when such seldom appears to us as a direct goal of our activities.[45]

Second, *the nature of values and the process of valuation*—topics we usually associate with ethics—concern the social psychologist as well. Language involves classification, the establishment of the identities of beings with whom or with which we interact, and this process of classification itself involves valuation, the assessment of the quality or worth of our experienced relationships. One social psychologist concludes (in words strikingly similar to relational ethics): "Value is not an element; it has to do with a relationship between the object and the person who experiences the object. This is just another way of stating that the 'essence' or 'nature' of the object resides not in the object but in the relation between it and the namer."[46] Since no identities are static, the process of valuation is continuous, a built-in feature of social interaction.

Further, there is an emphasis upon *the situational dimension of both identities and values.* In organizing our responses to situations, we not only classify and evaluate others (give them identities), we also establish our own identities. "Establishment of one's own identity to oneself is as important in interaction as establishing it for the other. One's own identity in a situation is not absolutely given but is more or less problematic."[47] This situational need to establish our own identities is a significant point frequently omitted from expositions of behavior, perhaps because it is only in the unusual situation that we become aware of identity confusion and paralysis of action. Yet our lack of awareness of this in the familiar situation does not mean that the process is absent—we are just not conscious of it.

Values, like identities, are not entirely habitual. They too must be continually established. Whereas commitment to certain values does, indeed, affect our responses to new situations, it is never quite as simple as merely applying these values in the decision confronting us. Another social psychologist observes, "Metaphorically put, the operation of values in the formulation of responses to situations is *advisory*, not *executive*."[48] The situations before us are infused with memories and hopes. Through language we can conceptualize remembered relationships as values and devise new and desired possibilities of relationship. But "without the binding thread of identity, one could not evaluate the succession of situations."[49]

Motivation is a fourth ethically significant theme in identity theory. As Mead observed long ago, we learn more roles than we actually use. We need to learn others' roles as well as our own, so that we can interpret the social interactions in which we are involved. However, we limit our own behaviors to a few roles that we define particularly as our own. Nelson Foote adds: "And [we] can only ascertain which role is [ours] in each situation by knowing who [we are]. Moreover, [we] must know who [we are] with considerable conviction and clarity, if [our] behavior is to exhibit definiteness and force, which is to say, degree of motivation."[50]

When we are confused about our identities in a given situation, our motivation becomes similarly confused and, in extreme instances, our ability to act may become paralyzed.

Max Weber's concept "vocabularies of motive" also assists us. Weber pointed out that a motive is a term in a vocabulary that appears to us or to an observer to be an adequate reason for our particular conduct. The social character of motivation becomes obvious when we realize that we use vocabularies of motives understandable and acceptable to persons (including ourselves) to whom we are explaining our behavior.[51] Nevertheless, Freud's question—Is this the real motive?—must still be faced. Hans Gerth and C. Wright Mills note that although there is often a disparity between the real motive and the person's conscious vocabulary of motives, "the more deeply internalized in the person, and the more closely integrated with the psychic structure a vocabulary of motives is, the greater chance that it contains 'the real motives.'"[52]

Motivated activity is always goal-directed activity in some sense, and it always has an important social dimension. Ends can be sought individually, but they cannot be sought individualistically. Strauss comments, "Notions of what constitute social or artistic success, how to get there, how to recognize the benchmarks of progress, whom to emulate and spurn, how to display to significant others the current point of arrival—all of these are widely shared by other persons who are anything but isolated from one another, communicatively speaking."[53]

Popular moral discourse abounds in suggestions that link identity and moral behavior closely together. "Big boys don't cry." "Good Americans support the President in foreign policy." "If I am a Christian, I must do this." There are, of course, legitimate and important distinctions between social psychology and ethics. Nevertheless, these identity explorations can help us understand how our identities are dynamically related to our decisional situations, to the values that we use, to the motivations that empower our acts—and, significantly, how all of these find their foundation in the groups of which we are part and that are part of us.

Part 3
ETHICAL REFLECTIONS

6

Dialogue on Community, Identity, and Morality

Beginning in the mid-sixties the Farmington Trust Research Unit (a British team of experts in philosophy, psychology, and sociology) began their work on problems of moral education. After considerable research, they arrived at a phenomenological listing of "moral components"—abilities that ought to be characteristic of every "morally educated person." They maintain that the morally educated person: (a) should be able to *identify with other people*, in the sense of having their interests and feelings count equally with one's own; (b) should have *insight into feelings*, one's own and those of others; (c) needs *a mastery of relevant factual knowledge*, including a reasonably clear idea of the probable consequences of one's actions in light of the facts of the situation; (d) needs the ability to combine the above—identification with others, awareness of feelings, and factual knowledge—into *formulations of principles* that relate to other people's interests and to one's own; (e) should have the ability to *translate these principles into action*.[1]

From a theological perspective much more needs to be said, yet Christian ethics must be concerned with no less than these components. Hence, this listing furnishes a useful springboard into our further dialogue with the social psychologists.

The Moral Community

Whatever else may be said about the church, it is by theological definition a personal fellowship, centered in the relations of personal beings, God and human beings. Its members are enmeshed in personal obligations. The rough parallel in the social sciences for such a relationship is, of course, the primary group. This leads us to the first affirmation of this dialogue: *the church functions as a moral community when it has a sufficient quality of primary relationship to nurture certain capacities needed in morally mature persons.* Perhaps this is so basic that it is just assumed in much Christian ethical reflection, yet a relational approach must insist upon its importance. The ability to identify with others, the capacity to have insights into personal feelings, the achievement of adequate personal security so we might use moral principles and rules without being enslaved by them—such capacities as these are developed only in certain kinds of interpersonal relationships. What we call these capacities is not in itself important. In the ethical literature they might be "virtues," whereas the psychologists of moral development might call them "moral preconditions." Whatever the name, any adequate definition of moral maturity assumes their existence.

If the church is to nurture such personal security, sensitivity, and willingness to identify with others, it is not enough simply to speak about these, important though their articulation. It is also necessary to *be* that kind of primary fellowship that affords ongoing and extensive personal communication in a framework of mutual trust and concern. Whether most Christian churches do in fact tend to exhibit this kind of community is a question we must face later; now we simply affirm this as a quality of moral community that Christians in common with all other persons need.

A second affirmation, and on the surface a very obvious one, is this: the church as moral community is *the bearer of a moral ethos and tradition.* Unlike the previous one, this affirmation is clearly emphasized in virtually all the literature of Christian ethics. Nevertheless, the social psychologists have now pointed out some ways in which moral ethos and traditions function, processes seldom examined by the ethicists.

One of these, taken from the studies of moral development, is the necessity of an articulated moral tradition for a person's growth toward moral independence and maturity. This affirmation is an important correction of Jean Piaget's thought. Piaget saw the stage of "heteronomy" in almost completely negative terms. It was a stage of unquestioning obedience to moral norms from authoritative sources—in the child's case, from the parents. Norman Bull rightly comments, however, "While Piaget borrowed the term 'heteronomy' from Kant, he did not also take over the philosopher's conviction that heteronomy is an essential apprenticeship in the moral craft."[2]

The Christian moral tradition may be used in an authoritarian manner, in which case it imprisons the self in a stage of immaturity. But this misuse should not blind us to the recognition that an articulated ethos, even a code of rules, is essential if there is to be any growth toward moral maturity at all.[3] In addition to its restraint upon our sin and its guidance in responsible behavior, the Protestant Reformers saw the moral law as driving us to repentance. It is significant that present-day psychologists link such repentance with the whole notion of moral identity: those who have not discovered the capacity to feel guilty have not discovered their own identities—the reality of themselves in relationship to others.[4]

Social science and Christian ethics agree upon a third affirmation: *The church as moral community contributes to the shape of its members' identities.* This takes us beyond the usual language of moral socialization. It is not only norms and principles that are internalized, important though these be. Nor is it even meanings and ethos. Beyond these, self-concepts and identities are crucial to our decision making. Indeed, our identities are problematical as long as any decisional situation is problematical. And personal identities are products of our relational and group experiences. Groups are not unconnected islands. Just as the family's impact as a socializing community depends upon its relation to other parts of society, so also does the church's.

The church lives in manifold interdependence with other groups, constantly penetrating others with its influences and being penetrated by them. If such were not the case, it would be difficult to see how the church could be a socializing community of any importance at all. If the sheer quantity of time spent by individuals in regular church gatherings is compared to that spent in other primary relationships (family, friendship circles, work groups, etc.), the church's socializing influence would seem severely limited. Yet this is true only to the extent that the church is isolated from such other primary groups. The manner of its interrelation with them and its consequent effect upon socialization and identity formation, then, become matters of considerable importance.

At least three affirmations, thus, can be made of the church when it functions as moral community: it nurtures certain relational capacities in its members, it bears a moral tradition, and it helps to shape its members' identity. As our inquiry continues we will keep these claims in mind, first testing them against the sociological evidence concerning what actually happens in churches, then submitting these claims to further ethical examination.

Along with these basic affirmations, the interdisciplinary dialogue raises several additional questions about the church as moral community. One, quite obviously, is this: *In what sense can the church be an* appropriate *object of loyalty for the Christian?* In light of the abundance of anti-institutional critiques and the fascination with spirituality as an alternative to institutional religion, this age-old question has been debated afresh in recent years. Relational theology, convinced of our social natures, is keenly aware of the necessity for churchly loyalty, yet, precisely because it is theology, it is aware of that loyalty's dangers. We cannot resolve the question simply by saying that since our absolute loyalty is to God alone the church can claim only relative allegiance. Of course this is true. But to say this much is not to say enough, because some of the very pressing questions about Christian moral existence are still left unclarified.

We know that our weightiest attitudes are usually linked with groups. We know that our various group memberships have differing degrees of importance to us and enter in different ways into our identities and decisions. Ought I then to identify more closely with my church than with my occupational group, nation, or family? Should the church function differently not only in degree but also in kind from my other reference groups? What of the dilemma that if the church claims anything close to our total loyalties, it becomes totalitarian and henotheistic, and yet without receiving our strong loyalties it can neither maintain itself as an effective group nor significantly influence our lives?[5]

Additional questions emerge from the interdisciplinary dialogue. *What accounts for the church's moral influence upon a person?* We have observed in reference-group theory that when the group has the power to reward or punish, it can exert a normative influence upon the person, and when the person uses the group as a standard for evaluation it has a comparison function. There are echoes here of H. Richard Niebuhr's insight: The authority in the ego-alter dialectic comes not simply from the other (or alter) but from the society of the self and the other. If this is true, the authority of Jesus Christ for the Christian ought to be considered not only by examining the intrinsic merits of Christ as authority but in addition by grappling with the meaning of the community between Christ and the self, which raises once again the question of the church.

Niebuhr further argued that our realization of another's authority stems from the positive attraction of maintaining and furthering the relationship with the other, an attraction that encourages us to accept the other's judgment. Similarly, both identity and reference-group theories maintain that one's willingness to accept a group's norms involves finding one's identity somehow defined (at least partially) as a member. Insofar as one's very self-understanding is tied to the group, the denial of group norms is a repudiation not only of the *relationship* between oneself and the group, it is also a repudiation of *oneself.* Thus, if one of my reference groups is the church, it would appear that when I am influenced by its moral norms I am affirming both my relationship with that body and the importance of my own self-definition as Christian. Or, negatively, if I reluctantly accept the church's norms on a given issue, I am at least affirming that this relationship and this self-definition are more valuable to me than the consequences of denying those norms.

This line of reasoning might suggest that insofar as the moral authority of the church is effective at all, it is both henotheistic and heteronomous. Yet need this be the case? Consider the Christian who, while valuing the relationship with the local congregation, cannot in conscience accept its homophobic and heterosexist attitudes and practices. The manner in which conscience functions in such instances, however, does not deny the reference group and social identity line of reasoning. On the contrary, it illustrates it. For what the person is doing is not only appealing to a higher norm of sexual morality than that represented by the local congregation, but also—and this is frequently neglected in ethical analysis—the member is challenging this congregation's finality as a Christian reference group. Further, the person is challenging the adequacy of a concept of "Christian identity" that makes heterosexuality a normative constituent of that identity. In such ways the social psychologists can illuminate a process to which relational Christian ethics points, for decisions are always more complex and more social than simply the applying of principles to situations.

How effectively can the church influence its members? Here is a related question, one on which there seems little agreement among those ethicists who take the Christian community seriously. Lehmann, for example, implies that the *koinonia* is the determinative context for the Christian's decision making, whereas Gustafson says that "for most of us, other communities are more determinative of our decisions than is our membership in the Church."[6] Reference-group theory, although it cannot exhaust the theological dimension of the church's influence, can be suggestive at this point. We learn that membership groups having more primary characteristics tend to be most significant. We learn, in addition, of certain related and important factors: the clarity with which membership is defined, the intensity of involvement, the breadth of the group's norms, the duration during which the person expects to participate, the relative size and cohesion, the strength of the group's expectations, the "visibility" of its norms, and the group's attractiveness to the member. Insofar as these are valid generalizations concerning group influence, we can expect them to apply to the church.

One last question might be raised: *Can we assume that a primary-type relationship in the church or any other group is always good?* Granted, there appears to be a positive correlation between the primary relationship and the *power* of the group's influence in its member's life. Yet what of the nature and effects of this influence? What if the more closely knit the group's internal community is, the more ingrown and exclusivist it also becomes? In his comparison of the strengths and weaknesses of both Judaism and Christianity on relational matters, Niebuhr's comments about Judaism are a case in point. While a greater degree of primary community ("intense incarnation") seems to exist in Judaism than in Christianity, and while the Jewish faith seems to embrace the member's life more completely, nevertheless Jews seem plagued even more than Christians by the temptations of particularism. The objective universal One with whom faith began recedes in favor of "that which makes them one and makes them different."[7] Many sociologists uncritically celebrate the primary relationship, but a few are more discriminating. Michael Olmstead, for example, writes: "A primary group may restrict, inhibit, or even smother the individual in its close embrace. The individual, in turn, is usually impelled to resist this pressure in some measure even while [welcoming] the gratifications which the group affords."[8]

Perhaps the same question, then, can be posed in different ways. In sociological terms we can ask, Can a primary group socialize its members into a universal identification? Can a group have the intensity of interaction and cohesion necessary for a strong reference effect and, at the same time, deny its own ultimacy? Theologically speaking, is the intensity of the church's community related positively to its members' loyalty to God's universal realm, or must there always be some "theys" over against whom the "we's" find their unity? Can intense communal incarnation be combined with "the Protestant principle"?

The Moral Self

Already we have seen points of contact between relational ethics and the social sciences on the nature of the self—its sociality, its historicity, the openness and indeterminacy of its identity. Now we can press the dialogue further.

Two basic questions (though seldom phrased in this manner) seem to emerge in current identity theory: *To whom am I related? How am I so related?* The questions are present in contemporary ethics as well, though seldom explicitly pursued. When Lehmann, for example, speaks of the interrelatedness and openness of persons for persons as understood and experienced in the *koinonia*, he points to both questions but without really exploring them. What kind of interrelatedness actually leads to openness?

Relational Christian ethics emphasizes the primacy of the indicative over the imperative: God gives before God demands. Although the tools of social psychology are not fashioned for describing divine grace, certain attitudes, qualities, and actions of those sorts which theology usually associates with the response to grace have been of interest to the psychologists. In Erik Erikson we have seen how the developing child can be nurtured in the capacities for self-acceptance, love, and cooperation. We have seen how certain family relationships if buttressed by supportive groups in the wider society can also help the developing child to avoid vindictiveness, suppression of others, and overcompensated moralism. Erikson's conclusions about the essential communal backgrounds to these manifestations of grace are supported by the major research efforts into authoritarian personalities and prejudice.[9] Our concern about the continuing incarnation of God's grace in nurturing the interrelatedness and openness of persons in community drives us to take these social psychological clues seriously.

Another point of contact with the social sciences is suggested by Niebuhr's assertion that in the midst of our many loyalties we seem to seek "a court of last resort" that will bring unity to the self. The question to be pressed further is this: Is this "court" to be found in the midst of our social relations, or does it utterly transcend the life of human groups? Although this complex issue cannot be illuminated adequately by any one conceptual tool, role theory can give us help.

Niebuhr himself is skeptical of the possibility of assistance from these quarters, however: "The sociologists who speak of the many roles a person plays in . . . relation to different groups do not seem to answer the question about the one self that is present in all the roles."[10] Peter Berger approaches the same problem from a different angle in speaking of the reification of roles and "bad faith."[11] The formula for role reification is this: "I do not have any choice in the matter; I have to do this because I am a parent" (or a bishop, teacher, member of Congress, or whatever). The bad faith is that we can use our roles as moral alibis. When we honestly come to believe that we *are* our roles, then we have willingly abandoned our moral freedom and our opportunity for responsible existence.

Is this an adequate judgment? It reminds us that roles are always "social fictions." They are constructs of society and subject to all the moral distortions of any human enterprise. Nevertheless, they are necessary constructs if we are to live in groups at all. They are necessary if we are to be socialized, indeed, if we are to be human.

Further, it is one-sided to suggest that roles are likely to be convenient escapes from moral responsibility. Of course they may be, but it is equally true that the failure to take roles seriously can be irresponsible. Parenthood, after all, is not merely a biological phenomenon. More fundamentally, it is a sociomoral role. The adoptive parent is much more truly a parent in fully assuming those role responsibilities with creative faithfulness than is the biological parent who sees the role involving obligations only as they are convenient and pleasurable.

This leads to the third observation: roles differ immensely in their importance to us, but certain roles are consistently more important than others to our self-definitions. A person may consistently find the role of parent more central for identity than the role as officer in the local civic organization. This does not mean that this individual is always more *conscious* of parenthood than of civic office. It does mean that in any conflict between the two roles, parenthood will clearly have more defining significance.

This still does not satisfy the question, however. Let us grant that our roles are important to our identities, that our roles are also situationally variable in their intensity, and that some roles are consistently more important to us than others. Granting all this, am I not more than my roles? Of course I am. But if it is an error to say that I am nothing more than the sum of my roles, it is also an error to think that my identity is what it is quite apart from my roles. Identity is not the sum of one's roles, nor is identity intelligible apart from those roles. Roles as our structured links with groups are indispensable to the identity of the social self.

What, then, of the relation between a person's church role and that individual's identity as a Christian? It may be questioned, of course, whether role theory can be appropriately applied to *church* participation. What, after all, is a "church role"? For our purposes, the inter-group role concept rather than the intra-group concept will prove most helpful. Hence, we shall think of "church role" not primarily as the particular positions a person may occupy within a church (e.g., church school teacher, trustee, etc.), but rather as the pattern of expectations perceived as the result of being a church *member* in comparison with those expectations which come from other group involvements.

Role theory reminds us that social structure and processes as well as personal choices enter into the determination of which roles will be most important to our identities. Compare occupational and church roles as a case in point. Through its values and its structure our society encourages the dominance of the occupational role, and the orientation of our educational system toward occupational preparation is but one vivid reminder of this.

Here is Jane Green, member of Community Church, vice-president of Acme Inc., spouse and mother, member of Metropolitan Athletic Club, past president of the Chamber of Commerce, and civic leader. Green's various roles intermingle in their influence. Some family pressures affect her business decisions, her business role colors her orientation to the church, she feels the weight of some expectations from her church life in her business and civic interests, and so forth. Occasional conflict among certain of her roles is probable. What then? She may, we have seen, attempt to compromise the role expectations, or to escape from the conflict situation, or to compartmentalize her roles so that she does not admit the conflict. More frequently, however, Green relies upon a major role, resolving the conflict in terms of that which provides her most significant frame of reference.

Although Green is a regular church participant on Sundays, her Christian beliefs seem to have limited relevance to her policy decisions at Acme on Mondays. Does she lack moral seriousness about the Christian faith, or does she simply fail to grasp the ethical significance of the gospel? Either or both may, of course, be the case. It is also quite possible that the centrality of the occupational role to her identity is an important part of the picture. She tends to interpret her church role in terms of her business role more than vice versa. How can we understand this?

While no one factor is a sufficient explanation, the combination of several may be important. What does role theory suggest? First, that role in which the person finds most sustained primary interaction often dominates. The structure of our society affords the business executive more sustained interaction with others through occupational role than through any other. Even leisure associations frequently are direct outgrowths of business relations. True, the interaction that some persons experience in their jobs is so impersonal and secondary that their occupational associates never become significant others for them, but not so with Green and "the Acme management team."

In a related manner, that role in which we find our prized self-image confirmed by significant others is often of more consequence. The image of "Christian" that Green perceives in her church is that of a pious, virtuous, self-effacing person. But in a sexist society and corporation, she has sacrificed much and proved much to get where she is at Acme. She prefers the self-image of a capable, confident, assertive, successful woman who is at home in the executive office.

Again, a role tends to be more central when it is more inclusive in its behavioral and attitudinal expectations. If Green has found that church expectations deal primarily with personal salvation experiences, proper doctrinal beliefs, certain private virtues, and appropriate acts of institutional loyalty, she has also found that such expectations are considerably more restricted than those of her occupational role. At Acme and among her other business associates she finds expectations that encompass a whole style of life including economic, political, and social attitudes as well as personal morality. Whether or not she accepts those expectations, they are there and they are powerful.

Furthermore, the vocabularies of motive that we use most consistently, other things being equal, are more likely to become integrated into our self-understandings. In a highly complex society, Green has internalized several. She has somewhat different vocabularies with which she interprets her motives to her family as compared with her business associates, and the motivational language she uses at Community Church's board meetings, though related to the others, has its own flavor. In spite of these differences in vocabularies, language appropriate to one institution can spread to others. In our own time, language once associated almost exclusively with economic activity has spread to other institutions. Thus the Greens' family language (by which, for example, they interpret their leisure activity to each other) is heavily impregnated with an economic vocabulary. The same is true of their church language. Her "vocabulary traffic" is heavier in the direction from economic enterprise to church than vice versa.

Thus, insincerity or ignorance concerning the Christian moral tradition may not be the sole or even the major factor in Green's case. For related though somewhat different reasons, her own moral identity may have become linked more directly to her occupational role and business reference group than to any other. We need not assume a deterministic operation of these social influences. Green makes choices at every step of the way, choices that have viable alternatives. The ethicist reminds us that action is always response to interpreted events. So also the social scientist insists that our interpretations are conditioned by our roles, our reference groups, and the manner in which these have become socialized into our identities. Social behavior is always dependent upon some degree of regularity and predictability in human relationships. Persons simply cannot consistently contravene the expectations of their key membership groups and find their limited societies remaining intact. We must have an ethos that makes conduct both meaningful and possible.

The Moral Pattern

Both role theory and developmental psychology furnish suggestive leads for the interdisciplinary conversation about the moral pattern. Dorothy Emmet, one of the few philosophers to use role theory in ethical reflection, recognizes that the notion of role "provides a link between factual descriptions of social situations and moral pronouncements about what ought to be done in them. It has, so to speak, a foot in both camps, that of fact and of value."[12] If what people think they ought to do depends significantly on how they perceive their roles and role conflicts then, she asserts, we need to inquire into the connection between roles and rules.

Emmet rightly argues that rules of moral obligation are closely connected to our social roles: roles create rules, and rules are parts of roles. We need, however, to expand our understanding of the nature of the rules that are involved. In addition to rules of moral obligation (the kind Emmet emphasizes, as do most role theorists), there are also rules of *permission* or *strategy* and rules of *meaning*.[13]

Many role expectations are rules of requirement. We expect parents to support their families; we assume that this is their moral obligation. There are also rules of permission. It is appropriate for parents to encourage their children to take music lessons, but this appropriateness has the nature of permission rather than obligation (though it may be differently presented to the child). Similarly, the football quarterback is obligated to follow the rules of the game, but there are also rules of strategy that are not obligatory regulations, but rather certain patterns of action that have proved useful in winning previous games. However, the line between rules of requirement and rules of permission is never hard-and-fast. Much depends upon the context of the situation.

There are also rules of meaning. Meaning is governed by rules in the same sense that language has rules. "A linguistic rule, as such, is not a rule which requires or permits a speaker to use a certain expression in a specified situation, but a rule which determines both for the speaker and for . . . hearers what [the] utterances can be taken to convey."[14] Actions as well as speech have rules of meaning. We dress differently for funerals than for picnics: we are following an understood rule that specifies that our clothing be appropriate to the meanings of those different occasions.

Thus, rules as mutual expectations are basic to social roles, and without some kind of rule consensus our common life would be impossible. There are different types, however. Some rules specify what we *ought* to do, some what we *may* do, and some *the significance* of certain kinds of behavior. The latter two types, although not moral rules in the narrower sense, often contribute necessary elements to moral actions. In fact, a relational ethics that emphasizes response to interpreted action must take seriously rules of meaning and strategy as well as rules of obligation. They too are important dimensions of our responsiveness.

Moral norms—rules, values, principle—are variously interpreted, however. Relational value theory argues that norms ought to be interpreted relationally (rather than objectively or subjectively) because this is more appropriate both to the radical monotheism of the Christian faith and to our actual moral experience. The social psychologist argues that norms are interpreted relationally by some and not by others—it all depends on both the stage of moral development and the communal experience of the person. Although psychologists of moral development vary in their descriptions of moral stages, we have observed a persuasive general consensus on three counts: that there are definable stages of moral growth; that the developing child typically moves from the subjective experience of values to objective interpretation and finally to relational understanding; and that the movement toward this relational understanding is intrinsically connected to the child's social development and experience.

Recall Piaget's developmental stages now in connection with value theory. The child's first stage has some affinity to value subjectivism: rules are interesting examples but not obligatory realities because the child claims his or her feelings and preferences as authoritative. The second stage (variously called the transcendental stage, the stage of heteronomy, or the morality of restraint) is quite clearly a period of value objectivism. The child perceives values "out there," in authoritative others, existing independently. The third stage, the morality of cooperation (subdivided into two developmental parts, reciprocity and equity) is clearly a stage of relational norms. Now values and rules appear less as objective and external things sanctioned by higher authority than as descriptions of valued relationships. And, importantly, this development into relational moral thinking is clearly associated with the child's development in social relations. When children's only significant social group is one of dominance and submission (the family), they will perceive values, rules, or norms differently from the way they do when they become experienced in the give-and-take of their peer groups. Both family and peer group are primary groups, but the authority patterns differ in them.

Is it true, then, that when persons actually make decisions they tend to act as value relationalists? Apparently it all depends on two interdependent factors. The first is the stage of moral development that one is displaying most characteristically in one's actions. Since we never completely leave our earlier stages behind, we usually have access to qualitatively different moral styles that we can use on different occasions. The second factor is the nature of the person's significant moral group and relationship to it. It is quite possible for an adult to perceive norms relationally in most situations but not in all. It all depends.

Emile Durkheim and Max Weber provide clues that help clarify these ideas. Noting that different groups had different suicide rates, Durkheim suspected correlations with the patterns of person-group integration and group structure.[15] Admitting that these factors alone do not constitute a complete explanation of suicide, Durkheim nevertheless found three broad types. *Altruistic* suicide resulted from such intense identification with one's major group that the group's condemnation was tantamount to self-condemnation. At the other extreme, *egoistic* suicide appeared to be linked with a lack of social integration, a lack of commitments and emotional relationships that would give one a sense of worth and deter one from self-destruction. The third type, *anomic* suicide, also resulted from low integration with the group. In this case, however, the group norms had been weakened to such an extent that the person lacked the security of guiding norms by which to live.

Durkheim's distinction between egoistic and anomic suicide is particularly suggestive. Persons committing egoistic suicide, though lacking those personal bonds which might have deterred the act, had not necessarily rejected the norms of the group. On the contrary, they most often were deeply concerned about their moral behavior but were oriented more to abstract principles rather than to emotionally felt commitments and loyalties. Persons committing anomic suicide, on the other hand, were quite involved in such relationships, but their groups were so morally unstructured that they failed to provide them with meaningful and limiting norms.

Durkheim's observations give additional weight to the case argued by the moral development psychologists: that there is a correlation between adequate integration into group life and relational value perception, on the one hand, and between inadequate social integration and either anomic subjectivism or rigid objectivism about norms, on the other hand. All of this is true of adults as well as in children. In addition, Durkheim's analysis of the third type of suicide, the altruistic, reminds us that close groups are not necessarily primary. Individuality can be smothered and personhood can go unrespected in certain close-knit groups.

In our actual decision making, then, we do not necessarily *perceive* norms and values as relational in character. We may, in fact, understand them as quite objective things or as subjective experiences. It all depends upon the social-relational patterns in which we are immersed. To put it differently, our perception of the nature of moral norms is significantly affected by the psychosocial distance we feel between ourselves and the source of obligation.

Max Weber's observations on bureaucratic development assist us here. Reviewing the development of canon law in the medieval church, Weber noted the coincidence of two factors: the bureaucratization and centralization of authority, and the rationalization of law. "The jurists of the church were not concerned with rendering opinions in individual cases and hence with developing a body of rules on the basis of precedents and logical articulation. *Because of the hierarchic structure of the church, they were interested rather in developing a body of laws on the basis of official decrees and conciliar resolutions*, and eventually they even 'created' such authoritative documents by deliberate forgery in order to resolve certain crucial issues. Consequently, the church lawyers furthered the separation of law-making and law-finding and promoted the idea that adjudication consists of the application of enacted laws."[16] Weber distinguishes between substantive rationality and formal rationality in law. The former, more characteristic of English common law, is the development of a body of law on the basis of cumulative decisions made in individual cases through the jury system. Formal rationality or authority, in contrast, tended to prevail in the medieval church because Roman legal studies (a deductive approach) were significantly conditioned by hierarchical church organization.

Thus our attention is drawn not only to the manner of the person's integration into the group but also to the structure of the group. Weber maintains that hierarchical-bureaucratic group structure encourages rational-legal ethical patterns. Conversely, we might expect that a group whose structure encourages more egalitarian communal interaction and in which the primary relationship is predominant over the secondary-bureaucratic will encourage a more relational perception of moral norms. If these propositions are true of human groups generally, they are of course true of the church.

The nature of the group and the manner of the member's integration thus affect his or her perception of the group's moral norms in these various ways. What more can be said about the interdependence of group life and the member's moral pattern through additional insights from the social scientists?

First, we are reminded that, in addition to the articulation of the moral norms, the community provides important *supportive* functions for its members. We can see this in families. While the degree of moral consensus within families varies considerably, some kind of agreement on norms is necessary if the family is to stay together at all. Norms are seldom discussed in the abstract, but case-oriented discussion of morality is common family fare, which in turn supports the upholding of family norms and censures violations. Something similar though sometimes more formalized occurs in the church. The member finds (often in informal and subtle ways) encouragement and approval in following the group's norms and disapproval of violations. While the methods vary considerably, any group has the power to reward and to punish its members, and the church is no exception.

Social scientists also observe that the very fact that a group has expressed its moral norms publicly tends to make the following of those norms easier for its members. Professional associations publicize their codes of professional conduct, a process that frequently anticipates and thus mitigates conflicting demands upon their members.[17] Because most people know that physicians are morally obligated not to reveal the confidences of their patients, the doctor is saved from considerable prying and many awkward situations.

Further, social scientists observe how groups, having some knowledge of the particular situations of their members, can make their principles relevant to those situations. Here we see not only support and encouragement in following the group's norms but also positive guidance in instances of role conflict. This minimizes the necessity of each person approaching de novo those situations in which the principles just do not quite seem to fit. Although this function is more easily observed in occupational work groups and professional associations (where most of the available studies have occurred), it also takes place in churches in spite of the greater role diversity in the congregation. In the church's adult discussion group, an insurance agent raises an is-sue: Is it appropriate for insurance agents to play on people's la-tent fear of death, not only to boost their own business but also to motivate clients to provide adequately for their dependents? But if agents play on these anxieties aren't they violating the meaning of Christ's resurrection? Although no one else in the group has exactly the same moral dilemma, many face analogous problems. Thus, a parent admits playing on the status anxieties of a teenager so that the youth will get the homework finished. In the ensuing discussion group members are not simply sharing their moral quandaries, they are also engaging in an important communal form of moral casuistry.

These, then, are several ways in which we can see more clearly how the nature of the group and the person's relation to it have pervasive effects on the ways a member understands and uses the group's moral norms. To the objection that we should not equate "*Christian* moral norms" with "*church's* moral norms," several things might be said.[18] In the "moral triad"—the interaction of God, the self, and the neighbor in every moral situation—it is, I believe, more fitting to associate the *formulations* of moral norms (though not the moral obligation itself) with the self-dimension more than with the God-dimension. "*More* fitting" suggests no ex-clusiveness, for the whole relational approach in ethics is based upon this interaction. Yet insofar as we associate the moral law *in the first instance* with God, we risk diminishing our ability to perceive freshly the activity of the living God. Subtly and unintentionally, though perhaps inevitably, we begin to respond more to order than to the One who orders, to moral guidelines rather than to the One who guides us.

Our principles and rules are not the laws of God so much as they are attempts of the faith community to articulate fitting human responses to divine activity. This perspective can help to keep us humble. Our formulation of moral norms is always necessary— and it is always inadequate. This perspective also help us us grasp why the social effectiveness of these norms depends upon both the community's relational structure and the member's communal involvement. When we see *community* as the bridge between the divine claim and the person's response, we are alerted to look for, to understand, and to cultivate the many ways in which the church is a crucial context of the Christian's moral life.

7

Moral Nexus:
The Personal
and the Universal

Homo Religiosus and Social Faith

In the foregoing conversation between Christian ethics and social science we have the ingredients for a tentative hypothesis. At
the outset, two preliminary issues need consideration. First, we
must look again at the questions, Is the human being essentially a
religious being? and its corollary, Does religion inherently involve
a social loyalty? Second, we need to define the dimensions of "the
personal" and "the universal" which will be the constitutive principles of the hypothesis.

Homo religiosus? In previous chapters I have assumed that this,
indeed, is the case about human beings. Numerous biblical and
theological arguments can be cited (and a few have been men-
tioned) to the effect that faith is not optional, that we worship either God or idol. Certain evidence from the social sciences appears to bolster this contention, but it is still a moot point in both
fields.

The debate in sociology continues. The great formative figures
of modern sociology argued for the indispensability of religion.
The sacred in Durkheim's view, charisma for Weber, piety for
Simmel—these thinkers argued that adequate understanding of
social phenomena is impossible without taking seriously "the un-
alterable, irreducible role of the religious impulse."[1] Nevertheless,
each of these sociological giants was an agnostic, and from that
fact if from no other we are led to suspect that although religion
may be indispensable to society, many individuals may function
quite happily without it.

Contemporary sociologists too are divided. The argument that, in Western society, instead of secularization we are actually seeing the replacement of old religions by newer religious forms, contends Bryan Wilson, assumes a more or less constant fund of human religiosity that we have no way of measuring or proving. Hence, "such a concept obviously draws more strongly on theological than on sociological assumptions about [human]kind."[2] Likewise, Peter Berger argues, "it is possible for [people] to live without worshiping anything. It is their own uneasiness and lack of imagination that leads religious critics to deny this possibility."[3] On the other hand, Thomas Luckmann asserts that the very process of objectifying a worldview and seeking meaning and integrity for the self—the very processes in which consciousness and conscience become formed and personal identity is given shape— are religious and universal.[4]

The debate in theology continues as well. Bonhoeffer's enigmatic statements regarding religionless Christianity can be interpreted in more than one way, and apologists for secular faith seem to waver in their judgments. Two theological assessments might illustrate. John B. Cobb, Jr., isolates four factors that, when all present and interrelated, characterize religion: concern with a world not given in ordinary sensory experience, a sense of absoluteness, cultic ceremony, and interest in psychic or spiritual states. He concludes that although religion is an important aspect of Christianity, Christianity must at the same time be understood in secular terms. Indeed, "the reason for being a Christian is *not* that one necessarily is or ought to be religious and that Christianity is the best religion."[5] On the other hand, after surveying contemporary theology Roger Shinn decides that "the evidence on the religious nature of [persons] is not all in. But thus far it makes difficult any conclusion that [humanity] has left the religious question behind."[6] Shinn suspects that *homo religiosus* is not an outdated characterization of the human.

Are we by nature religious beings? Everything hinges, of course, upon our definition of "religious." If we mean self-conscious worship or concern with a world not given in ordinary sensory experience, then the answer must be no. If, however, we mean an abiding tendency to direct our faith, hope, and love toward centers of value that themselves cannot be proved as worthful and yet are depended upon for the meaning and integration of our lives, then the answer would appear to be yes. For an affirmative answer we cannot find conclusive proof, whether logical, theological, or sociopsychological. But the most persuasive evidences are, I believe, in the direction of an abiding human religiosity.

The social dimension of the question is of particular importance to us. Human religiosity and human sociality go hand in hand. One important element of religiosity, for example, is faith. Doubt is less faith's polar opposite than cynicism, and although a person can undoubtedly live a cynical life in many ways, pure cynicism is destructive of all relationships and hence self-destructive. But the same thing may be said of social interaction in general. Complete social withdrawal (like utter and thoroughgoing cynicism) is impossible, since we carry in our selfhood all of society that we have internalized as well as that which we consciously remember. The various approaches to the social self—socialization, roles, reference groups, identity—argue persuasively that the practical question for us is not whether to have social loyalties but rather which social loyalties to have.

We human beings are religious and we are social. These are not two disparate qualities of human selfhood, for our religiosity is always socially expressed. Just as from a Christian viewpoint we can say that the religious and moral situation is always triadic—the neighbor is always involved in the self's relation to God, and God in the self's relation to the neighbor—so also we can say more broadly, with the lowercase *g*, whatever our god or gods may be, our social loyalties and relations will express these faiths, these hopes, and these loves.

The Personal
and the Universal

The interrelations among the Christian's moral identity, moral pattern, and moral community can be clarified through the use of two principles: the personal and the universal. The principles themselves are familiar ones, having been used in differing ways in a variety of moral philosophies and theologies. For example, Kant's categorical imperative of duty contains the maxims of universality and humanity. And Tillich's theological criterion, ultimate concern, carries with it the requirements that what is ultimate for us must be absolute and universal, and what concerns us must be existential and concrete. The personal and universal principles have been implicit in the preceding chapters. Now I must attempt to describe more carefully (even if I cannot, strictly speaking, define) what they involve.

John Macmurray's approach is particularly helpful. The personal, according to Macmurray, is "that quality or set of characteristics in virtue of which a person is a person; a property therefore which all persons share, and which distinguishes a person from all beings which are not personal."[7] Personal knowledge of another—knowing another as a *person*—involves entering into a personal relationship with that individual, without which only objective knowledge by observation and inference is possible. Personal knowledge thus contrasts to objective knowledge. The former assumes that we have meaningful freedom and responsibility, whereas the latter assumes that behavior follows from predetermined patterns of causation.

But personal can be contrasted with impersonal as well as with objective. When I treat someone impersonally, I regard the other not as a personal agent but as a thing with certain characteristics useful to my own ends. The other is, according to Kant, "a means merely," or as Aristotle phrased it, "a living tool."[8]

The personal principle is expressed also in the distinction between primary and secondary groups and, on a broader social scale, between community (*Gemeinschaft*) and society (*Gesellschaft*). The personal group acts together as a fellowship, whereas the impersonal group can act together without such communion. The personal group is constituted and maintained by personal relations. Its counterpart is constituted by a common purpose that is common only because the members, with their own interests, desire to achieve it and need the cooperation of the others for that end. The unity of the former group is personal rather than mechanical. Each member remains a person, a distinct individual who finds selfhood in communion with others. The unity of the impersonal group tends toward the functional with the member a function of the group, or toward the excessively organic with the group a fusion of selves in which individuality is lost.[9]

The universal dimension is not a second principle simply added onto the first. Rather, it is implied in the personal. If the members of a group see their relation to one another to be exclusive of those outside the group, they must defend themselves against intrusion. "Their friendship becomes a positive element in a motivation which is dominantly negative and this will destroy the realization of the exclusive relation itself. To be fully positive, therefore, the relation must be in principle inclusive, and without limits. Only so can it constitute a community of persons."[10]

Here, then, are descriptions of the personal and the universal. We can call them values, for they are expressions of the good that arises out of certain kinds of relationships. They are basic qualities or dimensions of relatedness, and as such it is appropriate also to call them principles. Although these biblical terms have additional meanings, we can say that the personal principle is expressed most pointedly in the concept of the *koinonia* and the universal principle in the concept of the realm of God. These also imply each other, for the *koinonia* has its universal implications and the realm of God its personal implications.

The personal and universal dimensions are thus appropriate principles by which we can measure the church, the Christian's moral identity, and the style or pattern of Christian ethics. They are also appropriate principles through which we can see the interrelatedness of these three elements. We can affirm this precisely because the personal and the universal have their roots in God. The principles thus speak of God's ways of relating to humanity and to creation. Accordingly, H. Richard Niebuhr can describe the church as "the community which responds to God-in-Christ and Christ-in-God."[11] When the church responds to God-in-Christ, it responds to the absolute in the finite. And to Christ-in-God, the church responds to the redemptive principle in the absolute. We can adapt Niebuhr's formulation, I think not unfairly, to speak of the universal-personal God. We respond to the universal in the personal in meeting God-in-Christ, and at the same time the personal in the universal, for the Holy One is Christ-in-God.

The Personal and Universal
Principles in the Church

The church is *koinonia*. It is personal community. These are important normative statements. They are also notoriously difficult for the social scientist, for empirically we must face such facts as these: local churches vary considerably in the personal nature of their congregational life; some members give evidence of intense and meaningful experience of the *koinonia*, but others appear only slightly affected; some folks who are unbaptized, unconfirmed, and unlisted identify closely with this personal community and speak of its effects upon their lives; Christian subgroups such as families and friendship circles frequently show much more personal community than the gathered congregations. Such realities pose difficult sociological as well as theological problems.

At this point, on the basis of the social psychological data, at least we can say this: to the extent that a church would be morally influential in its participants' lives, it must significantly express the personal principle in its internal relationships. Indeed, the degree to which a group is personal is one important element in the extent to which it will be an influential reference group, the locus of a prominent role, a moral socializer of some consequence, and a significant identity influence. These affirmations, it is safe to say, carry a strong consensus in social psychology.

From the theological side we can say that the personal principle in community will reflect both organic and covenantal elements. As organic, the church is a body with ethos and tradition. It has a givenness about it. The whole is more than the sum of individual members. We do not create the church, it is given to us. Yet personal community is weakened if its unity is only organic, for then the part is lost in the whole and the member's individuality is sacrificed. Thus the personal community is also the community of covenant, calling for acts of loyalty and responses of conscious fidelity on the part of its members. Without the organic the covenantal becomes contractual, just as without the covenant the organic becomes tyrannical.[12]

From both sides of the dialogue we hear it said that to the degree that the church is personal it cannot be a special interest group. If a group is personal or primary, it engages the whole person and not just one segment of that individual's life—on this the social scientists agree. From the theological side comes a similar insistence: however we might speak of the self's various dimensions, the person is first and foremost a unity, and it is the whole person who is called into the church. Therefore, the church is not concerned fundamentally about religious interests or "the spiritual side of life"; it is concerned about *persons*.

Similarly, the universal principle is basic to Christian community. Sociologically speaking, primary groups can be ingrown, provincial, and stultifying. Churches can be close fellowships at the price of being closed fellowships, strong on the "we-feeling" but at the expense of the "theys." Theologically, the church can easily slip into henotheism, the cult of the tribal god, whether the tribe is race, class, nation, or some form of traditional religiosity. But just as the personal principle cannot be truly personal without the universal, so also the *koinonia* cannot be *koinonia* without the realm of God. The church is not the realm of God, but it is a witness to that realm. Yet it cannot be servant of God's universal sovereignty unless that universal servanthood becomes part of its own communal life.

Using reference-group theory, let us put it this way: the church reflects the universal principle when it functions as a self-transcending reference group. To the degree that its community is personal, the church will be a significant reference group for its member. Yet the church when true to its calling does not try to monopolize the claim to community. To the contrary, it sees as part of its mission the nurturing of community wherever that is possible—in families, neighborhoods, leisure groups, factories, offices, the nation, the community of nations. However, community present in any human group can become truncated, restrictive, ingrown, and idolatrous. The church is clearly subject to each of these distortions. Yet there is a significant difference here: the universal principle is central to the church's self-understanding in a way not true of the Christian's other groups.

The family, for example, is more of a natural primary group than is the local congregation. As such, most families are important communities of loyalty and centers of value for their members. Yet the family can easily lose its rightful character as a relative value center, becoming the fiddler calling the tune for the self's other loyalties. What is best for my family becomes the highest norm of judgment. But when one relative group tyrannizes other loyalties, it not only distorts and devalues them, it also distorts and devalues itself.

The same can and does happen in churches, though with a significant difference. The church's witness beyond itself to the universal realm of God is *central* to its purpose. To be sure, the church is not distinctive because God is present there while absent from other human communities. Nor is the church distinctive because

it alone is true to its function only when it refuses to absolutize itself. Its distinctiveness lies in the fact that central to the church's
purpose, in a way different from our other communities of loyalty,
is the *consciousness* of God. God-consciousness is primary to everything else the church is and does.

The church is a community that knows and practices the presence of God to human beings and human beings to God. As such,
the consciousness of universalism can invade and pervade the
church in a manner somewhat different from other communities.
Think of the family. Relating its members to the wider community is part of its function, and we tend to measure the moral
health of families with this as one important criterion. Yet it is difficult to say that this is the *central* purpose of the family. Similarly,
when they are able to move beyond their own self-interest, other
groups also have causes that transcend the group itself—the labor
union in its press for social justice, the business enterprise in service to society, the nation in its historic mission to the community
of nations. Yet for none of these groups is self-transcendence central in its symbols or group language in the way that is true of the
church.

At the same time, by the grace of God, the church has no monopoly on nurturing the personal and universal community of life.
We need not look far to see other groups frequently putting the
church to shame in both of these dimensions. Nevertheless, the
church's central task is to be the servant of God's personal and
universal community wherever it may be nourished. Through its
interlocking memberships with other groups, through its own
corporate voice, through its example, the church is charged to be
a gadfly whenever other loyalties become narrowly provincial and
an agent of healing when other groups become depersonalized. In
doing so, it is the needed servant of the other groups of our common life. For no other community—be it a family, a community
of artists, a political party, an agricultural cooperative, or an international association—can fulfill its own distinctive purposes if
it violates the personal and universal dimensions of human life.

Let me emphasize once more: the church has no claim to moral
superiority here, as its past record and present condition make
abundantly clear. What it *does* claim is that central to its existence
is its consciousness of and its need to articulate in worship, in education, and in action the personal-universal One who is the

source of all true community—wherever such community exists—the One who is both Christ-in-God and God-in-Christ, the moral nexus.

The Personal and Universal
Dimensions of Christian Identity

If it is true that moral community, the self's moral identity, and the self's moral pattern are all internally related, then it is appropriate that we apply the personal-universal measuring stick to Christian identity. We have seen that the identity question always appears to entail a double relational question: To whom am I related? And in what manner? Now we can see that the universal principle is particularly involved in the first part of the question and the personal especially in the second. Through the Christian community somehow I experience the claim that in God I am related to the whole realm of being, and I am related to this universal community in a manner of faith, hope, and love.

But surely our experience in the church is far more partial and distorted than this! Both local congregations and larger church bodies are limited in hosts of ways in membership composition—racially, ethnically, sexually, economically. Churches are not microcosms of the macrocosm. The theological standards and moral expectations of the churches symbolize and undergird our divisions as well as our unity. Furthermore, even if the church were far more whole than it is, it would still be a community of human beings and thus limited in its representation of the universal principle. The universal includes the whole realm of creation, whales and ants, rocks and trees, stars and seas. Human communities almost invariably tend toward human-centered ethics, to the disvalue of other creaturely existence.

In actuality, it is true that in all these ways Christian churches deny universality. Nevertheless, insofar as the church keeps the reality of the realm of God central in its symbols and message, its own partial community stands under creative judgment. To that extent it is broken open to witness beyond the community of Christians of this denomination in this place, to the community of all Christians, beyond that to the inclusive human community, and beyond that to the community of creation.

If the universal principle is reflected in the inclusiveness of the community with which the self needs to identify, the personal principle is reflected in the manner of the self's identification. Earlier we considered the security and openness that enable the self to participate in the feelings of others. Yet another way of seeing this personal identification is the way in which the "burden of proof" is felt in different kinds of groups.

If in a primary group I were to evade a perceived responsibility toward another, the burden of proof would be upon *me* to demonstrate that some higher responsibility for the communal welfare made the performance of this particular obligation impossible. In the secondary group, however, the burden of proof is upon the *other*. It is his or her burden to demonstrate that the service is included in the contractual understanding by which we are bound together. Insofar as the personal principle is present in any group, the church included, the member experiences a primary relatedness and sense of obligation that goes beyond any specific terms of contract. It is a relatedness deeper than its conscious awareness or articulation.

When the universal and personal principles together are present in a marked degree in the self's identity, then the "we-feeling" is extensive in its reach. Why should I, a comfortable American, be moved by reports of hunger in Africa? The reasons may be varied, including of course my sense of guilt for my own material wealth. But even this sense of guilt is inexplicable without some kind of identification with the other. I simply do not feel guilty about the plight of those toward whom I sense no obligation. I may experience other kinds of sympathetic feelings, but I do not feel the guilt of evaded obligation.

Granted, the extent to which the universal and personal can be combined in identification with others is an unresolved question. Erik Erikson says, "To have the courage of one's diversity is a sign of wholeness in individuals and in civilization. But wholeness, too, must have defined boundaries. In the present state of our civilization, it is not yet possible to foresee whether or not a more *universal identity* promises to embrace all the diversities and dissonances."[13] Still, we have the examples of the saints—past and present, in the church and outside of it—whose identification with others exhibits marked degrees of both the personal and the universal.

Role theory provides another way that these principles can be observed in the self's identity. The most important considerations that affect the selection of the dominant role in times of role conflict, we have noted, are three: the role in the group that has the greater degree of primary relations; the role that confirms our desired self-image; and the more inclusive role with the more inclusive vocabulary of motive.

The first application to the church is obvious: when primary community in the church is strong, the member's church role will more likely be important in self-identification. But what self-image might that church role convey to the member? An authentic Christian self-image is one that somehow expresses both our human misery and our human grandeur. If it does this, it has the power of an attractive self-image. It is not appealing in a superficial sense of massaging the ego or titillating the sense of social superiority. Rather, it is attractive because it is a self-image that speaks honestly both to our deepest perversities of selfhood and to our deepest longings and capacities for wholeness and worth. Here is a self-image discovered in a community whose basis is not its members' abilities or virtues or social achievements but their identification with the One who calls forth repentance and gives hope of renewal.

In addition, the more inclusive role is likely to prevail in time of role conflict. Among all our various groups of loyalty, the church would seem to have the greatest possibilities for role inclusiveness. Its universal witness is central to its very existence as church. And its vocabulary is inclusive, for it is not limited to "religious interests" but embraces the whole range of human experience.

Certainly we are dealing here in ideal possibilities. Our actual experience in the church is much more ambiguous. Nevertheless, the directions seem clear: in role conflict those very qualities necessary to the integrating role are qualities which *in principle* are characteristic of Christian community.

Perhaps the most striking clues to the importance of the personal and universal dimensions to Christian selfhood come from identity theory itself. The two great threats to identity wholeness are diffusion and foreclosure. These seem to occur precisely in the inadequate experience of the two dimensions of relatedness—the personal and the universal. Lacking sufficient experience in personal community, I am more prone to identity diffusion and its correlate, moral polytheism. I may have many segmental loyalties, but in none am I involved with my total self. I have many relative centers of value, but none do I identify as central.

Correspondingly, inadequate experience of the universal community encourages identity foreclosure and moral henotheism. Here I may find satisfying communal involvement, but if my community is bounded by artificial walls of class or caste, then my answer to the question "To whom am I related?" is correspondingly foreclosed.

But to the extent that the church incorporates both principles into its life—to the extent to which it is both *koinonia* and witness to the realm of God—it offers the matrix for the development of an integrated moral identity that is neither diffused nor foreclosed. At the center of the self's integration is the personal-universal One, the One who meets us as Christ-in-God and God-in-Christ, the moral nexus.

The Personal and Universal Elements in Christian Ethics

Christian ethics frequently focuses upon the moral pattern so exclusively that inadequate attention is given to the moral self and the moral community. But as we look at the moral pattern with the personal and universal dimensions in mind, something becomes increasingly apparent. The very nature of that pattern is conditioned by its interaction with the structure of the self who uses it and by the community of the self's moral orientation.

Consider the common dichotomies in Christian moral patterns between sacred and secular moral issues and between personal and social moralities. Although these divisions are regularly criticized in treatises on theological ethics, they are steadfastly maintained by a host of Christians. For example, the fact that many still insist that individual honesty is an appropriate issue for Christian ethics whereas substandard housing is not, is usually attributed to basic theological errors reinforced by certain cultural biases. Such a diagnosis might be true as far as it goes. However, one's relation to the church as moral community and one's own sense of moral identity are likely involved in these dichotomies also. If I feel that my relation to the church is largely contractual in nature, this is bound to have a limiting effect on my moral judgment. For if the

relationship is based on religious interests, religious achievements, or religious concerns, then only part of my self is involved.
On joining the church and in making the ongoing affirmations of
my membership through various acts of participation, I have already drawn a dividing line: some things are religious and some
are not. It might make as much sense for my chess club suddenly
to evince a concern about substandard housing, for such an issue
(I have always assumed) lies outside the basis of contract by which
the chess group and I have joined ourselves.

If, conversely, the union between the individual and the group
is more organic and inclusive, if I feel myself involved in the
wholeness of my identity, then such prior limitations are not built
into my understanding of membership. It is significant that many
church members, when confronted by the claim that housing is a
legitimate part of the church's moral concern, do not react principally to the theological-ethical bases of that contention; rather,
their primary response is to the implied notion of church membership. The feeling (expressed or unexpressed) frequently is this:
"Unfair! After I joined the game, you changed the rules."

Paul Lehmann's fine concept—the church as a laboratory for
an ongoing experiment in human interrelatedness and openness—
is helpful at this point even though it needs greater explication
than he has provided. Perhaps some of the needed clarification can
come through such interdisciplinary dialogue as this. From the
viewpoint of faith, primary human interrelatedness must be expressed in theological terms. It is the union of spirits (enfleshed
spirits, to be sure) created by the Holy Spirit. But such theological expressions can be enriched by the sociological. Thus role theory brings to mind at least part of the social structure within which
God's Spirit may work. Here in the church are individuals whose
personalities and behavior are affected by the most diverse institutional roles—roles in a variety of families, occupational groups,
age and sex groups, educational and political institutions—all
bound together. Here is an interrelatedness not only of individuals, but also of social groups and institutions. Here is an interlocking of institutional roles within that institution whose basic
purpose is service, including the service of the true well-being of
other institutions.

One of the more important moral consequences of this interrelatedness is brought out in the literature on primary and secondary

groups. In a secondary relationship one takes cognizance of others in making a decision only insofar as they help or hinder the pursuit of one's own goal. This need not mean either selfishness or willful manipulation. It simply means that in a secondary relationship the focus is on the attainment of a certain end, and personal relationships are means to that end. By contrast, in the primary relationship one takes into account the effects one's decision might have on others in the group regardless of their immediate involvement in the issue itself. Again we are reminded of that simple yet important truth: the ability to empathize with others is a capacity that is nurtured in and sustained by community. When we take another into account in making a decision, the other being one with whom we identify, we decide on grounds far richer and more complex than impersonal means to impersonal ends. We have admitted other living persons into our decisional framework, persons who are not abstract individuals but who are what they are because they are social selves bound to us and to others in innumerable ways. How are we related to these persons, and how inclusive is this relation? Here again the personal and universal dimensions enter the decision.

Our ability and willingness to allow our identifications with others to enter into the decision-making process affects not only the decision itself but also the very style of moral reasoning by which it is made. It is increasingly difficult to reason primarily as "the self as maker" or as "the self as citizen" the more we bring living beings consciously into our ethical focus. The use of goals and of laws in moral reasoning is necessary, but goals and rules retain their rightful place only when they are constantly measured by the personal criterion as well as the universal. It appears that "responsibility" as the key ethical image both arises and is understood out of a certain communal context, one that nurtures the ability to identify with others.

There are other ways in which we can see how the moral pattern is conditioned by the nature of the moral self and the self's community. It can be seen in the perennial ethical tension between antinomianism and legalism. Hardly anyone consciously defends either of these extremes. Ethicists typically argue that their own positions maintain the tension between the poles of freedom and order, to which antinomianism and legalism are the respective aberrations. But the debate frequently remains on the level of moral pattern per se. Our awareness of the interaction among pattern, selfhood, and community, however, drives us to ask additional questions and seek additional relations. On the level of moral selfhood, is there not some connection between antinomianism and identity diffusion? Are not legalism and identity foreclosure connected? And, on the level of community structure, is there not a corresponding parallel with the polarities of anarchy and tyranny?

This use of the freedom-order polarity not only supplements our use of the personal and universal principles but also corrects an overly simplified division between them. We can see this in the problem of identity foreclosure. Earlier it appeared that such foreclosure resulted simply from the lack of the universal dimension of experience. It now appears that there is a corresponding lack of the personal as well. For the foreclosed self—the self with the tribal god, the henotheist—seems also linked with the experience of legalistic and tyrannical moral community. But such moral community is that in which there is distortion of *both* the personal and universal principles. We might have anticipated this. The universal principle, after all, is not a discrete dimension simply added onto the personal for balance. It is implied in the very nature of the personal and vice versa. This same interrelationship may be seen in the connections among antinomianism, identity diffusion, and anarchy.

The dimensions of the personal and the universal thus suggest two things. First, the interaction of moral community, moral selfhood, and moral pattern can be seen more clearly when we realize that both the personal and the universal (and their distortions) are present in *each* of these three interdependent realities. Second, when we use the personal and universal principles not simply as neutral measuring sticks but as basic criteria that arise out of a Christian understanding of God's relation to creation, we have a way of assessing the ethical adequacy of our identities, our churches, and our moral patterns.

Left at this point the reflections in this chapter would be unacceptably abstract and theoretically wanting. However, further attempts to refine them must await the addition of other ingredients to the mixture: sociological interpretations of community, identity, and morality in American society and in our churches. To those we now turn.

Part 4
PERSPECTIVES FROM SOCIOLOGY

8

Groups, Values, and Persons in Contemporary Society

Moral Community
in Contemporary Society

On few themes in the history of sociology has there been such widespread agreement as on the movement of western society from the dominantly communal to the dominantly associational form. This polarity pervades the works of the early giants of modern social thought—Comte, Weber, Durkheim, and Maine. It is Ferdinand Tönnies, however, who gave it a lasting articulation in the "ideal types" *Gemeinschaft* and *Gesellschaft*, concepts that can be translated as "communal society" and "associational society."[1]

Tönnies isolated several major contrasts between the two types: (1) In the communal society, relationships are valued as ends in themselves, whereas in the associational they are characteristically viewed instrumentally, as means to other ends. (2) In the communal society persons feel unlimited obligations toward the other members, obligations that are typically unspecified; in the associational, obligations are typically specified in agreed-upon contracts. Thus, the burden of proof in the communal society is upon the one who would avoid responding to an obligation implied in the nature of the relationship, whereas in the associational society one is obligated only if proven so by the person making the claim. (3) All this implies a fundamental difference between the two types: the unity or the separation of persons. In the communal society "they remain essentially united in spite of all separating factors," but in the associational society "they are essentially separated in spite of all the uniting factors."[2] (4) Attitudes and meanings are central to the former relationship, whereas legality, rationality, and action are central to the latter. (5) Tradition and symbolism are also much more important in communal society than in the associational. (6) Finally, there is the element of time. Associational society, based on the notion of limited contracts, also involves the understanding that the time of mutual obligation is terminated when the goals for that instrumental relationship have been reached. The communal society knows no such temporal restriction.

In all these characteristics we see decided parallels, though now on a society-wide basis, with primary and secondary groups. It is obvious that though the formative social theorists recognized the gains of associationalism—such as modern liberalism, the refinements of modern culture, and advanced technology—they had a strong moral bias, even a romantic nostalgia, for the communal society. They were sure that in the movement toward associationalism moral community had become more problematic.[3]

What of contemporary American society? Certainly the associational process has continued, and there is a widespread sociological consensus about its manifestations. The recurring themes in the literature testify to this:[4]

1. The relatively slight development of stable primary groups is accompanied by an ominous preoccupation with community in both modern thought and mass behavior.

2. Symbols and rituals have lost power. While an earlier society found social and public ways of dealing with individual emotional problems, now the burden falls primarily upon the individual.

3. There is an enormous proliferation of formally organized special interest associations. Even though urban people experience daily an incredible number of "contacts" (the word itself is significant), there is a profound difference between these functional liaisons and the groups to which persons relate in their totality.

4. Large-scale, centralized organizations have become powerful influences in all areas of social life. These formal organizations—political, economic, religious, educational, military—all have similar traits: minute specialization of individual roles, formal and explicit organizational norms, patterns of deference and social distance among the various organizational positions, and the need for numerous coordinating and mediating structures. Though they may be headquartered great distances away, these centralized organizations permeate local groups and communities with their influence.

5. The rate of change in virtually all areas of society has accelerated enormously. This involves an accelerating frequency in geographical relocations, in occupational changes, in alterations in organizational structures, in technological innovations, in the pace and volume of the information explosion. All of these have been gathering speed, with profound consequences for social and personal life.

6. Subcultures—informally organized, rapid in growth, sometimes transient—are multiplying at a heretofore unseen rate. Retirees, bikers, environmentalists, Black Muslims, survivalists, youth, and countless other subcultures express distinctive lifestyles and provide opportunities for personal identification.

These characteristics of our increasingly associational society, however, are not evenly or uniformly experienced. In the city the breakdown of natural areas and natural subgroups under the impact of urbanization has long been underway. In spite of deliberate attempts to preserve and foster neighborhoods, it is an uphill struggle against the leveling processes of a mass and mobile urban culture. A corollary to the disappearing sense of localized community is the necessary growth of secondary agencies for maintaining urban social order—movement from informal to formal controls and from localized to more distant controlling authority. The mass communications media, urban in origin, tend to reflect urban ways and values. The electronic media have contributed to the dilution of localized communities and increasingly enter into our perception of the realities of our environments and our identities. Occupational work becomes increasingly removed from the family, both geographically and psychically, and the nuclear family has to bear a greater emotional burden of its members' communal needs. Such conclusions as these pervade the studies in urban sociology.[5]

Some have argued that in the suburb the greater homogeneity, the greater emphasis upon child socialization, and the larger amount of informal neighboring all mean that here the associational process has made fewer inroads than in the core city.[6] The more illuminating suburban community studies, however, clearly indicate that associationalism is very much a suburban fact, although with a somewhat different coloration. Conscious of their transiency, suburbanites frequently withhold themselves from deep personal relationships, and antagonistic cooperation is present in the ways "people and friendships are viewed as the greatest of all consumables."[7] Nor is moral community nurtured in the suburban organization where "human contacts are . . . generally organized around some activity or 'cause,' preferably one which will also advance or make plain the social standing of the participating individuals."[8]

Even the small town, the last outpost of resistance to associationalism, feels the impact. "Neighboring" and community solidarity decline, secondary special-interest groups proliferate, and distant centralized organizations exert fragmenting controls over local life in ways that local residents themselves resist recognizing.[9]

Alvin Toffler captures the broad trend that affects our entire society: "What is involved . . . are the abilities not only to make ties but to break them, not only to affiliate but to disaffiliate. Those who seem most capable of this adaptive skill are also among the most richly rewarded in society."[10] To be sure, the decline of holistic relationships means also the increase of freedom—at least in the sense that regimentation and control by social conventions is significantly loosened. It may also mean, however, the attrition of supportive moral communities, which themselves are essential to the individual's moral freedom.

Moral Patterns
in Contemporary Society

A relational understanding of value carries the assumption that values arise in, and only in, the relationships of being to being. Any discussion of values apart from the relationships in which they emerge is unduly abstract and misleading. Thus, as we look at the value patterns in our society, we must do so in dialogue with the evidence on our social structures and relationships.[11]

In the extensive sociological literature on values in general and on American values in particular, scholars have concentrated especially on two aspects.[12] The first is those value orientations that people actually hold. These, however, are of less immediate concern to us than the second focus—the social processes that give certain shape and character to the consciously held values in a society. Examining the revolutions of technology and political democracy in modern society, Robert Nisbet finds several basic processes that condition the ways in which we perceive and hold our moral beliefs.[13]

1. *Individualization.* Individuals are separated from communal structures, becoming discrete units of a population more than parts of an organic system. This is part of the associational process that we have been observing.

2. *Abstraction.* Norms that earlier arose in clearly recognizable social contexts and values once linked with particular social groups have become abstract. Because the norms of science and technology are abstract and impersonal, they tend over time to influence our ways of perceiving other norms. As a result, other values also seem less urgent and sacred, more like propositions of utility.

3. *Generalization.* Hand in hand with the separation of individuals from local groups has come the broadening of loyalties to larger social units. Family and local values give way to national values. Another sort of generalization occurs when people begin to see each other less as individuals and more as members of general aggregates or classes. Industrialism opened the door to this phenomenon, with the manufacturer perceiving those who toiled in the factory as only workers (a mass) and the workers associating their employer with the idea of a capitalist (a category).

4. *Rationalization.* Areas of thought and behavior traditionally the provinces of individual and informal decision making have been brought under formal controls, formal rules, and hierarchical administration. With rationalization comes increased efficiency and productivity, but also augmented controls and rules and a diminished sense of the morally creative and responsible individual.

With these processes in mind, we can turn to two sociological characteristics dominant in our associational society to illustrate the interdependence of our social structures and our values: urbanism and bureaucracy. Louis Wirth's classic essay of years ago, "Urbanism as a Way of Life," still provides the basic outline of the principal impacts of urbanization on relationships, and his observations connect with Nisbet's.[14]

First, Wirth observes, although urbanites are associated with more organized groups than their rural forebears and depend on more people for their daily needs, they typically meet each other in highly segmented roles. Accordingly, we have been emancipated from the controls of many intimate groups but have also lost the sense of belonging and emotional support. Our moral norms thus become more abstract.

The urban relationship is utilitarian as well as segmental. "Our acquaintances tend to stand in a relationship of utility to us in the sense that the role which each one plays in our life is overwhelmingly regarded as means for the achievement of our own ends."[15] Values become increasingly individualized, perceived less in terms of a group's relationships and more in terms of an individual's interests.

Furthermore, a fairly broad tolerance of conflicting opinions is encouraged by the juxtaposition of divergent modes of life experienced in the urban area. Values become generalized. Our moral reasoning is oriented toward categories and classes, with less attention to specific relationships.

But, observes Wirth, along with toleration and generalization comes the need for a broad system of formal controls. "The close living together and working together of individuals who have no sentimental and emotional ties foster a spirit of competition, aggrandizement, and mutual exploitation. To counteract irresponsibility and potential disorder, formal controls tend to be resorted to."[16] Our social environment then nurtures moral formalism more than moral creativity and responsibility. And when large numbers of persons begin to reject such formalism, social stability is threatened precisely because their social environment has not been conducive to nurturing responsibility without fixed rules.

Hand in hand with urbanization has come "the organizational revolution." The individuated-entrepreneurial style, characteristic of early associational society, has gradually given way to "the welfare-bureaucratic style" of organizational life. Max Weber's analysis has provided the generally accepted framework for interpreting bureaucracy.[17] It is a formal, rationally organized structure involving a series of hierarchically arranged statuses and offices. Based upon a technical division of labor, bureaucracies have standardized administrative techniques and frameworks of rules that prescribe the relations among their personnel. The organization is self-perpetuating because authority adheres to the office rather than to the person. All these factors result in a considerable degree of formality and rather clearly defined social distances among persons at different levels.

Bureaucracies are designed for the efficient accomplishment of complex tasks, but this capacity is purchased at the expense of interpersonal spontaneity. Personal attachments are discouraged, clients of the organization tend to be treated as cases, and strict adherence to regulations is prized to such a point that the rules become transformed from utilitarian regulations into symbolic absolutes.

The career bureaucrat develops a stylized behavior involving specialization and routine, impersonality (keeping personal attachments to a minimum), and a basic conservatism that defends her or his own interests against threatened changes. True, not only do organizations shape people, people also shape organizations. Nevertheless, there is recognizably such a thing as "a UAW leader," "an IBM executive," or "a Methodist bishop."[18]

To be sure, executives of large organizations increasingly interpret their tasks more as the management of change than the management of production, placing a higher premium upon innovation with people and not only upon innovation with production processes. Toffler is right in claiming that the old Weberian bureaucracy is in transition, and now decisions must be made more frequently "within a kaleidoscopically changing organization structure built upon highly transient human relationships."[19] Nevertheless, the "bureaucratic style" has made a deep impact not only upon personalities intimately involved with large organizations but also upon the values and the ways of perceiving values in our society.

Abstraction, generalization, rationalization—these are processes that still shape bureaucracy and are given impetus by it. The bureaucratic personality is not just the IBM executive, the UAW leader, or the Methodist bishop. This personality and this way of looking at value patterns have now become in varying ways and degrees a part of most of us. To the extent we see relationships as instrumental, virtually all obligations as having strict limitations, actions as more important than attitudes, rationality as inherently superior to tradition—to the extent that these are characteristic of our way of looking at the world—bureaucracy has made its impact. The revolt of many youth and the attempts of numerous countercultures to establish new relational styles simply testify to the pervasiveness of the bureaucratic phenomenon.

Moral Selfhood
in Contemporary Society

The types of social relationships that dominate a society inevitably affect the identities of that society's people. Less prone to identity confusions, the person in a strongly communal society also has less opportunity for the development of individuality and a sense of responsibility. The opposites tend to be true in a strongly associational society. In the medieval village of western Europe, persons knew one another. They also knew one another's station in life. "In a society where roles are stereotyped and each [person] 'knows his [or her] place,' as do others, there is not much chance for differences to arise between self-images and the images others hold for [that person]."[20]

But the development of responsible moral selfhood requires the opportunity of detachment from one's roles. It requires the possibility of some distance from the expectations that others hold for one in role enactment. If I simply cannot conceive of myself apart from my prescribed roles and self-image, neither am I likely to develop a high degree of self-criticism or a sharply honed sense of responsibility. Things just seem fated to be as they are.

If in traditional society personal identity was achieved largely through identification, the identification with a given role or status in the scheme of things, in modern associational society identity is much more frequently sought through individuation, the attempt to find ourselves in freedom from our social claims.[21] With more roles and a greater range of alternatives, we have the possibility of more growth in the capacities of moral judgment and discrimination. On the other hand, if the conflict of expectations is too severe, integrated selfhood and responsibility are undercut by confusion.

The computer engineer whose suburban home is miles from her office, who is uncertain about her future with the company, whose child aspires to be a teacher of romance languages, and whose minister and church members know next to nothing about her highly specialized computer engineering is in one situation regarding identity integration. The medieval shoemaker, whose workbench was in his home, whose adolescent son worked at his side, and whose priest regularly assured him of his divinely ordained status, was in another. Role conflicts are simply more numerous in associational societies, and the more role conflict one experiences, the more likely one will have difficulty in identity integration.

The same phenomenon can be seen through the "vocabulary of motives." The shoemaker had a vocabulary of motives that showed striking continuity between his youth and his adulthood, between his family life and his occupational life, between his church life and his community life. The computer engineer may use different motives for roles involving her husband than for those involving an acquaintance she sees occasionally on the commuter train. It is not simply that conduct is compartmentalized into the various roles played by the modern person. It is also a separation in the reasons one gives for one's conduct. The person must keep secret from others a set of motives that are appropriate only for some; what is meaningful to some may be just silly to others.[22] Our roles are our links with institutions. Institutions develop vocabularies that we adopt and internalize in order to be effective in our roles. Yet in a complex and competitive society where institutional conflicts are numerous, we are more likely to internalize these conflicts themselves, finding identity integrity more difficult and diffusion more tempting.

In Erik Erikson's view, identity diffusion is most common during adolescence, when the individual finds difficulty linking childhood identifications with future adult roles. But, as we have observed, such diffusion may persist into adulthood, and contemporary society increases precisely that possibility. Thomas Luckmann observes, "In comparison to traditional social orders, the primary public institutions no longer significantly contribute to the formation of individual consciousness and personality, despite the massive performance control exerted by their functionally rational 'mechanisms.' Personal identity becomes essentially a private phenomenon. This is, perhaps, the most revolutionary trait of modern society."[23]

The terms vary. To David Riesman it is "the other-directed personality," C. Wright Mills speaks of "the personality market," and Erich Fromm talks of "the marketing personality."[24] But each of these social analysts maintains that contemporary selfhood involves more than simply taking cues from one's environment. It also involves learning to manipulate the images that the self presents to others. Manipulation may be for sheer acceptance. It may be for financial gain and success. In any event, the individual fails to establish a distinctive personal identity. Even when one affirms "individuality," this means "being different," and the ways of being different themselves become standardized and stylized.

The achievement and maintenance of a satisfying identity requires both identity models and confirmation by one's social environment. The lack of these nurtures identity diffusion. The problem of models may be acute for an assembly line worker, for example. He or she does not typically foreclose identity around the occupational role in the way frequently seen among professionals. Indeed, as Harvey Swados argues, a "myth of the happy worker" is held by many in the middle class: the assumption that because blue-collar workers have higher real incomes and have adopted many middle-class tastes, therefore they have middle-class attitudes toward their jobs. To the contrary, "the worker's attitude toward . . . work is generally compounded of hatred, shame, and resignation."[25] Although the diffusion of middle-class tastes and values has softened the worker's earlier sense of mission, assembly-line work has become no less monotonous and depersonalizing, and certain types of work simply do not provide enough role satisfaction and role models to play a dominant part in one's identity. In such cases, persons often turn elsewhere for their satisfactions, frequently to the mass media. But, as Stein maintains, "identity models provided by the mass media which cut across class lines and sub-cultural lines are usually so abstract and fantastic as to become little more than outlets for wish fulfillment rather than workable alternatives."[26]

Diffusion is nurtured also when there is a lack of real identity confirmation by one's significant others. "Springdale," the small town studied by Arthur Vidich and Joseph Bensman, provides a case in point. Springdale makes a vigorous, even vehement, attempt to maintain an image of independence, self-determination, and rural virtue when actually the forces of mass society are shaping much of the town's life. The town's own self-image simply has become internally inconsistent with social reality. In the face of inconsistencies, a tacit public agreement insists that only the positive things be emphasized and all public statements of disenchantment be eschewed. Individuals reinforce the evasion by techniques of self-avoidance, externalizing themselves through long hours of work, through a sociability that remains at the level of small talk, and by automatizing and ritualizing the personality. "In these types of adjustment, loss of self becomes the price one pays for attempting to maintain one's equilibrium in an alien world."[27]

In addition to these particular examples of identity diffusion in contemporary society, other pervasive symptoms are present. Our conflicts over the use of time are one. There simply does not seem to be time for all the multifarious demands upon us. We may be saying that because everything is equally meaningful for us, we cannot choose, and, paradoxically, overactivity itself may be a way of avoiding the very kinds of deep commitments and relationships essential to adequate identity integration. Even more broadly, we can point to what Toffler calls "future shock." "The striking signs of confusional breakdown we see around us—the spreading use of drugs, the rise of mysticism, the recurrent outbreaks of vandalism and undirected violence, the politics of nihilism and nostalgia, the sick apathy of millions—can all be understood better by recognizing their relationships to future shock. These forms of social irrationality may well reflect the deterioration of individual decision-making under conditions of environmental overstimulation."[28]

It is now evident that identity diffusion and identity foreclosure, although opposite in appearance, are closely related. When the adolescent finds diffusion intolerable, the temptation toward premature closure is strong. This is true of adults also, and for reasons frequently linked with society's relational patterns. In this regard Toffler's reference to the politics of nihilism and nostalgia rings true. The super-patriot, for whom a fixated image of the national society has become the definitive reference group, seems to say, "I may not be sure of much else, but I do know *I am an American*—and this helps everything else fall into place." Likewise, the white racist seems to say, "Other things about me are confusing, but I do know I'm free, *white*, and twenty-one, that's what I am."

In spite of increased job mobility and organizational changes, however, occupational identity foreclosure for many in professional and business groups remains one of foreclosure's most common manifestations. One sociologist summarizes the evidence: for most persons one's work is the dominant clue to the course of one's life, one's social being, and one's identity.[29] Another writes, "Of all the activities of life that shape the human being after initial socialization has occurred, preparing for and carrying on one's occupation is probably the most potent. . . . Occupation gives the readiest index for social identification—therefore, self-identification."[30] "What do you do for a living?" is no longer just a male-oriented question. It is generic. We have discovered through previous experience that, as we try to locate a stranger in our minds, occupation is our best clue to a host of related attitudes, values, and interests in that person.[31]

Even more telling is the question we put to children: "What do you want to be when you grow up?" It is obvious to the child that we view occupation as a matter of *being* as well as doing. We expect an individual not only to learn certain skills for work but also to learn a self-image appropriate to the occupation, complete with personality traits, behavior patterns, and, frequently, a way of looking at the world.

Identity is never fixed once and for all. It is a lifelong process. It is a process in which there may be growth, regression, relative stability, or even dramatic changes. And though foreclosure and diffusion appear to be polar opposites, they are not simply the extremes at either end of the continuum. In the political community anarchy and tyranny seem to be opposite, and yet the one nourishes the other. So also in personal identity the continuum bends in ways that bring apparent opposites close together. The anxieties of identity diffusion press us toward foreclosure, and the constrictions of foreclosure tempt us back toward diffusion.

As we turn to the sociology of church life we will find all the issues raised in this chapter present. But now we will look at community, moral style, and identity in more specific Christian contexts.

9

Churches, Members, and Moral Styles

The Church as Community

A persistent theme in late-twentieth-century sociology of religion has been the decline of the church's influence both on its members and on society. Jeffrey Hadden's analysis is representative. Hadden contends that the churches are faced with a threefold crisis—the crisis of meaning and purpose, the crisis of belief, and the crisis of authority. In each of these interrelated ways strong evidence points to a growing division between clergy and laity, a crisis that in the foreseeable future may seriously disrupt and significantly alter the very nature and structure of the church.[1] For those of us personally committed to the Christian faith and its community, the sociological evidence is disturbing, but it also may contain elements of promise.

What is the evidence regarding the *diffusion* of Christian community? Although sociologists differ in their prognoses for organized religion in America, they agree that the quality of religious affiliation and experience is changing. There is an attenuation of corporate feeling within churches, obviously related to the associational process in society as a whole. Over a generation ago H. Paul Douglass observed, "One finds the local urban church in complete theoretical harmony with the newly developing principle of association by selective affinity. . . . In its actual organization, the church tends to subdivide the universe of the religious into independently numerous bits, each commanding a piecemeal attachment of some of the church's adherents, whose loyalties are to those attenuated secondary interests rather than to any closely knit whole."[2]

This process has continued in suburbs and small towns as well as in the central city, as the community studies indicate. In suburbia: in a manner similar to the rigid schedule of the service club luncheon, "the same emphasis on precision, overshadowed by a general atmosphere of haste, may be noted in the fashionable congregations of the churches which circle Crestwood Heights."[3] In the small town: the churches of Springdale are so highly organized and subdivided that their meetings constitute 50 percent of all organized social activities in the town.[4] Within most congregations in whatever location the selective affinity principle is obvious. Age groups are separated, spouses are in different groups, and parents and children are separated in the Christian education process.

While the associational tendencies in the local congregation are most visible, the organizational revolution in denominational structures lies importantly in the background. Denominations, like other large organizations in our society, have become increasingly bureaucratized. Rationally organized and hierarchically administered, they bring together into a coordinated structure a complex multiplicity of different activities, each requiring functionally specialized staffs and each attempting to use objective criteria to gauge the performance of organizational goals.[5] While most members of local congregations are not intimately aware of or perhaps even concerned about the bureaucratic structure of their denominations, the very fact that (particularly in Protestantism but also in Catholicism) the structure of the larger institution and its agencies depends upon the local unit for both support and effectiveness means that a certain institutional ethos is difficult to escape in the local church. Instead of seeing the church most fundamentally as a community of faith or as a worshiping and serving fellowship, the majority of members may look at the church in basically institutional terms. It is an organization whose leaders, they believe, are most concerned about institutional success, structural efficiency, and organizational loyalty.

Also contributing to community diffusion are those very factors which help explain the large numerical participation in American churches. Although church attendance has demonstrably declined in the last decades, the United States continues to have a dramatically high rate of religious participation compared with Western Europe. Will Herberg's argument—that in a melting pot nation the major religious groups have functioned as ways of expressing identification with America—helps to explain this.[6] Also pertinent is Robert Bellah's exposition of the American civil religion, in which biblical imagery has been used both to interpret our society's historical experience and to express the nation's "obligation, both collective and individual, to carry out God's will on earth."[7]

Furthermore, one of the best-documented observations in modern sociology is that participation in voluntary associations generally increases as persons move higher on the socioeconomic scale. Increasing affluence and upward social mobility for numerous Americans in recent decades have strengthened church rolls as well as membership lists of other voluntary associations in our society.[8] Yet these factors which appear to contribute to relatively high numbers in religious organizations are not the factors that nurture internal community. Each of these explanations also suggests acculturation—a phenomenon that hastens the attrition of church identity.

The homogenization of religious distinctiveness, although undoubtedly contributing to the ecumenical movement, likewise suggests the diffusion of internal community in the churches. Robert Lee has argued that the emergence of a common-core Protestantism (reflected in growing doctrinal consensus, interchangeable memberships, and similarity in organizational structure) has been nurtured in large part by the churches' interdependence with an increasingly homogenized cultural ethos.[9] Likewise, Victor Obenhaus and Widick Schroeder argue from their Corn County studies that the minimal cognitive content of the Christian faith in these churches suggests "a uniformity of religious belief and practice fostered by the same forces that make for uniformity in the rest of American society."[10]

Some of these developments may well have very positive effects for the churches themselves and for their contribution to society. Increased organizational sophistication can bring increments in effectiveness. Surely the ecumenical movement has been furthered by growing similarities of religious groups. Cultural assimilation may also mean enhanced opportunities for influencing the culture. However, my point here is different. The processes of associationalism are not community-strengthening processes. Segmental participation, selective affinity in membership, bureaucratization of denominational structures, numerical abundance at the expense of

depth involvement, minimal cognitive grasp of religious traditions—each of these processes points toward the diffusion of community, and their influence in combination with one another is unmistakable.[11]

Similarly *foreclosure* of the Christian community is evident as we
examine the sociological literature. Institutional segregation is one
type. The internal differentiation and specialization of institutions
is a major fact of modern social life. In economic life production
has become separated from consumption and the family separated
from the productive enterprise. Education has become an autonomous institution. Examples could be multiplied, but the point
is, of course, that the same process has been going on in the
churches. Once the church was the center of culture and learning,
the major source of social welfare, the focus of domestic and international political decision making, the social source of physical and
emotional healing, the judiciary for moral law, and the nucleus of
social control. Now other institutions have assumed these functions. Although the process is not entirely one-directional, the
functions gained by the church are minor in scope compared with
those which have been assumed by autonomous institutions.[12]

Institutional specialization has brought with it great social gains.
Indeed, a strong theological case can be made that the church
should pioneer unmet social needs and at the same time encourage
the development of new institutions that will subsequently assume
those responsibilities. But one of the prices of such specialization
is a strong tendency toward institutional segregation and a narrowing of the church's concerns. Even in their first Middletown
study, Robert and Helen Lynd noted that "other activities of the
community as they become more secularized are forcing upon religion a narrowing place and time specialization."[13]

In an associational society other reference groups compete with
the church not only for the time and interests of its members but
also for influence over moral values and style of life. This is another form of foreclosure in Christian community. In the rural lo-
cality, for example, the town itself can be a powerful reference
group. The authors of the Springdale study report, "In the final
analysis religion serves to accentuate and emphasize the public
values of the community and to surround those values with a
framework of church activity which further accentuates participation in and commitment to those values."[14] The nation too can be

a strong reference group. Then "the American way of life" becomes a frame of reference in competition with that of the church, and the church as an attenuated reference group becomes, at least in part, an expression of the American ethos—performing the functions usually attributed to the established churches of Europe.[15] Thus the church's community becomes foreclosed. It becomes narrower in its focus and more limited in its reference-group effect than either the town or the nation. It becomes their religious specification.

The reference group on which most sociological effort has been expended in its relation to the church is socioeconomic class, and this research also helps us to understand church identity foreclosure.[16] Socioeconomic class is highly influential in church selection, and changes in church membership are recognized symbols of upward social mobility.[17] Class influences the content of religious belief at times more than does denominational orientation.[18] The amount and intensity of church involvement is connected to class: though lower-class persons are less inclined to be church members, those who are tend to be more intensely involved in the church's community.[19] Further, the manner of religious expression frequently correlates with class membership: although middle- and upper-class persons tend to "do" their religion through ritual participation, lower-class members tend more to "feel" their faith.[20] Moreover, the prevailing moral outlook in different denominations and local congregations is most often closely associated with their dominant social class.[21]

Related to both class and ethnic factors, foreclosure in Christian community can be seen in the closely knit religious "subcommunity." Lenski argues that we cannot simply equate religious groups with formally organized churches. Religious groups are basically endogamous, and religiously homogeneous families and other primary groups frequently function as significant subunits of churches, exposing their members to daily influence in a variety of social relationships. Although these communal groups are important agents of socialization and ongoing attitudinal influence, they are also frequently narrow in outlook. "Though the churches have often been accused of fostering intergroup tension and hostility, our evidence indicates that actually the subcommunities are the primary source of this in Detroit at present. . . . Those who were most involved in the subcommunities were a good bit less likely to express favorable views of other groups than those who were not so involved."[22]

The foreclosure of the church's community, although very different in appearance, is closely related to the community's diffusion. Indeed the two terms may describe different dimensions of the same processes, two sides of one coin. The foregoing sociological research largely emphasizes the "Durkheimian" conclusion—that religious expression derives its content from general cultural forms. As we turn to the focus upon Christian identity, the Durkheimian emphasis is still present in much of the reported research. However, the "Weberian" thesis—that religious expression, while conditioned by its surrounding culture, also has a relative autonomy—is not absent.[23]

Christian Identity

In recent years one of Max Weber's primary sociological concerns has been revived: the manner in which religious groups affect the orientations and personalities of their members. The measurement of various dimensions of church participation has been the major research method used for this purpose. Typologies have been devised to measure the *intensity* of involvement: nuclear, modal, marginal, or dormant members.[24] Other typologies are designed to assess the *manner* of participation: communal or associational participation; organizational, intellectual, devotional, and doctrinal involvement.[25] At the risk of oversimplifying some of the data, we can see certain directions emerging, directions that at times are contradictory in emphasis.

Much of the data suggests that *both* identity diffusion and foreclosure are present in Christian identity. First consider diffusion. The sociologists discover that there are, indeed, some church members whose church role appears to integrate and define their other various institutional roles. These are the nuclear members, the core of their churches' communities. However, their percentages are small: Joseph Fichter found 5.7 percent of urban Catholics to be nuclear and the Glock-Ringer-Babbie sampling of Episcopalians disclosed 8 percent.[26] The much larger number of fairly regular church participants in these studies do not find their attitudes and self-definitions as closely tied with the church as with other groups to which they belong. Similarly, mainly negative conclusions emerge from the Schroeder-Obenhaus study. Though Corn County churches were of four different theological types and religious styles, no significant differences were found between Protestants and Catholics or among the several types of Protestants in psychological characteristics or basic personality patterns.[27]

The most obvious sociological explanation for this diffusion of Christian identity may lie in the lack of sufficient primary community within the congregation. Associationalism and bureaucratization undoubtedly have affected the images that persons have of themselves as church members. With the social distance among persons, coupled with behavioral expectations carried over from their experiences in a host of other institutions, it is not surprising that many church members adopt the role of the spectator.[28] Whereas many churches make strenuous efforts to involve their members in small, primary group life within the congregation, they often succeed with only a fraction of those who attend Sunday services. Perhaps even among the active members there are many whose ongoing experiences in a bureaucratized society have simply not prepared them for the kind of interpersonal involvement that such group life demands but that, in their understanding, public worship does not.

Involvement in small-group life within the congregation, however, is no guarantee of greater self-identification as "Christian." Sociologists have noted that the proliferating subgroup activities within the American congregational structure frequently mean that many of these groups are so vaguely connected with the central purposes of the church that even frequent participation in them can easily leave the member without a strong sense of being identified with and influenced by the church.[29] The man who finds the men's club his most significant church involvement may discover that his memories of the World Series are regularly refreshed by the usual films and his pancake-frying is approaching expertise, but he may find little to nourish a vivid sense of Christian identity.

The diffusion of the *Christian* dimensions of identification actually may be unconsciously encouraged in some church situations. Such appears to be the case in Springdale, where Vidich and Bensman note that the energy poured into such church activities as suppers, fund raising, and guilds supports the process of "externalization" of the self. A focus upon the theological dimensions of church life could force introspection. But this in turn might threaten the self-image by which Springdale lives and to which most residents cling in their own identities. Hence, "in order to avoid such confrontation of the self, the purely religious aspects of religion are avoided and de-emphasized while the social and administrative aspects are accentuated."[30]

Luckmann suggests another interpretation—the autonomous consumer orientation nourished by contemporary society.[31] Various churches provide various models of truth, and none is given clear support by the other major institutions that impinge upon the church member's life. Furthermore, church members find a host of secondary institutions catering to their religious needs through prepackaged bits of truth in advice columns, inspirational literature, popular psychology articles, and even the lyrics of hit songs. Modern social conditioning does not particularly equip contemporary people, in contrast to their ancestors, to find religious identity irrevocably enmeshed with one religious group. Much more likely, society conditions them to see themselves as consumers in a buyer's market, selecting elements from a variety of competing sources for their identities.

If Christian identity diffusion seems evident in a majority of church members, we might suspect that foreclosure would be seen only in nuclear or core members, those who are most intensely involved. Or, if mainline churches tend toward diffusion of community, it might be reasonable to look at the sects for evidences of group foreclosure and thus personal foreclosure. These suspicions may have some truth, but they assume that foreclosure and diffusion are simple opposites, which we have seen is not the case. Foreclosure and diffusion in fact seem related in a more complex manner, and they often appear in the same persons and groups.

There are various forms of Christian identity foreclosure. One type is illustrated in an old youth group song: "Methodist, Methodist is my name / Methodist 'till I die / Been baptized in the Methodist Church / Gonna stay on the Methodist side." In another denomination, some still resist the name United Church of Christ, insisting that they be called Congregationalists. Or, instead of foreclosure around a denominational identification, the self-understanding can be narrowed to one particular expression of the Christian life: "I'm a born-again Christian, and that's the only kind."

Possibly most common, however, is the foreclosure that simply equates "Christian" with "religious" and restricts "religious" to a certain segment of life or experience. The "religious" can refer to the church's cultic activities in such a way that they have little to do with the member's intellectual interests or social concerns.[32] Or religious foreclosure can suggest that the "sacred" functions of church life are concentrated in the hands of the clergy, whereas the social, administrative, and organizational work becomes the proper domain for the laity, in which case the layperson may willingly accept a second-class religious self-definition compared with that of the pastor.[33]

Another foreclosure type is suggested by sociological interpretations of the "familialization" of the church. Now the religious sphere is restricted to those matters that particularly pertain to family life, and thus the full Christian identity is available only to those for whom traditional family roles have major significance in their self-concepts.[34] For some who are without a traditional family the church can be a "family surrogate." Here they find compensatory gratifications, for "the identification with an institution whose value system is rooted in the family, whose symbolism, imagery and programs are closely associated with the family enables them to experience vicariously the family life they either miss or find incomplete."[35]

In either case, Christian identity is restricted to the roles (whether presently experienced or absent but desired) in the nuclear family. For many church members, the family imagery that pervades their church life seems to relate much more meaningfully to the nuclear family as a subsystem of society rather than to the organic, universal family of creation. The former, then, becomes the realm of the sacred, and the individual daily involved in the impersonal functions and superficial contacts of the associational society may find that experience providing little basis for extending the sacred-family imagery to the world of power structures and institutions.

The foreclosure of Christian identity also frequently occurs in churches composed largely of single ethnic groups, in religious groups set off from the wider local community by social pressures, and in those sect groups wherein through doctrinal affirmation and intra-group lifestyle members are set apart from "the world." In these instances (as in the intense religious subcommunities Lenski studied in Detroit) the attitude "to be a Christian means to be one of our kind" is not uncommon.

Frequently the same major processes at work in modern society encourage *both* the foreclosure and the diffusion of Christian identity. Institutional specialization, for example, affects the way in which we perceive all institutions. Though they make claims to possess all-encompassing significance, we frequently dismiss these as public rhetoric, knowing that the organization in question really has competence and authority in only a very restricted, specialized area. Thus the church's claims that the gospel applies to all of life, not just one segment, may be either consciously or *unconsciously* neutralized through the individual's mind-set, the bulk of whose cultural experience has been that "everything is specialized these days—that's just the way things are." The specialty of the church, "of course," is the private life.[36] This specialization mind-set is surely one reason why, even in those denominations with long histories of social action emphasis, a majority of members identify the private life as the rightful domain of the church, and hence see their own "private" roles as the appropriate ones to link with a Christian identity.[37]

Although the bulk of the sociological evidence thus points to both diffusion and foreclosure in Christian identity—frequently because of nonchurch cultural factors—important data strongly suggest that this is not the whole story. Lenski's findings, we have seen, emphasize the Weberian possibility: the "religious factor" does indeed significantly influence participants (particularly in communal-type religious groups) in ways that broader cultural conditioning does not fully explain. Yet Lenski, while pointing to the independent influence of the religious group, still concluded that (in his Detroit study at least) the results tended toward foreclosure.

More important are the data from the Thomas Campbell–Yoshio Fukuyama study of the United Church of Christ. This study substantiated several "cultural conditioning" conclusions also found elsewhere. For example, church members from privileged social groups tend to choose religious orientations that reflect dominant American values, whereas the socially deprived choose other and compensating religious orientations. Further, privileged members tend to express their church involvements in ways that emphasize organizational matters and religious knowledge, whereas the less privileged are inclined more toward devotional and doctrinal-belief orientations.

Their crucial finding, however, is that church participation in organizational, religious knowledge, and devotional ways (thus, in every way except commitment to orthodox belief structures) tends to have a positive effect on social justice attitudes. And these effects go well beyond those that can be explained simply by nonchurch social influences on the member. For example, a devotional orientation even reverses the social conditioning that white members experience outside the church, inclining them toward positive racial justice attitudes.[38]

These findings shed important light on the widely publicized conclusions of Charles Glock and Rodney Stark about church member prejudice—that those who are "most religious" by usual measurements are in fact most reactionary and bigoted on racial and other crucial social issues. The "usual religious measurements" that significantly correlate with prejudice, however, are high orthodoxy in belief and high rates of church attendance. Glock has since speculated that these factors may say more about authoritarian personality structures than about religious maturity.[39] Thus, since moral attitudes are important clues to a person's identity, the Campbell-Fukuyama conclusions strongly suggest that for many members church participation can and does lead to styles of Christian identity that are neither foreclosed nor diffused.

Christian Morality
and the Church

Much of the evidence for both the diffusion and the foreclosure of the church's *morality* is similar to that which we encountered in examining the church's *community* and the Christian's *identity*. In recent years many sociologists and numerous Christian ethicists have, in essence, charged the church with moral diffusion. The major themes are familiar: the church is filled with comfortable parishioners sitting in comfortable pews receiving the assurance that theirs is "an O.K. world"; religion-in-general has replaced the cutting and saving Word; the church has become more concerned with social adjustment than with social transformation.

Like the patterns of diffusion to which they are closely related, patterns of Christian moral foreclosure have provoked considerable sociological and theological analysis. While a diffuse Christian ethic blends with the cultural ethos to a point wherein it is virtually indistinguishable, a foreclosed ethic is clearly recognizable but with well-defined and truncated limitations. The *institutional* and the *individualistic* seem to represent the most common types of Christian moral foreclosure.

While many church members are understandably concerned about strengthening and preserving the institutional church today,[40] institutional moral foreclosure is as old as the church itself and is only accentuated by certain societal conditions. We observe it in communities where, in spite of recent ecumenical developments, Protestant clergy are still mobilized into action on virtually the same issues that draw Catholic priests, only for different reasons: abortion, birth control, gambling, public aid to parochial schools.[41] We can see it not only in the restriction of Christian concern to a narrow range of public issues but also in the avoidance of issues that might disrupt congregational harmony. A recent study of church conflict over community organization depicts one church in which the members reported approvingly "that apart from the Alinsky proposal there has not been a single emotionally charged conflict in the congregation's history," and the pastor was proud to say "I never heard a heated word."[42]

Individualistic moral foreclosure, the second general type, finds a variety of expressions. For many members the sum and substance of the Christian life is that each person respect her or his own conscience. While the definitions of what constitutes virtue and sin may vary among and within the churches, a common thread binds many together in this foreclosure: Christian ethics appropriately has to do with the purity of the self, and issues that are not "obviously" connected with this are secular. A certain social strategy and view of the church are usually coupled with this: changing individual character is the only way of changing society, and since the church is simply instrumental to the needs of its members, its moral concerns ought to stay within private boundaries.

One other and somewhat more subtle type of moral individualism bears mention. Even many whose definition of Christian moral concerns takes them beyond personal and into social matters assume "that they are making judgments about politics from the perspective of an established and assured system of natural and divine laws or ultimate ends. The substance of these ends and laws is known prior to one's involvement."[43] There is no intrinsic connection between one's ongoing involvement in the faith community and the social situation, on the one hand, and one's understanding of Christian moral imperatives, on the other. It is a type of individualistic foreclosure, not because it separates individual from social moral questions, but rather because "the Christian answer" to any question is fixed and clear in advance of the situation.

These comments on the diffusion and foreclosure patterns of the church's morality do not represent the whole picture, to be sure. We have seen evidence that certain kinds of church involvement do broaden and intensify moral concern. Nevertheless, moral diffusion and foreclosure are common enough Christian phenomena to warrant our focused attention.

When we seek possible reasons for such moral patterns, it is important to recognize at the outset that ideas are not merely epiphenomenal. Ideas and beliefs shape as well as reflect social conditions. Hence part of the explanation for such moral patterns lies in the realm of theological and cultural thought patterns, and our emphasis upon the other side of the coin should not blind us to this. However, the sociological influences are important.

The diffusion of Christian morality into cultural morality has its modern aids—those leveling forces that erode group distinctiveness in mass society and nourish the growth of "value abstraction." The same leveling processes are also individuating forces. Not only do they diffuse Christian morality but also they nourish individualistic foreclosure—the notion that the Christian life can be summed up by respecting one's own conscience.

The ethics of personal purity has sociological as well as theological roots. In our own society a vivid illustration lies in the geographic coincidence between the Bible Belt and the Black Belt. Historically, Protestant fundamentalism has supported certain racist social structures without directly legitimating them, simply by focusing upon limited areas of "sin" that are irrelevant to social change.[44]

Limiting the church's social concern to changed individuals is also encouraged by social forces—the church's bureaucratization importantly among them. Church structures do not yet have built-in rewards for the professional leader's effective fulfillment of the prophetic task, though such rewards are plentiful if the leader increases the church's roll, budget, or properties.[45]

Further, it is difficult to appreciate fully the exaggeration of "denominational moral issues" without understanding the contributing sociological forces. Thus Catholics know their church's official position on abortion, members of certain Protestant bodies know their group's position on alcohol, and neither know their denomination's stand on migrant labor.[46] Since churches do not have a monopoly on concerns for social justice (as in the migrant labor issue), they can rely on other agencies to help represent such concerns. But certain churches do have monopolies on certain "sectarian" issues, and no other group can be counted upon to represent their concerns adequately. This phenomenon is understandable enough in ideational terms alone, but when we add to this the impetus for denominational survival in a time of cultural consumer mentality, it becomes even clearer.

Finally, individualistic foreclosure through moral absolutes has sociological as well as theological-ethical causes. The bureaucratic ethos that permeates both church and society contributes to foreclosure by nurturing the attitude that the institution's expectations can be fulfilled through specific and particular requirements. Just as we are conditioned toward a consumer mentality, we are also immersed in a social ethos of specific behavioral requirements, and it ought not surprise us that Christian ethics is frequently apprehended in this way.[47] Unpredictable and open-ended responsibility ethics are simply less likely to thrive in such a rationalized atmosphere than are ethics of specific and limited obligations that the person can fulfill.

Church and Sect Revisited

We have examined some tendencies toward diffusion and foreclosure along with the sociological realities that contribute to them. Now we can now look more directly at the interrelationships of Christian community, identity, and morality with the help of the familiar (and frequently debated) church-sect typology.[48]

Consider the usual distinctions made among the types. The *church-type* is typically portrayed as an institutionalized, hierarchically organized body. Ideally, its membership is co-extensive with society. Persons characteristically become members at birth. The church-type is a grace-administering, objective institution involving a religious division of labor, and it has a *modus vivendi* with the secular society.

The *sect* characteristically sees itself as limited in membership, recruiting its members on a voluntary basis and insisting upon certain standards of religious experience, belief, and morality. It emphasizes an equalitarian, subjective fellowship of love as opposed to an objective, grace-dispensing hierarchy, and it believes that this disciplined fellowship must stand in opposition to the worldliness of secular culture.

Denominations, a third type of religious organization, are found at various midpoints on the continuum between the church and the sect. Often (though not always) born of sectarian parentage,[49] they have an uneasy truce with the world, are less rigorous than the sect in membership standards without purporting to be inclusive of all in society, and they recognize the legitimacy of other religious movements.

The *sects* that particularly concern us are those which B. R. Wilson calls "conversionist" sects (fundamentalist, evangelical groups principally concerned about converting nonbelievers to their truth) and "introversionist" sects (which, in withdrawing from the world, cultivate their own inner holiness).[50] Both emphasize the close community of members with one another and the radical fellowship of love. As such we might expect them to be strong member reference groups. This, indeed, is usually the case. While the intensity with which the sect holds its common faith must not be minimized in assessing its reference-group strength, there are other factors as well. One is friendship patterns. Sectarians (as is true of others from the lower socioeconomic groups) tend to have a narrower range of personal friends than those higher on the social scale, and the sectarian's friends are most likely concentrated within her or his own religious group.[51] Furthermore, it is a sociological commonplace that groups for whom "overagainstness" is important in their self-definitions tend to have more sharply drawn lines of group identity and have an internal unity born of self-defense.

Earlier we noted in the work of Piaget and others that there appears to be in both children and adults a correlation between a strong sense of personal community and a relational style of ethics. Insofar as one senses the bonds of community with others, one is more likely to guide one's own actions by attention to the meaning and quality of relationships with others than by rigid adherence to authoritative precepts. But such hardly seems the case with the sectarian. Indeed, the various types of moral foreclosure—privatistic, institutional, and legalistic—seem to apply to most sect groups to an even higher degree than other Christian bodies. Distinctions between sacred and secular, personal and social, are sharply drawn; engagement in worldly activities is carefully restricted, and moral laws are interpreted with certainty and precision.

Does the sect, then, by its very existence disprove the correlation between interpersonal community and ethical relationality? Not necessarily, for several factors actually mitigate interpersonal community and the sect's "radical fellowship of love." One, quite obviously, is individualism in doctrine: personal religious experience, individual sanctification, and the individual moral life are emphasized. Troeltsch did not see a conflict between individualism and community: "This does not mean that the spirit of fellowship is weakened by individualism; indeed, it is strengthened, since each individual proves that he [or she] is entitled to membership by the very fact of his [or her] services to the fellowship."[52] But Troeltsch and most subsequent interpreters have not fully appreciated the way in which primary community is always compromised by such contractualism.

Indeed, the very basis of the sectarian relationship frequently becomes more contractual than organic. Initiates must prove their worthiness for membership, and once admitted they must maintain that membership through appropriate religious experiences and righteous behavior. Individuals are ultimately alone in their weakness. They are separated from the group when conditions of the contract have been violated and fully accepted only in their strength. In this sense the sect is not primarily a community of persons whose need for each other is an *essential* part of the religious experience. It is more a group of individuals whose entrance and continuance in good standing is determined by individual experience and achievement.

The intensity of sect group life, then, should not blind us from seeing the extent to which individualism and contractualism are woven into the group's fabric. Nor is it surprising that a nonrelational ethical style is quite characteristic of sectarian experience.

The point is not, of course, that primary community is absent. The frequency of face-to-face interaction and, at least as important, the presence in the sect of the member's closest friends suggest otherwise. Yet even face-to-face interaction is, we have seen, more an "accident" than an "essence" of the primary relationship. The point is that the primary group quality of the sect becomes diluted and qualified in important ways through the individualistic and contractualistic basis of its community.

To cast doubt upon the primary quality of sectarian community may appear an injustice to its obvious cohesion. Yet that cohesion actually appears to be more dependent upon a variety of other factors: the unity that "the disinherited" feel in opposition to their oppressors;[53] frequently, the resistance of an ethnic group to acculturation;[54] the absolutistic understanding of religious authority;[55] and the fact that sects often socialize their members in attitudes and traits that assist their socioeconomic rise, thus necessitating greater authoritative control in order to preserve the group's cohesiveness.[56]

Yet this very cohesion itself can sow seeds of its own disruption, as Wilson observes: "So strong is this aspect of sectarian life, and perhaps of all community life in which bonds are tightly drawn and the boundaries well-defined and the demand for allegiance total, that there is little doubt that a principal cause of schism and disruption in sects is disagreement about power and status."[57]

Troeltsch's description of the sect as a "radical fellowship of love" thus needs qualification, not simply because of the inevitable distortions of every human love but also because of peculiar factors in the structure and inner dynamic of the sect itself. Though more intensely involved in their congregations than many other Christians, sectarians may still lack the very kind of communal experience necessary for a relational ethics. Rather than locating themselves in a universal community, they foreclose their identities within the boundaries of the saved, and even this identification is mitigated, for by their beliefs and actions they must qualify to be and to remain among the elect.

Troeltsch's model for the *church-type* of religious organization came from the medieval Roman church. In most societies, including the United States, the Roman Catholic Church continues to be its closest approximation, though the picture is rapidly changing. In manifold ways the Catholics are moving toward the denominational type. As long ago as the end of the 1960s, a perceptive church historian observed: "The revolt in Catholicism was so widespread on so many issues that . . . disunity and not unity, divergence and not convergence characterized life in the church body once pictured as the most unified and most potent as a symbol for larger Christian and human unity."[58] All of this, indeed, sounds strangely distant from Troeltsch's description of "that type of organization which is overwhelmingly conservative, which to a certain extent accepts the secular order, and dominates the masses."[59]

Nevertheless, there are still continuities with the recent and distant past. Sociological studies of the church in the 1950s, a period of religious stability, may seem dated now. But since they bring into clear focus certain church-type elements, those studies are instructive for our problem. How did the pre-Vatican II, pre-*aggiornamento* church in the United States look?

Kenneth Underwood's characterization was typical: "The institutional attachment of the Catholic produces an assurance about the precise content of religion which the Protestant cannot or does not gain from his [or her] church. . . . The Catholic's role . . . is to live by the rules—chiefly the religious precepts stressed by the priests and the hierarchy to love and care for the institution, to defend it when it must be defended and to advance its religious influence when the opportunity is available."[60] In spite of significant differences, there were also important parallels in this church-type to certain sectarian patterns. It was a strong reference group for most members.[61] Its ethics were tied closely to the structural pattern of the group. There were numerous signs of individualism, legalism, and members' proclivity toward identity foreclosure.

Why were these characteristics so marked in this period? For one reason, the universal principle in American Catholicism was attenuated by a type of we-they thinking. Whereas the sect defined itself over against the world, this church-type organization, seeking to be universal, defined itself over against *theological and moral error* in the world. The ethos of universality was also undercut by a defensiveness that Catholic sociologist Thomas O'Dea described: "This factor derives from a long history of minority status, disability, prejudice and even persecution, and it tends to produce rigidity. . . . However, such defensiveness is fast becoming an unworthy sectarianism."[62]

Further, it was difficult for the church to reflect the universal principle in its ethos because of the very uneven representation of the social classes in its makeup. "American Catholics, despite observable gains, have not shared in the general social mobility to as great a degree as have American non-Catholics. The evidence suggests that Catholics are heavily concentrated in the lower levels of the social pyramid."[63] As remains true of most sects, the church's reference-group power was enhanced by social class and ethnic factors. Support for this contention comes from evidence that the more highly educated Catholics and those who were more expansive in their associational experiences were becoming less dependent upon the church in doctrinal and ethical matters—a situation that, again, has been accentuated in the intervening years.[64]

The individualism that we found prevalent in the sectarian ethos was also marked in the midcentury Roman Catholic Church. Fichter observed that urban American Catholics tended to think of Catholicism as a universally operating spiritual agency through which they could satisfy their religious needs rather than in terms of specific parish congregations in which they were integrated members.[65] Moreover, the stress upon fixed and objective standards for Catholic thought, worship, and morality was compounded by what O'Dea called the "basic characteristics of the American Catholic milieu"—defensiveness, authoritarianism, clericalism, and moralism.[66]

These are fairly representative sociological estimates of the American Catholic Church in the decade preceding Vatican II. In spite of certain continuities, there have been startling changes since that time bringing an accelerated movement toward denominationalism. For this very reason it is instructive to look back at these earlier appraisals for a somewhat sharper picture of that group which has most closely approximated the church-type in our society, and to see within that picture elements that constitute significant parallels to the sect in its impact upon Christian identity and moral style.

Historically, the *denomination* is a much later phenomenon than either the sect or the church-type. Not simply a midpoint on the church-sect continuum, this form of organization depends upon the emergence of religious toleration in society together with the possibilities for social mobility. The denomination has become that form of the church particularly characteristic of modern industrial society.[67]

As with the sect and the church-type, much has been written about the denominational church's evolution and its relationship with the world, but comparatively little about how its internal structure and community interact with its ethics and its member's identity. Yet a number of clues are available. Since the denominational church is the major focus of our entire inquiry, we can look at these clues in reference to the two guiding principles—the personal and the universal.

While most *sects* claim to express the absolute truth of the Christian message, they do not see their religious communities as universal in the sense of inclusiveness. Rather, they are particularistic. The universalism of the *church-type* carries with it the intention of embracing all of humanity within its community and within its own structure of polity, doctrine, and ethics. But for this very reason it is led to its own kind of particularism: with its own absolute definitions, the church-type sets itself over against theological and moral error in the world.

Insofar as the *denominational church* manifests universalism, its expression differs from those of both sect and church-type. Unlike the sect, it does not see its community as existing in radical discontinuity from the world. There is an uneasy accommodation, uneasy in its attempt to maintain some tension with the world, but accommodating in the recognition that the world is in the church as well as vice versa. Hence, the denominational church witnesses to the truth, but understands its own formulations of the truth as relative. Its universalism also differs from that of the church-type. Characteristically, the denominational church does not assume that its ideological and polity structures ought to be embraced by all people. Rather, it believes that through its relative structures it witnesses to the God who cannot be encompassed in finite forms.

Furthermore, the modern denominational church typically affirms that through God's own action a universal church has been created, and this inclusive community, known in faith, ought to be expressed in the churches' relations with one another. An early statement of the Central Committee of the World Council of Churches conveys this conviction well: "The member churches recognize that the membership of the Church of Christ is more inclusive than the members of their own church body. . . . They know that differences of faith and order exist, but they recognize one another as serving the one Lord and they wish to explore their differences in mutual respect."[68]

Denominational churches appear to express the personal principle also in a manner distinguishable from both sect and church-type. Sociologically speaking, if a major characteristic of personal community is *ascribed* status as contrasted with achieved status, membership in such community does not rest fundamentally upon what individuals do. Their acceptance is given to them. Theologically speaking, *grace* is an essential Christian expression of the personal community, for part of its meaning also is that acceptance is given, not earned. While the message of grace is preached, taught, and given liturgical expression in all three types of Christian groups, it is expressed differently through their understandings of community.

Because the church-type, while desiring to include all people, must define itself over against error in the world, it insists on correct belief, the performance of prescribed cultic practices, and adherence to authorized moral standards. The sect's claim to the absolute truth of its particularistic community leads it to a communal self-definition over against the world. This, in a manner not unlike the church-type, leads to an insistence upon correct belief, proper religious experience, and the maintenance of the group's moral standards. However, the very fact that an essential condition of the development of denominationalism is the recognition of religious relativity suggests that the same inhibitions of the personal principle are not *built into* its communal identity. Accordingly, denominational members are not faced with the same kinds of demands for correct "works" if they are to be accepted and maintained as members. Such appears to be the case, in principle at least, following from the different self-understandings of the three types of religious groups.

If both of the fundamental principles—the personal and the universal—are integral to the self-understanding of denominational churches, then we might expect to find fewer evidences of diffusion and foreclosure in their communities, membership identities, and moral patterns. Yet we have already observed manifold expressions of both distortions in such religious groups. Why? These distortions undoubtedly express "bad faith" in a variety of ways. But more is involved. Diffusion and foreclosure in the churches cannot be understood adequately apart from the social processes we have examined.

The question remains, Do the two principles suffer equally? Niebuhr observed that the dilemma of Christianity, in contrast to that of Judaism, was that intensity was sacrificed in order to achieve universality: "If every[one] is to be included in the community of faith, not all of [oneself] can, it seems, be so included. As Judaism has tended to become a faith culture so Christianity has tended to become a faith religion and a faith belief. . . . It is more relevant to describe a Christian as one who goes to a Christian church for worship than to describe a Jew as one who attends a synagogue. The word 'church' means for us a place of worship more frequently than it means a people, a community."[69]

If this is true, the universal principle fares better than the personal in most churches. Indeed, it frequently seems that foreclosure is less evident than diffusion in contemporary Christian life. However, if the personal and the universal necessarily involve each other, and if diffusion and foreclosure (although apparently dramatically different) are also strangely linked, appearances may be deceptive.

While my emphasis in this chapter and the preceding one has been sociological, my ethical concerns obviously have been in the background, informing the organization and interpretation of the data. In the remaining three chapters my emphasis will be directly on the ethical. But let me repeat that the advocacy of certain perspectives on Christian community, identity, and morality depends to no small degree on the dialogue between ethics and the social sciences. As a discipline Christian ethics is admirably suited to this kind of midwifery.

Part 5

FURTHER
ETHICAL REFLECTIONS

10

The Church and
Moral Community

The great sociologist Durkheim was convinced of the human need for viable moral community. He was also profoundly skeptical about modern Christianity's power to provide that community. Having lost its communal power, he believed, Christianity was highly unlikely to regain it.[1] Indeed, our own survey of both American society and the church has given us ample reasons for pessimism. Paradoxically, the denominational church in no small measure is dependent for its emergence as a viable form of the Christian church on the very processes of modern society that also tend to dilute and fragment community life. But Christian faith affirms today as it has throughout its history that the church is not simply subject to the social forces of its environment. Very much in the world, the Christian community also celebrates the Center of its life who enters these very relationships to transform and give new shape.

The Triadic
Personal-Universal Community

Whereas classic Protestant definitions of the church centered on the preached word, the sacraments, and the discipline, much contemporary theology rightly insists that behind all of these lies the basic reality of community.[2] The church is people involved in community created by God in Jesus Christ. All community is triadic in nature, but Christian community is conscious of this fact. While social scientific analyses of community are extremely helpful to us, we must reject any of their pretentions at completeness. Community cannot be exhaustively described without the fullness of the triad—God as the "in-betweenness" of the self and the neighbor—as Martin Buber has assisted a generation of Christians to understand. Human selfhood is indeed thoroughly social in its nature, but essential to its sociality is the eternal Thou, the Reality of communication between person and person, who makes both community and selfhood possible. "The community is built up out of a living mutual relation, but the builder is the living, effective Centre."[3]

The Christian affirms with many others that we become truly personal only in community. But Christian affirmation says more, for the needs of human nature are not simply determinative. More than a structure for personal self-fulfillment, community is God's will for creation. And however fractured existing community may be, its reality is not only a *telos* or goal but is also in some sense present, making our existence, communication, and intelligibility possible. This we know fragmentarily in our experience. Beyond our immediate experience, we affirm it in faith. With the writers of the New Testament we affirm this triadic community as a sharing of life in Christ. It is our sharing in Christ's life, death, and resurrection. It is our participation through Christ in the lives of others. As the resounding theme of Colossians puts it, all things hold together in Christ.[4]

Together with the triadic nature of community, we have affirmed two principles as central to its meaning: the personal and the universal. These principles characterize all authentic community, for they express the very nature and the intention of God, the personal-universal One. Conscious of these two dimensions, Christian community expresses them in the terms "*koinonia*" and "the realm of God," terms that do not exhaust the theological description of the church and yet are central to any ecclesiology.

The church is called to be the *koinonia*. The word itself has a variety of meanings in the New Testament, some emphasized by certain exegetes, some stressed by others. Yet "there is a fundamental residue of agreement among them as to the *koinonia* experience of the early church. The strong . . . feeling so real among them was not a solidarity necessitated by their circumstances, by the persecutions they suffered . . . but was due to the positive bonds of love which derived from God, who gave the gift in [the] Spirit."[5] Indeed, *koinonia* is God's gift of and intention for personal community.

The church is also called to express *the realm of God*. Although Jesus' own ministry centered on the proclamation of this realm, he nowhere defined the term. Contemporary interpretations range from that which is realized in Jesus' person to wholly futuristic expectations of God's sovereignty. Perhaps most adequate is a "both-and" interpretation: "Thus the [realm of God] 'comes,' but its final manifestation remains a future hope."[6] Just as *koinonia* clearly expresses the personal community intended by God, though its meaning has additional connotations as well, so also the realm of God clearly points to God's active reign in universal community, though its meaning has other dimensions too. As Tillich describes it, it is God's universal community involving the fulfillment of life under all dimensions.[7]

Just as the personal and the universal principles imply each other, so also there is no realization of *koinonia* that does not also embody the will to God's inclusive realm and vice versa. George Webber expresses this well: "Normal human communities are characterized by a clearly defined restriction on membership, by a definite limitation on the commitment required of its members, and by demands which are quite explicit and acceptable to those who join. In God's church [human beings] are called to go beyond this and to find intimate community with people who are incredibly different, with whom they have no natural human homogeneity, and whom they usually would have no other occasion to know."[8]

The New Testament is fully cognizant of the weaknesses of the empirical church, plagued not only by false teachings, quarreling, dishonesty, and lack of mutual love but also by restrictiveness, divisiveness, and class distinctions. Thus, when we speak of *koinonia* and the realm of God we are not speaking of qualities of life fully present in the empirical church. But neither are these ideal mental constructs. We are pointing to realities, present in the intention of God, present in our partial experience (else we could not understand them), but surely future in their final manifestations.

The "yes-and-no" of this eschatological perspective is unavoidable. Tillich expresses this: "The paradox of the churches is the fact that they participate, on the one hand, in the ambiguities of life in general and of the religious life in particular and, on the other hand, in the unambiguous life of the Spiritual Community."[9] We too can say that our experience of *koinonia* and the realm of God is, under the impact of God's Spirit, partial yet un-ambiguous even in the midst of the appalling ambiguities of our churchly life. Indeed, the church is called to be a paradigm of God's new community of creation, a community at once personal and universal, for it is the community of God-in-Christ and Christ-in-God.

Other pairs of polar terms can and should be used to express this personal-universal community. *Organism* and *covenant* are one pair.[10] The community is like an organism in several ways. Its life is more than just the sum of its parts, and there are different functions among the parts of the body. Like a living organism, the community has both continuity and constant interaction with its environment. There is an organic ideal of integration, harmony, and wholeness. The New Testament's use of "the body of Christ" suggests all of this. The covenant figure is equally important, con-veying the relationship of promise and response between God and the people. It suggests the ongoing conversation between the covenanting parties, the freedom of personal beings to interact with one another. More than the organic symbol, the covenant points to the fulfillment of the divine-human relationship in the *eschaton.*

The church needs both metaphors. The body of Christ and the people of the covenant are one community. The entrance cove-nant does not establish a relationship that was absent before, yet that organic relationship requires the conscious acts of promise and faithfulness. Without the covenant, the organic understand-ing leads to the imperialism of group over individual; without the organic understanding, the covenant can become little more than a contract assumed to be created by the promises and interests of its members.

The personal-universal fellowship must also maintain the ten-sion between *community* and *institution.* This complementarity can be seen in the organic metaphor: the community as the living or-gans and lifeblood of the group yet needing the skeletal structure, the institution, for support and shape. Since community has en-gaged our major attention, the oft-criticized institutional side of the church deserves special comment. Institution points to the structured ways in which a group relates internally and externally, hence ways the church patterns its tasks of enhancing communal life and fulfilling its mission in the world. Institutional framework is essential to the community's continuing identity. It preserves the very symbols of an identifiably common life—the Bible, sacraments, confessions, polities. By holding to these symbols, however distorted their interpretation may be at any given time, the church maintains those very channels which God so often uses to break in and transform our human relationships.

Bureaucracy, though often interpreted as conservative, inefficient, and self-perpetuating, is not necessarily an inhibiter of communal life and mission. In fact, the bureaucracy often can exert prophetic leadership and give the local church an "independent base" in regard to the local situation. Thus, denominational staff specialists in social action can do the background research for a policy pronouncement on racial justice and then interpret that statement to the churches; the statement, in turn, can both nudge the local congregation to examine its own racism and be used by it as a significant tool in that congregation's witness in its local community.[11] The emphasis upon community in the definition and analysis of the church, then, does not require us to deny (as Emil Brunner has mistakenly done) that the true church is also institutional.[12] Nor does it require us to agree with the critics who find institutional and bureaucratic structures inherently destructive of genuine community.

Freedom and *order* are polar values, and likewise both are essential to the personal-universal Christian community. Waldo Beach puts it well: "The centrifugal drive 'out' for individuality and separateness" must be combined with "the centripetal drive 'in' for cohesion and order."[13] Anarchy or tyranny can easily result, in subtle or blatant ways, when this tension is lost.[14] Freedom is found in the tolerance of and sensitivity to individual differences, needs, and interpretations of truth within the community. But order is also expressed in the common loyalty to the group's transcendent good.

Paradoxically, Christian community has both *intrinsic worth* and *instrumental worth*. If the community is conceived of only as a means to another end, then its unity is not so much a unity of persons as a unity of actions and functions, and persons themselves are used as means to the group's goals.[15] But if the Christian community is thought of only as an end in itself, it quickly becomes self-satisfied and defensive, losing its vision and universal thrust. This in turn is destructive of the personal as well. Ultimately, this paradox (as is true of the others) is held together by the unity of the One who is both God-in-Christ and Christ-in-God. The Holy One wills the church as an instrument for the universal community of all being, and at the same time as a valued relationship itself.

Numerous other theological-ethical polarities commonly have been used to illuminate the dynamics and functions of the church, and many of these would be germane to our concern.[16] But perhaps the point is clear: the personal-universal dimensions, although crucial to the description of Christian community, are incomplete and even misleading without expression through a host of other polar tensions.

The Church as Socializer

Doubtless, more intense community is felt and more powerful socialization occurs in Christian subcommunities than in congregations as such. The family, in Cooley's phrase, is still "the nursery of human nature," and neighborhood, school, friendship, and work groups in some instances are significant Christian subcommunities. Indeed, the recognition of the congregation's limitations as a socializer has led some Christian educators to insist that the church school would serve its function more adequately if it concentrated upon honest instruction and admitted that nurture must take place elsewhere.[17]

Nevertheless, the subcommunity is ill-equipped as a Christian socializer without its effective integration into the church, for the congregation and the larger church are socializers in different but vastly important ways. The first way, reflecting the *universal* principle, has already been suggested negatively through Lenski's findings: without vital ties to the congregational structure, the religious subcommunity actually tends to nurture a provincial, foreclosed view of the world.[18] The Christian subcommunity easily becomes ingrown in its outlook and exclusive in its socialization without the continuing input of the universal dimension, which the church can give through its symbolic participation in the universal family and its conscious articulation and celebration of the universal God.

The second and *personal* dimension of the church's socializing capacity is suggested by Erikson's thesis on trust: the experience of basic trust is crucial if a child is to be nurtured into healthy autonomy or independence, but this is mediated in the family setting only if the parents' own lives are involved in a wider communal framework of trust, a framework outside the family itself. "Trust, then, becomes the capacity for *faith*—a vital need for which [persons] must find some institutional confirmation."[19]

Trust underlies not only the capacity for faith but also that sense of relative autonomy and personal security that are crucial elements of moral freedom. The freedom of the Christian is, to be sure, freedom *from*—from the law, from principalities and powers, from "the ethics of death." It is also freedom *for*, and for that the person needs sufficient personal security to become involved in the needs of the neighbor, near and far. Ultimately such freedom comes from God through our confidence that in the divine presence the universe is trustworthy. But such faith is not discarnate; it is mediated through fleshly communities.

Using a psychotherapeutic model for clarifying certain processes in the church, James E. Dittes makes important contributions at this point.[20] The congregation, he maintains, can be a crucially important social locus for the nurture of freedom precisely because (like the psychotherapeutic experience) it is structured to be "not of the world" as well as within the world. Relationships experienced within the congregation are different enough from those the member experiences in other groups, so they do not carry the usual rewards and punishments of "worldly" life. The person can feel a moratorium on the pressure to produce, realizing that busy efforts in the church, by the grace of God, are not of ultimate significance. The member finds the freedom of stark focus in self-confrontation, introspection, and confession. The congregational community is "more casual, less intimate, less intense than the primary relationships which a person has in . . . family, among peers at work."[21] But it does not by that fact lack the qualities of primary community. Indeed, the freedom from constricting behavioral pressures and the relative absence of confining rewards and punishments *are* marks of personal community wherein persons are valued quite apart from their functions and usefulness.

Furthermore, because the nature of community in the congregation is different and freer, the member can meet the same persons he or she encounters daily (as well as others), but now in new role relations. This is not an argument for a sectarian withdrawal from worldly involvement. To the contrary, the Christian is better equipped for worldly responsibilities if typical "outside" behavioral pressures do not dictate the structure of relationships within the congregation. Surely "without this firm rooting in 'home base,' [one] may be buffeted about by these elements of the public sphere without purpose, direction, integrity, or effectiveness."[22]

The Church
as Reference Group

If the church embodies personal-universal community, can it at the same time be a strong reference group for its members? Some of the characteristics that sociologists associate with strong reference groups seem to pose no problem: the group's attractiveness to its members, its size, its cohesiveness, the duration for which members expect to belong, and the breadth of its behavioral norms. However, when the sociologist says that strong reference groups also define their membership with some clarity, expect conformity to the group's norms, and are marked by the visibility of a member's norm performance, then it would seem we are slipping into certain aspects of sectarianism that undercut that very personal-universal community we seek.

Yet this problem may be more apparent than real. For example, the sociological phrasing "expected conformity to the group's norms" itself suggests heteronomy—external authority imposed on the individual. But everything depends upon the nature of the community itself. Clues from social scientists and theologians alike assist us at this point. The developmental psychologist observes that we perceive the group's norms as heteronomous only insofar as we have not yet developed genuine social reciprocity with the group members. The social psychologist points out that when our sense of identity and deepest satisfactions are closely involved with a group, we do not characteristically perceive its norms as being coercive and external; they are internalized and part of us.

In a theological frame of reference something parallel can be affirmed. According to Tillich, we see moral law as imperative only to the extent that we are estranged from our essential law, the law of our own being. But when grace creates a reunion in which the cleavage between our true being and actual being is overcome, even if fragmentarily, the rule of the commanding law is broken.[23] And Karl Barth interprets the divine law not as command but as permission, as the form or structure of the gospel, because it is given in Jesus Christ.[24] If God is the in-betweenness of members of the church, and if grace is not received apart from the neighbor, then theonomous moral authority *can* be experienced (even if fragmentarily) in the moral expectations of the community. Indeed, it is only to the extent that adult children feel alienated from aging parents that the obligation to support them becomes a "commanding" law. It is only to the degree that the marital relationship is distorted that the prohibition of adultery is perceived as a heteronomous burden alien to one's self-expression. So also, to the extent that the church embodies personal-universal community its norms are not only moral claims on the member, they are also descriptions of the very relationships that give one personal wholeness.

Similar arguments that need not be detailed here can be made for other indicators of reference-group strength, such as the manner in which membership is defined and the visibility of the member's moral life. Surely in the sect we have seen that strong reference groups may well violate heteronomously the qualities of *koinonia* and the realm of God. The point is, however, that the reverse is not true. In fact, it is precisely the personal-universal community, wherever it is embodied, that combines the possibility of reference-group strength with that of theonomy.

Scarcely beneath the surface of any discussion of the church as a reference group, and implied in much I have already said, is the question of homogeneity or heterogeneity.[25] At the outset it would seem that the homogeneous congregation—involving commonalities of socioeconomic class, racial uniformity, sexual orientation, and so on—would be the stronger reference group. Yet this would suggest that the congregation that can include within its membership a heterogeneous diversity reflecting more of the realm of God's inclusiveness, will *ipso facto* be weaker in its moral influence upon the member. Moreover, the problem of homogeneity-heterogeneity is not exhausted by matters of class and caste. It is also a question of Christian commitment and part of the whole church-sect issue. Can the church be a viable reference group and "a community of moral discourse"[26] while embracing these internal differences?

The heterogeneity of class and caste, to be sure, can bring difficulties in communication, internal social differentiation, and leadership. And the heterogeneity of Christian commitment can tempt the church to seek a middling compromise between sectarian exclusiveness and the false inclusiveness of formless capitulation to the world. But while it would be fatuous to suggest that the answers are easy, it would surely be faithless to assume that the personal-universal God is unable to create community in the midst of diversity. Precisely because the structures of the congregation's relationship do not need to recapitulate the rewards and punishments of "worldly" role structures, such community is possible. And precisely because church and world need not exist as two spheres in mutual hostility, nor need the church simply express a "religious aspect" of the world, such community is possible. The church is a slice of humanity that consciously confesses and celebrates the One in Jesus Christ who is seeking to realize the divinely intended community among all.[27] Sociological and even spiritual variety can be a source of the church's strength if the members together can make this basic confession.

The Church, the Burden of Proof, and the Vocabulary of Motives

A sociological study of two rural towns in the Southwest provides intriguing illustration of differences in how "the burden of proof" can be felt in local communities. "In Rimrock . . . the expectations are such that one must show [others] or at least convince [oneself] that [one] has good cause for not committing time and resources to community efforts, while in Homestead cooperative action takes place only after certainty has been reached that the claims of other individuals upon one's time and resources are legitimate."[28] In spite of notable similarity in other sociological ways, the essential difference between the two towns is that Rimrock is entirely composed of one religious group, whereas in Homestead there is vigorous competition among ten churches. Although Rimrock's unity is purchased at the price of sectarian and heteronomous social controls, there is here, nevertheless, a striking illustration of how religious communities can shift the burden of proof away from the direction normally felt in an associational society.

In the Christian ethical tradition it is abundantly clear that we bear the burden of proof in regard to the neighbor. We have responsibility to the neighbor's need without having to be convinced that the obligation is specified in some sort of contract. And this responsibility is not essentially a burden. It is not the oppressive heteronomy of the external law—"for my yoke is easy, and my burden is light" (Matt. 11:29). Presumably, the message of responsibility to the neighbor was preached in Homestead churches, but in that town the ethos was divisive and competitive. In Rimrock, by contrast, responsibility was consciously experienced in the fabric of an inclusive moral community.

It is true that the internal fragmentation of Homestead is more typical of our social life than is the cohesion of Rimrock. It is also frequently true that even when the burden of proof is experienced in a more inclusive way that sense of inclusiveness still has very definite boundaries. Thus in Rimrock the keen sense of responsibility to the entire community was coupled with feelings of superiority over and distance from the folks of nearby Homestead. Even so, this sociological illustration persuasively argues that moral motivation is quite incomprehensible apart from the social relations in which and through which it is felt and experienced.

Regarding Christian motivation, it is clear that the church is never immune from the fragmenting forces of mass society. Neither is the church simply shaped by those forces either in the quality of its own community life or in the relatedness it feels beyond its boundaries. F. D. Maurice was surely right that we are called to be "diggers rather than builders," seeking to express the reality of the divinely established human relatedness rather than trying to construct communities with materials of sociological or religious similarity. If our universal relatedness is not only an eschatological hope but also a present fact perceived in faith, a reality that transcends the apparent facts of our divisions, then the sociological burden of proof argument makes remarkable theological sense.

The vital significance of *relationships* in motivations does not mitigate the importance of motivational *language*. Rather, it places such language in its proper relational perspective. As Weber has reminded us, a "motive," among other things, is a term in one's vocabulary that appears to oneself and to others to be an adequate reason for one's behavior. We want others to understand why we act as we do, and the vocabularies we use for interpreting our actions are rooted in our communities.

The church, like every other human community, is a community of language. It maintains its own identity and inner unity in no small measure through the internalization of meanings represented in various linguistic forms: chiefly the Bible, but also liturgies, creeds, hymns, and the language of the church's history. As with every other human community, an important part of the person's membership in the church is learning and using the group's distinctive language.[29] Language is not simply a tool we use in order to communicate. It is the very ether in which we communicate. Because one is a member of a community, one "re-presents" the community in speech and action.[30]

But the language of the church is affected by the change of social structures. It is true of the "family" imagery, for example. The modern family—mobile, separated from many traditional functions, less inclusive in its relationships, varied in its forms— scarcely carries the experiential weight it once did as a metaphor for the church. Thus, the church is affected not only directly by the weakening of natural and traditional communities on which it has depended. It is also affected indirectly by the dilution of key images it has used for its self-interpretation.

The terms "brother" and "sister" in the early church usually expressed an intense we-consciousness and a deeply felt sense of obligation for the other's well-being. Today they are rarely heard outside of sectarian groups and certain black churches. In these groups the terms are still meaningful because of particular theological heritage and stylized habit. They are also meaningful as terms that reinforce the we-consciousness of people who still experience racial or economic oppression. However, the embarrassment most "mainline" church members would feel on being called "sister" or "brother" indicates more than theological and social differences from these other Christians. It also indicates the inappropriateness they may feel about the terms as describing their own communal experience. Lacking a strong sense of particularity and lacking the daily experience of hostility from the outside, these church members feel little need to use such language. The words do not seem to fit their communal experience. But as a result, they also lack verbal tools of this sort that might both express and nurture Christian community.

The church's vocabulary of motives must be both personal and universal in its power. The language must be personal: "The human situation demands language that encourages people to become involved with others, to feel as well as to know. This kind of language has its roots in tradition, in 'the language of the people.'"[31] The language must also be universal. When persons of other faiths are called "non-Christians," the clear implication is that "Christian" is the proper standard of measurement for all human beings. When those of other faiths are deemed "pagan" or "unsaved," the we-they division and the assumptions of Christian imperialism are blatant. When they are "children of God," not only are different moral attitudes conveyed but we are also moved to different styles of moral action.

Christian Community and Human Community

An intensive community generates a moral ethos that pervades the daily lives of its members, but such community does not necessarily lead to inclusiveness of concern or a universal sense of responsibility. This we have seen in a variety of ways. Now the question is, can the Christian community be sufficiently personal and cohesive to afford security, freedom, and the basis for personal identity, and yet be sufficiently universal to relate its members to the inclusive commonwealth of God?

The evidence from social scientists concerning group self-transcendence is both suggestive and inconclusive. Some assume that increased harmony and cooperation *within* a group will automatically foster the desire for *inter-group* harmony, but abundant evidence also suggests the very opposite. One of the most widely heralded studies of intergroup relations concluded that—more than the presence of a common enemy, or the correction of stereotypes about other groups, or appeals to individual action, or increased intergroup contact—the discovery of "superordinate goals" that could be attained only by the combined efforts of several groups was the most reliable method of reducing hostility and increasing positive relations.[32]

At the same time, there is no conclusive evidence that inner cohesion in and of itself actually fosters hostility toward those outside the group. Gordon Allport, summarizing the data on prejudice, concludes: "The principle states that concentric loyalties need not clash. To be devoted to a large circle does not imply the destruction of one's attachment to a smaller circle. The loyalties that clash are almost invariably those of identical scope."[33] In other words, it is the bigamist or the traitor who is in trouble.

To the extent that Christian groups feel themselves superior to or threatened by others, their universal dimension of course will be distorted. But so also will their personal existence. In any group that becomes exclusive, defensive against the outsider and fearful of intrusion, the negative motivation will strongly affect the internal relationship. Inner *unity* and exclusiveness may be compatible, but true *community* and exclusiveness are not. There is no genuine *koinonia* without the realm of God.

The church's superordinate goal is its mission toward God's universal reign, God's commonwealth. The goal is not to make Christians of all persons. The presumption is not that others can participate in universal community only if they first become Christianized with the church's distinctive language, forms, and traditions. But if it is not served by an aggressive posture, neither is universal community served by a submissive and contemplative church that expects a universal community it does not in fact intend.[34] Rather, the church speaks of, points to, and works for that universal community which it knows decisively and particularly through Jesus Christ, but which is not without God's witness elsewhere.

Numerous Christians have discovered their profound unity with folk of denominations other than their own as they have struggled side by side against racism, war, and poverty. They have demonstrated that the ecumenical recasting of doctrine and polity often follows investment in common mission. Far beyond Christian unity, however, we are called to human unity. And the mission of humanization must by its very nature be undertaken in partnership with those who do not consciously confess Jesus as the Christ.

If the church is not the community that must organize society, neither is it simply one community among others for the Christian. It is rather a community intended by God to live in conscious and articulate faithfulness to the world's true Center. In so doing, it witnesses to those qualities of relationship fundamental to the world's existence and fulfillment. It would be difficult to improve upon Canon Wickham's words: "It is the situation where the Church is acutely conscious of belonging to the world, subject to the conditions of the world, yet a catalyst within the world which is its only sphere of obedience. It seeks neither to manipulate nor dominate the world, nor to escape from it, nor merely to reflect a voluntarist religious aspect of it, but to understand it, prophesy within it, interpret it and stain it."[35]

But the personal-universal community is never simply that of human beings joined through God. It is a community of creation. It is the community of human beings bound to the birds of the air, the teeming life of the seas, and, indeed, to the acid-rained lakes and polluted atmosphere. Though we can speak with some justified focus on the human community, it is partial. Our slow awakening to the environmental, ecological crisis should make us realize that Francis of Assisi, far from being a mere romantic, was a thorough realist when he spoke of "Brother Cloud" and "Sister Moon." Somehow we too must find a larger vocabulary of motives and a larger community of creation that bear to us the burden of proof, for unless we do so, "humanization" will become simply one more partial and hence ill-fated expression of that community which is, in God's intention, inclusive of all being.

11

The Church
and Moral Ethos

"If there is one fact that history has irrefutably demonstrated," wrote Durkheim, "it is that the morality of each people is directly related to the social structure of the people practicing it. The connection is so intimate that, given the general character of the morality observed in a given society . . . one can infer the nature of that society, the elements of its structure and the way it is organized."[1] While Durkheim was prone to overstate the dependence of religion and ethics on social structures, his insistence on their inescapably intimate connection is utterly important.

Assuming this interdependence of the patterns of social relationships and the patterns of ethics and morals, we have looked at American society. We have seen the social dynamics that encourage "moral foreclosure": instrumental affiliations, the sense of limited liability, the subtle transformation of organizational rules into symbolic absolutes, and the elevation of technique over attitude and rationality over tradition. Not surprisingly, there are at the same time evidences of "moral diffusion": the common feeling that "everything nailed down is comin' loose," the revolt against encapsulating traditions, and the restless quest for a new moral consciousness.

As in society, so also in the mainline churches there are obvious pulls toward moral foreclosure and diffusion. Foreclosures around institutional and individualistic ethics exist hand in hand with the gnawing sense that the church's moral witness has become diffused, an uncertain trumpet. And in this situation a gathering storm has developed between those wanting a comforting church and those seeking a challenging church. Although the winds of the storm come from markedly different directions, perhaps they are similar at least in this respect: the experience and the ethical expression of mainline Christian moral community appear weak in all the divergent currents.

Christian Ethics as
Personal and Universal

While relationships rather than principles or rules are the basic "stuff" of ethics, the latter are indispensable tools of the Christian moral life. Though the literature of contemporary ethics displays varied definitions, there seems to be a growing consensus about the meaning of principle and rule.[2] Principles are more general than rules, pointing to certain qualities or dimensions that ought to be present in moral acts regardless of the situation. Principles are not characteristically enforced by social sanctions. Rules, on the other hand, are more specific, articulating what is required or prohibited in particular situations. Though both principles and rules are socially based, it is more obvious in the case of rules inasmuch as rules reflect the obligations of members of certain social groups or the expectations associated with certain social roles. While many groups have rules that members would have difficulty tracing to moral principles, in a well-integrated ethics rules will express the general principles that lie behind them.

In interpreting the interdependence of moral ethos, moral community, and the person's moral identity, I have relied most heavily upon the principles of the personal and the universal. Certainly, Christian ethics is appropriately expressed in additional major principles as well—love foremost among them, but also justice, faithfulness, mutuality, nonviolence, and so forth. Frequently, ethicists single out one such principle, claim its centrality, and interpret all else in its light. For example, one might argue that the personal and the universal principles are simply dimensions of love. But if they are merely "sub-principle" dimensions of this more traditional and substantial principle, why bother to emphasize them so? Why not simply speak simply of the centrality of love—love that must be expressed in both personal and universal ways?

In fact, there are several reasons for the importance of the personal and the universal principles. They describe important aspects of the activity of God, the personal-universal One, in creating, maintaining, and renewing the possibilities of authentic community in the midst of life. This communal activity of God is the basic relationship that Christian ethics attempts to clarify and, through such clarification, to evaluate and to criticize morality as we seek to participate in the divine action.

Christian ethics then finds its starting point in the church not because God is uniquely present here, but because it is here, not elsewhere, that we who are Christians become conscious of the Source of *all* true community. It is here in the church where we celebrate the Center of all community, here we find the criteriological symbols by which to evaluate community wherever it may be, and here we are shaped to participate in God's worldly activity. Others may and will find these things elsewhere, but Christians find them in a particular historic community of faith. The personal and universal principles thus have particular usefulness not only as the criteria of authentic community but also in clarifying how existing human communities in their varied distortions and possibilities are interrelated with the varied shapes of personal identity and moral ethos. Such clarification is aided by the very polarity of the principles themselves, for that suggests an inner dynamic and tension that single ethical principles may not convey.

For example, the Christian personal and universal principles shed needed light on current humanistic ethics. Though the language of humanization has certain advantages over the language of natural law, an uncritical baptism of secular humanism by some Christian moralists has been fraught with problems. For one thing, secular humanism, for all its advances over the ethics of closed societies, still tends toward a premature foreclosure of its own: humankind itself. Roger Shinn says it well: "In closed humanism [we are] militantly loyal to [humankind] simply because, within the context of the universe, [humankind] represents 'our side.' . . . The nonhuman world is the field of conquest; its only value is its value for human beings."[3]

In contrast, the reign of God expresses an inclusive *universal* community not limited to human beings. How we might more fully experience our community with the beasts of the field, the birds of the air, and the soil and the sea is an extraordinarily important, complex question, but one that goes beyond my present focus. Suffice it to say, unless we can realize our kinship with all of creation, a relationship beyond utilitarian advantage for human beings, our conception of universal community is still foreclosed and the ecological crisis will deepen. Put in H. Richard Niebuhr's words, radical monotheism goes beyond the religion of humanity, as admirable as that is; it even goes beyond the religion of life to an understanding of community that excludes no realm of being from the sphere of value. "Its two great mottoes are: 'I am the Lord thy God; thou shall have no other gods before me' and 'Whatever is, is good.'"[4]

But secular humanism needs transformation by the Christian *personal* principle also. Shinn sees this as the movement from a self-confident to a graceful humanism, from singular confidence in human capacities and potentialities to trust in a grace that is given us for our fulfillment. In a more political theology, Rubem Alves sees the same need: that humanistic messianism, "born out of a historical experience in which only the statistically and quantitatively tangible resources of [our] freedom and determination are available," be transformed into messianic humanism, "created by the historical reality of liberation in spite of the collapse of all human resources."[5]

None of the above theologians explicitly uses the personal and universal principles, though surely the norms are implicitly present in their work. Implicitly so, for these theologians are concerned about a genuinely human existence, but such existence in fact comes only through the reality of personal community. But here in this personal community we are also given the security that breaks us open to the great community, the realm of universal being. And it is the great community, through its universal God, that shatters the pretensions of our little self-enclosed societies.

It is neither necessary nor desirable to argue that the personal and universal principles are the keystone of Christian ethics. It is sufficient to contend that Christian ethics must come to grips with these important realities given in revelation and human experience, for consciousness of their importance brings great gains in our attempts to interpret the moral life.

The Importance of the Moral Tradition

The polar tension between freedom and order in Christian community is crucial to remember in assessing the place of moral tradition, for though such tradition can be used tyrannically, there is moral anarchy without it. We can see this in a variety of ways.

One is in the moral development of the child, concerning which both developmental psychology and ethics have warned of twin dangers. One peril is denying growing children a moral tradition. The other is imprisoning them within an absolutized tradition. For adequate moral development they need to be confronted with a body of moral norms and interpretations. They may accept or reject the norms, and it is important that they sense some freedom in this regard. But in the absence of any fairly clear moral tradition not only are children subject to anxiety and insecurity, they are also denied a crucial developmental experience that is necessary for their later, mature use of normative ethics. This developmental process, obviously, is inconceivable apart from community.

Other more frequently heard arguments for moral rules should be seen in a communal context, also. Rules, it is often observed, are necessary moral habits. They are necessary for the convenience of the decision maker; our lives would be paralyzed had we to reflect ethically on each new moral situation. They are also necessary for social existence; the very communities essential to our being are inconceivable apart from the cement of expectations and obligations that hold them together. Rules are, as Luther often said, "dikes against sin," but the power of restraining our sin actually lies in those relationships to which the rules give expression.

We see the communal nature of rules also in the connections between roles and rules, connections we have noted earlier. All roles involve several different kinds or functions of rules, and a person's role in Christian community is no exception. There are rules of obligation, for example, "A Christian ought to show active concern for the dispossessed in society." There are rules of permission or strategy, for example, "Since those in positions of power seldom voluntarily extend their own privileges to the have-nots, community organization of the dispossessed may be an important activity for the Christian." And there are rules of meaning, for example, "When I march in this demonstration, my actions express my faith's convictions about justice in employment practices." All communities tend to generate these three types of rules. Through participation in the community a person learns them, internalizes them, and understands their appropriate uses.

Not only the functions and types of rules but also their authority must be seen in the communal context. Three ways of understanding their authority are common,[6] but the discussions of these usually abstract rules from their social networks. The first possibility is that of treating a rule as a moral absolute, a context-invariant, morally binding in all situations regardless of different and changing circumstances. Already we have seen that this posture is theologically untenable. What now must be said is that any absolutizing of rules is also and inevitably the absolutizing of the community of which the rules are a part. But such is a henotheistic perversion of the community.

Second, a rule may be used strictly as an illuminative maxim. As such it may or may not give appropriate guidance in the situation, and the rule may be disregarded without hesitation if the person's central moral principle (e.g., love or justice) appears to be better served by doing so. This attitude, though correct in its refusal to absolutize rules, fails to take the moral tradition seriously enough. Consequently, it also expresses a rather cavalier attitude toward the moral community.

A third possibility, however, sees the appropriate rule as always relevant to the situation, though not necessarily decisive. These are prima facie rules. They are not to be disregarded even though they may be overridden. We assume in advance of the situation that the rule ought to be followed, and the burden of proof is upon us when we decide against it.

This third possibility most adequately reflects an appropriate seriousness about the moral community. Christian moral rules are humanly made. At best, they are the community's attempts to articulate appropriate patterns of response to divine activity. Because they are human constructs they are also subject to all the distortions of our sin and finitude. Yet there is reason for a presumption in their favor. The church is the place where we consciously affirm the God whose will is personal-universal community. And the very structures of that consciousness—the Bible, doctrine, symbols, history—provide means of rule correction and rule revision. Just as the moral community creates a presumption in the neighbor's favor (the burden of proof is upon the one who would deny the neighbor's need), so also the same burden of proof applies to the moral tradition. To treat all rules as rules of permission or strategy is to take community with less than the seriousness it deserves.[7]

The question of church pronouncements on social issues is germane to the discussion of rules. The debate is not only between the "comfort" and "challenge" factions in the church. It is also between those who argue for specificity in pronouncements and those, like Paul Ramsey, who would restrict the church's role to the more general cultivation of society's political ethos and to informing the leader's conscience.[8] Ramsey's caution against ill-informed, naive, and theologically presumptuous public statements is well taken, but his general conclusion goes too far.

A well-informed Christian specificity, conscious of its own relativity in the grasp of both social problems and God's truth, is necessary. The church, after all, is not called to perfection but to faithfulness. Such specificity, moreover, is as important in the moral education of church members as in its impact on public policy. We have seen reasons for this. The presence of a moral code (dealing with public as well as with more private issues) is important for our ongoing moral development, whatever our chronological age. Without it we are subtly convinced that such issues are not really important. So also, the public elaboration of moral guidelines makes their following easier for group members. This is true, we saw earlier, in professional associations. It also holds for Christian churches. Surely the processes that change social structures and those that change individuals are inseparably linked.

Community, Institution, and the Uses of Moral Tradition

In contrast to deductive ethics and also to certain types of individualistic existentialism, a social-relational approach can elucidate the intimate interdependence between "the medium and the message," between the Christian community and the moral tradition it carries. Social scientists have helped us understand how a group's institutional structure and its communal life interact, each facet affecting the other. Such clues actually provide parallels to the interaction of the community and its moral tradition, inasmuch as "institution" means not only a group's organizational structure but also the structure of its normative expectations.[9]

While "moral tradition" is much richer and more variegated than a body of moral rules, for the sake of simplicity I will focus on how the community-institution interaction affects the ways that moral rules are interpreted and used.

First, *the community is the foundation of both institutions and rules, not vice versa.* As the sabbath is made for persons, so also institution is made for community, not the other way around. Nowhere ought this to be more apparent than in the church. Likewise, the communal relationship has both a temporal and a value priority over moral rules. It is true in the body politic. "The community," writes a legal philosopher, "is the matrix of its own law; without it there would be no law at all. Law takes its origin in the community, it grows *pari passu* with the community, it functions in the community, it is renewed and sustained by it, and it is directed toward the end which is the community."[10]

So also Christian community is not simply the place where moral rules are taught. More fundamentally it is the basis of such rules and the matrix of their development. Biblical laws did not originate as disconnected bits of revelation; they grew out of the experiences of the covenant community of Israel and the covenanted body of Christ. Moral law presupposes social existence, and Christian moral law presupposes Christian community.[11]

Second, and following from this, *existence in community is necessary if we are to understand and to use properly both the institutional structure and the moral tradition.*[12] For example, the institutional structure of the church is built upon specific obligations—the members' obligation of financial support, the officers' defined responsibilities in guiding the work of the church, the local congregations' duties to denominational structures, and the like. On the other hand, the church's community involves not formal and specific obligations, but indeterminate and general obligations. Unless members perceive and feel these, they find it quite impossible to grasp the necessity or the meaning of specific institutional requirements. This is why, after all, we usually try to elect to crucial church offices those who have more experienced deeply an internalized Christian community. This same interactional pattern applies to moral rules. They convey specific obligations (or prohibitions) that can hardly be understood and appropriately used without a grasp of the relational context of the situation and its implications for community. "You ought not to commit adultery" is lacking both in meaning and moral power apart from some internalization of the marriage relationship.

We can see the same interdependence of factors in the matter of moral knowledge and relational distance. Neighbors' needs—as the neighbors themselves see them—do not constitute all the "facts" of the situation, but they surely are of tremendous importance. Yet this specific moral knowledge of needs comes only as a relationship of understanding is somehow established between the parties. And it is a relationship that is essentially communal and not created by either rules or institutional structures. Josiah Royce saw this in Paul's ethics: "As to the question: 'What shall I do for my brother [or sister]?' Paul has no occasion to answer that question except in terms of the brother's [or sister's] relations to the community. But just for that reason his counsels can be as concrete and definite as each individual case requires them to be."[13] So also, in the attempts of well-intentioned middle-class Christians to assist welfare families: the differences in moral knowledge and effectiveness are immense between those few who have communal ties across class lines and the many who do not.

Third, *community and institution judge and correct each other; likewise the community and its moral tradition stand in this relationship of mutual tension.* The informal obligations of community not only are the basis of institutional requirements, they are also a source of the institution's reformation. The ecumenical movement has provided examples of this when institutional reform has followed the development of informal interdenominational community. In a similar manner, the communal experience judges and corrects its own moral tradition. Thus, the reform of oppressive religious attitudes toward sexual minorities comes not only as scientific knowledge increases, but also as personal relations develop between persons of differing sexualities.

But this process is a two-way street. Though the institution is founded on community, it also becomes semi-independent of it. For this reason institutions can furnish correctives needed to transform and enlarge communal life. The same is true in regard to moral tradition and community.[14] Thus local churches often need the prophetic word on racial justice that can come from the upper reaches of the denominational structure where pressures of the local situation are less intense.

Fourth, *the community is prior to both the institution and to the moral tradition, for norms must be internalized before they become effective and are transmitted to others.* This conviction, especially, in regard to the moral tradition, underlay Horace Bushnell's conception of Christian nurture: "What is wanted, therefore, is not merely to give a child the law, telling him [or her] this is duty, this is right, this God requires, this [God] will punish; but a much greater want is to have the spirit of all duty lived and breathed around [the child]; to see, and feel, and breathe . . . the living atmosphere of grace."[15] This general insight is true of adults, as well. Again Bushnell: "Certain it is that we are never, at any age, so independent as to be wholly out of the reach of organic laws which affect our character."[16]

Moral norms not only are *transmitted* through their incarnation in community, they become morally *effective* in this manner as well. While Christian ethicists too often neglect this fact, it is well recognized in sociology. The sociological insight into the connection between norm commitment and social roles is an example. The significance of socialization is not only in the person's acquiring a commitment to the norms (internalizing them) but also in "that he [or she] accepts the rightness of applying a particular norm or norms to a specific situation. This acceptance is, in turn, based upon an important characteristic of the socialization experience, that the censure and rewards of socialization focus on the role relationships as a unit, far more than on conformity with a single norm."[17] We can see the reasons for this in the socialization of the child. The child cannot see specific moral norms, but can understand concrete roles ("girl," "daddy's helper," etc.). Further, many moral norms must be modified to fit particular role relationships: "Respect your elders" may differ depending upon whether one is relating to parents or to aunts and uncles. Also, the rewards and punishments are centered on role relationships more than on discrete moral norms. "The norm has no independent, original source of power other than persons, and their spontaneous censure usually focuses on the role relationship."[18] Since socialization is not simply a childhood experience but a lifelong process, these observations are applicable to all ages.

The intimate interconnections between the moral tradition and the Christian community is thus another way of pointing to the profound moral significance of this community for its members, and we can thank the social sciences for additional insights about this interdependence. Any Christian ethics that limits its focus to the norms themselves has done only part of its job, for the very manner in which such moral norms function is deeply conditioned by the communal relationships that surround them.

Christian Community
and the Source of Moral Norms

Though we might argue that relationships are the basic stuff of ethics, the social sciences have already suggested that whether or not we actually *perceive* the relationality of norms is quite another matter. When we experience a close sense of community, we do tend to see norms relationally. Where community is not so experienced, the norms appear much more objective. To put it in another way: the greater the psychosocial distance from the source of obligation, the greater the objectivity with which the moral norms will be perceived.

Relational Christian ethics affirms that we always meet and experience God, self, and neighbor interdependently. But, it can be argued, many people neither consciously recognize nor believe this. What of those who affirm no faith in God and who believe that when they meet the neighbor they meet only the neighbor? Or those who would see the neighbor simply as an extension of the self's desires? Or those who believe that only in drawing apart from the neighbor do they really meet God?

Nevertheless, the triadic structure of relatedness seems built into human existence even when it is not recognized. If we are inherently religious, the way we meet the neighbor inescapably expresses the object of our deepest faiths, hopes, and loves. The self's god cannot be escaped. And if the self is inherently social as well as religious, neither can the neighbor (except in our deluded imaginations) be dissolved in the egoism of our self-seeking or in the 'purity' of our religious withdrawals. Nevertheless, the *consciousness* of this triadic reality is of immense ethical-moral importance, and the Christian community's function in keeping such consciousness always before us can hardly be overemphasized.

The same problem, however, crops up in traditional theistic ethics. James Sellers has correctly observed that when it turns from theory to concrete problems conventional theistic ethics usually builds on some scheme of divine-human polarity. Ethical orientations that may differ quite widely in other respects converge in their attempts to construct various devices for relating the divinely given norm and the problematical human situation. But this bifurcation is no longer satisfactory. "We can no longer be content with a description of the norm as divine and of the problematic situation as human. Rather, the norm is divine and human at once, for we see real [human beings] as *imago dei* in Jesus Christ. And the situation is human and divine at once, for we see [persons] becoming real and reflecting the divine in their actions."[19]

The social psychologist affirms that when people experience close community they also tend to understand moral norms relationally. Theologically expressed, when Christ is recognized as the in-betweenness of the self and the neighbor the moral norm loses its heteronomy and participates in theonomy. Barth is right: in this situation the law is changed from command to permission, and this transformation comes only by grace. But grace is inconceivable apart from community and the mediation of others. In all of this it is in community that the divine-human norm becomes real.

This does not reduce the moral claim to subjectivity. "Love," as Niebuhr discerns, "is reverence: it keeps its distance even as it draws near; it does not seek to absorb the other in the self or want to be absorbed by it."[20] Furthermore, God works through secondary groups and institutional structures, not only through communal relations. Fairness in human relations is frequently safeguarded by the former against the misplaced subjectivism of the latter. Yet unless the source of the moral claim is perceived in communal experience, its relationality will be missed. When that happens the heteronomy of the distant lawgiver or the autonomy of self-realization seems to dominate the encounter with the other.

We who are Christian perceive the relationality of the moral norm in a Christian community bound by Christ to the world. The ethical bifurcations that plague the churches—personal ethics versus social ethics, the sacred versus the secular—express at one and the same time distorted conceptions of the church's Head, of its community, and of its relation to the world. These bifurcations depend on belief in One who is not both Christ-in-God and God-in-Christ. They build on the experience of a community that is not both personal and universal in its present life or future hope. They rest on a church posture that attempts to withdraw from the world, to express a religious aspect of the world, or to seek dominion over the world.

But insofar as the church is that conscious servant of God's personal-universal community wherever such community may be found, its ethics reflect the oneness of reality. And just for this reason, Bonhoeffer reminds us, the Christian is no longer the person of eternal conflict. Our worldliness does not divide us from Christ, nor does our Christianity divide us from the world. When we belong wholly to Christ, at that precise time we stand wholly in the world.[21]

Ethics of Christian Community and Ethics of Human Community

The emphasis on the intimate connection between the Christian community and Christian moral norms may lead some to suspect that this is an inside ethics for the church alone. If it is this, it will not engage Christian life with the world. Nor will it provide guidance for common human action on common human problems. Surely such Christian failure frequently occurs. But it is only secondarily the failure to discover those moral norms that can be held in common by all people. More basically, it is the failure to discover the human community itself. Whenever we experience the reality of the personal-universal community, we will also discover norms adequate for cooperative moral action. Without this experience, however, the availability of formalized norms will be of little help.

In some sense, of course, the relationship is dialectical. Our acceptance of common moral norms also facilitates our realization of human community. This latter emphasis is more prevalent in ethical reflection. Without some agreement upon, for example, the ethics of race or of war, how can the human community be more fully realized? There is truth here. But if these very norms themselves are relational, priority must be assigned to the other side—community. Without some realization of community, how will agreed-upon norms emerge? The problem is primarily *relational*; it is secondarily *rational*.

This perspective, of course, suggests an attitude toward natural law. The usual criticisms of traditional natural law are well taken—that it is overly rationalistic, often too specific, and tends to be time-bound, culture-bound, and static. Even the recent attempts to place natural law into a more dynamic framework seem to emphasize the intellect. Yet it is the functional prerequisites of society and the lessons of social experience more than the possession of an innate common rationality that best explain the phenomena to which natural law theories point.[22] Indeed, most evidence from the social sciences, especially that concerning the interdependence of socialization and moral cooperation, points in this direction.

Consider, for example, the shift in attitudes of church leaders toward war between World War I and World War II. Roland Bainton notes that during both wars all three traditional responses to war were present: pacifism, the just war, and the holy crusade. Yet the dominant note sounded by American church leadership during World War I was clearly that of the crusade, whereas in World War II it was of the justified but mournful war. Typical of World War I was this: "American church [people] of all faiths were never so united with each other and with the mind of the country. This was a holy war. Jesus was dressed in khaki and portrayed sighting down a gun barrel. The Germans were Huns. To kill them was to purge the earth of monsters."[23] When World War II broke out, however, "if pacifism largely collapsed, its place was not taken by a crusade in which the knight could fight without qualm, assured that the cause was holy. . . . Such a mood recurred but slightly this time and chiefly in secular quarters. Practically every church pronouncement was replete with the note of contrition."[24]

What accounted for the change? Bainton's own treatment deals mainly with the theological climate during these periods. From our perspective, however, an additional question emerges: Was there a change in relationships among Christians and others during the interwar period, a change that not only was effected by theological attitudes but also affected them?

At this point the conflict theory of sociologist James S. Coleman is illuminating.[25] Though developed from his studies of local community (i.e., town or city) conflicts, his theory has wider applicability. According to Coleman, four variations in the social relations of the community appear to be the most crucial in affecting the course that a controversy will take: (1) When individuals identify their own well-being with the community itself, they are less likely to engage in personal attacks on others, more likely to keep the debate focused upon the issues, and more likely to seek reconciliation. (2) High organizational density usually means that conflicts quickly involve the entire community, but because most organizations help their members to identify with the entire community the conflict is regulated and contained. (3) Those persons most involved in the town's organizational network are more quickly drawn into the conflict, but when the organizationally uninvolved are drawn in they are less constrained and quickly leave the issues to engage in personal attacks. (4) When individuals have many interlocking organizational memberships, the community is more closely knit and the conflict is constrained, but when group memberships are confined to discrete divisions, the conflict tends to become polarized.

It is significant, though perhaps not surprising, that the characteristic responses to international war are similar to the typical responses to local conflicts: going all out against "the enemy" (the holy crusade), refusal to participate in the conflict (pacifism), and a restrained, reluctant participation that takes sides but also seeks reconciliation (the just and mournful war). Inasmuch as the sociologist finds such responses regularly and closely tied *to the relational patterns* of persons in local communities, it seems possible that something similar might hold true in the international example.

Of particular interest to us is the shift away from the holy crusade orientation in World War II. The parallel phenomenon in a local conflict is seen in the individual whose group loyalties are spread throughout the community and who identifies with the community itself as well as with its subgroups. In a conflict situation one then experiences "cross-pressures." Less able to commit oneself fully or enthusiastically to a certain side of the conflict, one will either withdraw, or one will take sides, reluctantly refusing to go "all out" against "the enemy." In either case, having internalized the conflict, one is eager for reconciliation.

What happened to relationships among Christians of different nationalities between the two wars? The increase in communications of all types across national boundaries was considerable. Furthermore, within the church the international ecumenical movement had taken several giant strides. On this latter point, another church historian writes: "Nevertheless, both this [the Edinburgh

Conference] and the Oxford Conference did much to cement the bonds between the leaders of the Churches that were so soon to be engulfed in the war and to be cut off from communication with one another. Relations between Christians on opposite sides of the conflict were never embittered in the Second World War as they had been in the first, when preachers and theological professors had presented arms with shocking slickness."[26]

To be sure, the general increase in communication, the peace movement, and the developing international ecumenical movement are themselves all examples of the interdependence of relationships on the one hand, and beliefs, values, and ideas on the other. But this interdependence is exactly the point. The movement away from the holy crusade position did not occur because of ethical thought in abstraction from experienced relationships. It occurred rather because of the *interaction* of new relational patterns and ethical reflection.

By the time of World War II, church leaders were less able to externalize the conflict. More than previously they were bound to "the enemy" in ways that had become part of their own self-structures. The personal and universal dimensions of their identities had grown with increased involvement in the personal-universal community. To the extent this happens, these same dimensions inevitably will be expressed in moral norms. It is difficult, indeed impossible, to assign any clear priority to the several factors in this process. But to recognize their interdependence is an important part of ethical analysis.

This example of changes in war attitudes is, of necessity, oversimplified. Other elements, of course, entered in. Nor does the example do justice to the complex issue of Christian ethics and the wider community. It may, however, suggest that a relational approach affirming that the fundamental nexus lies in God's personal-universal community can be illuminating. For then the development, the efficacy, and the adequacy of our moral norms all are seen through those particular and concrete relationships that bind us to the *koinonia* and the realm of God both in actuality and in hope.

12

The Church
and Moral Identity

The contemporary Christian serious about the faith faces the same identity pressures in our society as any one else, experientially knowing that which the sociologist describes: "We have created the disposable person: Modular Man [People]."[1] Seeking refuge from the perils of identity diffusion, we are tempted to find self-definition in a foreclosed group—whether family or work group, subculture or class, race or nation.

But the Christian is also faced with identity perils in the church, the very body that voices the promise of wholeness. Only a minority of Christians apparently find their church roles central for self-definition, and even for those escaping the diffusions of cultural Christianity, the foreclosure perils of "the organizational church member" and a narrowly defined religiosity are tempting. Of such features is composed that social context in which we must affirm who we are.

The Christian as
Personal-Universal Self

In contrast to every form of individualism or mysticism, relational theology does not find the solitary, worldless self standing before God, but always finds the self with the neighbor and the self in the world. Some theologians have viewed our dependence upon human relationships as temporary and childish. Wilhelm Herrmann, for example, exclaimed, "Even in respect of our faith in God we outgrow our dependence on our surroundings."[2] Such individualism seems to operate with a mathematical formula of inverse relationships: the more there is of God, the less there is of the self and the self's relations.[3] But the Bible speaks of the One who meets us in the midst of our relations, the One who gives us the neighbor, and in that gift we find our humanness.

The gift comes as and in community. It is true for all people. Christians, however, articulate the nature of that community and that gift in particular ways. We affirm that the personal and universal dimensions of Christian community express and nurture the necessary dimensions of both Christian and human identity. They do so because they point to the nature and activity of God, the personal-universal One. When the personal principle is slighted, identity diffusion results, and when the universal is lacking, identity foreclosure appears.

But we can know ourselves related to the universal realm of being through God-in-Christ. And we can experience the manner of that relationship in love, faithfulness, and hope through the community of Christ-in-God. Such relatedness can transform our moral polytheisms and henotheisms. Indeed, "transform" is the proper word, since we are not removed from the normal relationships and roles of life. Our roles are neither replaced nor dissolved, but we can perceive them and act in them in a new light.

Personal-universal selfhood is, to be sure, an ideal in the sense that we realize it only fragmentarily in this life. It is constantly being retarded and deformed by our sin. In another sense, however, it is not an ideal to be sought. Jesus' paradox of losing and finding life is entirely applicable here. If the personal-universal state of the self becomes that goal sought above all others, then paradox is denied and the quest is in vain. Such a quest involves seductive self-righteousness and is an implicit denial of God's grace. It uses both God and the neighbor for the self's own achievement. All of this distorts and disfigures the very selfhood desired. There is a risk, then, even in attempting to describe Christian identity lest it be interpreted as the goal to be achieved. Yet the risk must be taken, for the task is ethically important.

Moral identity has been described normatively from a variety of perspectives. The philosopher, we have seen, can speak of "the morally educated person." This person, according to John Wilson, can identify with other people. This individual has insight into both the self's and others' needs. Such a person has adequate factual knowledge of the situation and is able to use reason to formulate both rules and principles on the basis of that knowledge.

He or she is committed to carrying the rules and principles into action.[4]

We can also turn to psychologists for their assessment of the "healthy" or "mature" person. Accordingly, healthy adults, says Marie Jahoda, are able to master their own environments, to demonstrate unity in their personalities, and to perceive themselves and their surrounding worlds correctly.[5] Or, says Gordon Allport, the mature person is characterized by expansion (an enlarged scope of interests and concerns), by objectivation (knowing oneself and being able to objectivize oneself fairly easily), and by integration (being unified into a dynamic synthesis).[6]

From the philosophers and psychologists who speak generally of moral identity, we can turn to those concerned more specifically with Christian identity. A psychologically oriented theologian, David Duncombe, cites the following marks of the Christian's shape: a freeing sense of security (that enables one to live with inner freedom in the face of uncertainty or threat); self-knowledge (ability to recognize and acknowledge one's important feelings and acts); honest expression (ability to express one's feelings, thoughts, and doubts); accurate perception (sensitivity to others and to the world in its varied experiences); and adequate response (ability to respond appropriately to the particular situation without being rigidly constricted by social expectations or personal scruples).[7]

Finally, we can turn to the Christian ethicist who describes various components of the Christian moral life. According to James Gustafson, it is a life characterized by a certain perspective and posture toward the self, others, and the world, evoked by confidence in God's goodness through Jesus Christ. It is a life marked by certain dispositions or persisting tendencies to act in particular ways (such as hope, freedom, love, trust, boldness, and humility). It is a life characterized by certain intentions and purposive orientations that, like dispositions, give shape to the self whose basic trust and loyalty are in Jesus Christ. And it is a life whose guiding norms are subject to Christ.[8]

All these descriptions have merit and appropriateness to our concern, not in the least the latter two, which speak particularly of Christian identity. My intention is not to duplicate such efforts. Rather, it is to affirm that *both personal and universal principles un-*

derlie each of the various qualities of the authentic Christian and human moral self.

For example, when we speak of accurate perception of others and of the world about us, we refer to that sensitivity born of personal community and to the universal inclusiveness of that sensitivity. If we speak of dispositions, we refer to qualities or virtues that are both personal and universal in their dimensions. Thus, the virtue of freedom is inner release from excessive concern over the self and others' expectations, release from crippling anxieties and scrupulosities. Such freedom is nurtured in personal community. But it is freedom *for* the other as well as freedom *from* that which constricts the moral life, and this is a dimension of the universal.

If we speak of the self's integration, we are referring to the self's ultimate loyalty, for a person has one self insofar as he or she has one god. But the God of Christian loyalty is the personal-universal One, and the self's integration displays the manner in which the personal and the universal are implied in each other. We cannot be truly personal if we deliberately exclude others from our realms of concern, nor truly universal if we see those others as objects or things. If we speak of the self's intentions and purposive orientations that are shaped by Jesus Christ, we mean that the self's governing direction is the personal-universal community—for surely this is the intention of God-in-Christ and Christ-in-God.

Thus, my aims in describing the nature of Christian identity are both limited and inclusive. They are limited because I offer here no detailed description of the many facets and qualities of Christian moral existence. By the same token they are inclusive, for here is the claim that whatever these facets and qualities of Christian identity may be, they characterize the individual who authentically even if fragmentarily participates in personal-universal existence.

The Church Role, Freedom, and the Prophet

The issue of determination and freedom—important as it is to this entire inquiry—needs further examination. The problem is raised, for example, by the observation that some persons seem to be dominated by their occupational roles. Actually, however, it is inaccurate to speak of a role dominating the person. Roles do not rigidly determine actions and attitudes. People do. This realization reflects the important distinction between the "I" and the "me." The irreducible "I" is never completely determined. My roles (part of "me") are, indeed, highly significant for my behavior, but they are significant because they figure prominently into my interpretation of situations. And it is *I* who must interpret, *I* who must decide, *I* who must act.

To be sure, some of the social scientists on whose insights we have drawn do not exercise sufficient care in this regard. Even George Herbert Mead, whose "I" and "me" distinction is so crucial, slipped into an unacceptable behaviorism and was prone to "the oversocialized conception of the self," a problem implicit in a great deal of contemporary social science.[9] Such a perspective assumes that the self is little more than an acceptance seeker, and this view moves toward a theory of motivation in which social approval and social harmony are pivotal. This is one of the dangers of sociological functionalism, a pitfall we recognized earlier. Relational Christian ethics is not immune from this danger, yet it is quite possible to use these social science insights while interpreting them through our own assumptions about God and human existence.

A relational account of the prophet or reformer is a case in point. Community in Jesus Christ always stands in judgment on the partial and distorted expressions of that community in the Christian churches (as well as elsewhere). Indeed, one of the key marks of the church's participation in personal-universal community is its capacity and willingness to act as a fountain of its own self-criticism. It nurtures the healthy restlessness and fresh imagination of the prophet within its midst. Here is the reformer who brings to bear the eschatological community on the existing community, and can do so precisely because of conscious participation in both and in the tension between them. The prophet is not an unrelated, rugged individualist, but rather one who lives with vivid awareness of her or his own multifaceted sociality. Standing within the prophetic tradition, Jesus did not preach the infinite value of the individual. Jesus proclaimed the realm of God and its implications for human existence.

Friedrich Schleiermacher and Josiah Royce both exhibit this understanding. Both saw the prophet and the reformer not as exceptions to basic human sociality but as instances of it. Schleiermacher, discussing the determinations of self-consciousness, delineates a twofold movement in "purifying or restorative activity": church discipline and church reform. Church discipline means, in part, that one cannot mold one's own spirit. This molding is done by the Divine Spirit that Christ imparts not to the individual as such but to the entire Christian community. Nevertheless, church reform is as essential as church discipline. The reformer calls the church back to its true nature when the church distorts the reality of Christian community. Thus, it is a two-way movement.[10]

Royce, acutely sensitive to the distortions and sins of individualism (which, he observed, feed collectivistic fires), was keenly aware that true individuality can grow only in community. The affirmation of true individuality over against person-stifling collectivism is possible, he contended, not as a protest on behalf of the unrelated individual but as a protest of loyalty to the universal community, the body of Christ.[11]

In this entire exploration of the moral nexus, I do not believe I have artificially grafted theological perspectives such as these onto an alien trunk of social science. Or vice versa. The assumption in such a procedure would be that only in theology is there room for freedom, whereas in the social sciences everything is socially determined. One can, of course, postulate (as some do) a narrow social scientific frame of reference wherein it is impossible to speak of personal freedom. But the logic of the social sciences does not require this.[12]

If we affirm that freedom is subjectively real to us, if we affirm that part of freedom's meaning is precisely the ability to contribute to a predetermination of the social future, then we also see society neither as a prison nor as a puppet theater but as a drama, a stage filled with living actors. The players have been shaped and guided by the scenario, but they also have the liberty to play their roles with inner conviction and role distance. They have the option of giving ultimate significance to their immediate social environment or, without transcending their own sociality, gaining transcendent perspective on their immediate communities through their participation in the reality of the great community.

Such is the role of the prophet. Indeed, it is the calling of every human being.

Christ as Role Model

Since our identities and key social roles are always closely intertwined, one of the major ways we learn to be Christians is through our observation of role models. Another member of the congregation, a modern Christian hero, a saint from the church's past—each may function as a role model, for good or for ill. In a normative and somewhat different way Jesus Christ himself is the role model for Christians.

Much of the reaction in contemporary Christian ethics against interpreting Jesus as a pattern and moral blueprint is well taken.[13] Yet the notion of role is not quite the same. Role is basically a concept that focuses on relationships and on the context of expectations rather than on character traits, specific attitudes, or actions. These latter factors obviously accompany roles, but they follow in the wake of role interpretation.

Niebuhr's remarkable description of the image of responsibility exhibited by Jesus Christ is to the point: "The responsible self we see in Christ and which we believe is being elicited in all our race is a universally and eternally responsive I, answering in universal society and in time without end, in all actions upon it, to the action of the One who heals all our diseases, forgives all our iniquities, saves our lives from destruction, and crowns us with everlasting mercy. The action we see in such life is obedient to law, but goes beyond all laws; it is form-giving but even more form-receiving; it is fitting action. It is action that is fitted into the context of universal, eternal, life-giving action by the One. It is infinitely responsible in an infinite universe to the hidden yet manifest principle of its being and its salvation."[14] Applied to this description, "role model" seems an appropriate term. Niebuhr is not describing actions to be imitated or specific moral beliefs that may or may not be relevant to social situations two millennia later. Rather, he is describing the basic relationships and context within which the responsible self, seen decisively in Jesus Christ, exists and acts.

But Christ does not exist for us without community. Of course the style of life the congregation inevitably communicates to its members and the world around it is often at variance with the role-ship we see in the Jesus Christ of the New Testament. His role-ship stands in judgment on every such distortion. There is always a tension between the eschatological Christ and the Christ existing as community. But unless there are fleshly embodiments, roles lack efficacy. In that case they are not really role models but ideals, and, in theological language, there is no continuing incarnation.

Persons in contemporary society are unusually aware of the importance of role and identity models. They are also unusually aware of the difficulty in finding adequate models. As Marshall McLuhan reminds us, the movement from the linear to the electronic stage accentuates the significance of models and images, while at the same time an associational mass society makes meaningful models and their community contexts more difficult to find. All this suggests something to the church—for Christ as role model must have continuing incarnation.

The Church as
"Role Budget Center"

Socialization and identity are not fixed states but ongoing processes. The church, to the extent it is a significant influence for its members, does not merely socialize the person toward a certain moral identity and then recede from this function. Rather, it continues as a living moral center. Its ongoing communication of role models is one way of understanding this. Another is its function as "a role budget center."

Sociologist William J. Goode has developed this provocative notion in regard to the family.[15] Goode bases this concept on his theory of role strain, which assumes that persons desire integrity and freedom from destructive role conflict (assumptions congenial to our perspective). Each person's total role system is unique. Moreover, it makes more demands than one can fulfill, and it makes demands that frequently conflict with one another. For many adults and children alike, the family is in a key position to assist in solutions to such role strain and conflict. "Most individuals must account to their families for what they spend in time, energy, and money outside the family. And ascriptive status obligations of high evaluation or primacy are found in the family. More important, however, is the fact that family members are often the only persons who are likely to know how [one] is allocating [one's] total role energies, managing [one's] whole role system."[16]

Here in such a family, then, are important role budgeting resources. Here the person is known more completely in varied role obligations and pressures, fulfillments and failures. From this communal background one can gain perspective and support in working out role strains. Here one's role is more ascribed than achieved, more given than earned. One knows one's own family role well. It has the comfort of an old shoe. Regularly the person finds that in this role and this community he or she can lick the wounds inflicted by role conflicts elsewhere. The member is indeed held to standards in the family. But the very fact that roles here are ascribed more than achieved means that one is not judged by the same fine distinctions of accomplishment encountered in most other roles. Here one finds more flexibility, more room for individual differences, and a "role cushion" in regard to one's other groups.

To be sure, Goode's theory is based upon certain assumptions about the family that are not true of many families in our society and, indeed, seldom fully experienced in any. Yet I believe his theory is valid precisely to the degree that the family participates in personal-universal community. And if the role budget center is an appropriate clue to a process that goes on in personal-universal community, it is an instructive notion to apply to the church.

The church role is more comparable to a family role than, for example, to most occupational roles. In the church as in the family there are standards. But, insofar as the community is personal, the ethos is one of grace more than law, of ascription more than achievement. It is role ascription but not in the medieval-hierarchical sense of recognized status compared to superiors and inferiors. It is rather the ascription of one's ultimate status as a free and beloved person—a gift. And here the universal principle is expressed in the range of moral concern that extends to and encompasses all other roles and relations.

Yet few congregations offer the interpersonal intimacy that the family can afford. Even so, as Dittes observes, the very fact that the congregation may be somewhat removed from the intense relationships experienced elsewhere gives it the opportunity to provide a "moratorium." Such moratoria, Erikson also has argued, are of crucial importance for adolescent identity establishment. But an ongoing moratorium experience is vital for the maintenance and transformation of adult identities as well. Thus Dittes is right in noting that "it is good and necessary . . . for churches to have in their parish life struggle and stress, even demands and pressures, a true slice of life as it is lived outside. But the suggestion being made here is that these pressures and stresses not be accompanied by the desperate, sometimes almost life-and-death sanctions which they have outside."[17] This grace gives "playfulness" and leisure in the life of the congregation that allow reflection and perspective upon other life roles.

If Christian community is to function as role budget center, it seems likely that this must happen in a church-subcommunity combination. For some the subcommunity will be the nuclear family. For others it may be a friendship group, for still others a group expressing a distinctive subculture. The church and the subcommunity need each other, for we need both. We need intimate community with acceptance and knowledge of our role-sets. But the intimate community must be personal or it will constrict the self instead of freeing us. And it cannot be personal without the thrust toward universality, in this case the concern for our integrity in the whole range of our role commitments. The church's symbolization and public celebration of the Source of *koinonia* and the realm of God thus assists the particular subcommunity as well as the congregation itself to be an effective role budget center. Thus, the role budget center as a moratorium for identity shaping is another way that the ongoing interdependence of Christian identity and community is expressed. And ongoing it must be, for the Christian's identity is never finished, never static, and seldom free from internal strain and conflict.

Christian Community and Role Transformation

Christ came and comes in the form of a servant. This is the clue for the church's stance toward the world. And if so, it is also the clue for the relation of the member's church role to other roles. The church role is to serve and transform. To do this it must retain its distinctiveness, for otherwise there is only Christian identity diffusion. But the integrity of nonchurch roles must be respected also, lest Christian identity foreclosure be the case.[18]

We have seen some of the nontransformative ways in which people often use their church roles. They can be masks or shields wherein church participation is a busy escape from unpleasant realities. They can give uncritical support to other major roles, as when the church role provides some security for the rootless young executive without raising serious questions about the occupational climb. The church role can be misused in a host of other ways as well, but such need not be the case.

A sociological study of different orientations to bureaucratic roles in the federal government is suggestive at this point. Just as the church role need not function uncritically or in an escapist manner, so also the civil servant need not develop a "bureaucratic personality." Leonard Reissman has discovered four basic types of orientation to similar bureaucratic roles.[19] First is that of the person oriented primarily toward a professional group outside the bureaucracy. This is "the functional bureaucrat," one whose major concern is the professional quality of one's own work. "The specialist bureaucrat" is similar, but this person exhibits a greater identification with the bureaucracy. Third, "the service bureaucrat" is one who utilizes the framework of the bureaucracy as that through which he or she can best realize certain personally held goals of service to a group outside the structure itself. Last are those entirely immersed in the bureaucratic structure, finding their aspirations, goals, standards of achievement, and satisfaction all in the organization itself—"the job bureaucrats."

It is "the service bureaucrat" who provides a promising model. Here is the person who is "in but not of" the bureaucracy. This person is immersed in the bureaucracy's functions and necessities, but does not depend on it for major goals, satisfactions, or sense of worth. This person sees the bureaucracy's necessity and value without absolutizing it. Nor is primary value placed on the quality of the work or achievements. Rather, this person uses the bureaucratic role and achievements as means of rendering a needed service. It is quite possible that a civil servant's church role can make the crucial difference in seeing his or her work in this perspective.

The church role can be instrumental in serving and even transforming one's other roles in a variety of ways. In the gracious community of Christ-in-God we can face our own sin, our illusions about the world will be fewer, and our questions more penetrating. Here we can recognize God's Spirit at work in the world, and can then discover that our hopes for that world are greater and our sensitivities sharpened. And in this community, which is also the congregation of God-in-Christ, we might realize the universal context of our relatedness and responsibility.

These dimensions of the church role go far beyond the common notion that the Christian occupational responsibility is to exhibit those virtues typically associated with "the Christian moral life." Not that such virtues are unimportant. But they become important when they are not pieces of an exhibit of "the virtuous self" but rather characteristics of the relationships of those who can ask the right questions, who can bring the penetrating perspectives, and who have insight into the possibilities and responsible uses of the occupational roles in which they are involved. Indeed, a certain identity style can come through the church role. It is the style of those who have not given their hearts to the world but who care about it so deeply they may lose their lives for it.[20]

How completely can the church role and the Christian identity transform our other roles and identifications? Regarding this difficult question, racial identity is a case in point. Some years ago, early in the days of the civil rights movement when racial segregation in the churches was even more obvious than it is now, a suggestive debate occurred between two Christian ethicists. Kyle Haselden argued that within the Christian fellowship (as we know it from the New Testament) there can be no ethnic or racial distinctions. If one applies for membership in the church, one applies as a Christian and not, for example, as a black person. Any discussion of that person's admission on the basis of race is simply evidence that both the conscience and the church have surrendered their right to the name "Christian." Haselden concluded: "In the Christian community divisive differences remain only as a phantasm of deluded minds and prejudiced hearts. When [one] sees [another] Christian as anything other than a Christian, [one] has called forth a specter which has its embodiment only in [one's] own mind and heart, an apparition which fades and disappears as [one] is lost in Christ."[21]

Paul Ramsey countered with a plea for greater realism, maintaining that the church member "who saw only such Christians around . . . on Sunday morning would be seeing specters."[22] In the flesh-and-blood people for whom Christ came, differences among persons do not fade into phantasms. To be sure, it is in the church that the tension between what we are and what we are to become ought to be the greatest. Nevertheless, argued Ramsey, as we try to make ideal Christian descriptions of perfect community regulative of the actual community of the church, the results can be disruptive. This is because we are living between the times, and the reality of the community in Christ is relevant primarily as an eschatological standard of judgment, a standard that radically criticizes all actual churches and societies. Here then was the debate: Are other roles and identities "lost in Christ," or does Christian identity exist more as eschatological hope and critique than as empirical possibility?

Neither of these emphases, however, really does justice to the transformative possibilities in Christian identity. If the former too easily assumes that racial identity is replaced rather than transformed by Christian existence, the latter too easily concludes that Christian identity leaves racial identity essentially unchanged, even while it brings awareness of the gap between what is and what ought to be. Here are the ingredients of those ancient but ever-relevant debates about eschatology and sanctification, though now cast in terms of identity.

On the one hand, it is true that race is never simply blotted out. In part this reflects the depth of our moral problem, and in the years since the above discussion we have seen ample evidence of the stubbornness of white racism. But the tenacity of racial identification needs to be recognized for its positive side as well. Toward the end of the 1960s an emerging black pluralism and the rise of the Black Power movement were both significant and positive. So also were certain changes in racial justice strategies in dominantly white denominations. Whites had begun to realize what many people of color had long known: that the vicious denial of the black person's right to a positive racial identity had produced incalculable human suffering in both identity diffusion and foreclosure, and that one oppressed because of race simply could not experience self-respect and authentic humanness without also experiencing an affirmative blackness confirmed by the environment.[23]

Events in succeeding years have tutored us in some of these things. Our racial roles and identities do remain and must remain with us; they are not simply dissolved in Christ. But neither must nor need they remain paramount. True, we live between the times, but the great community is more than eschatological judgment and hope. Social psychologists teach us that our identities are never utterly fixed. More fundamentally, this is the message of the gospel.

But this larger, transforming human identification—wherein racial identification takes its positive but subordinate place—is scarcely possible apart from a mediating community that effectively incarnates the personal and the universal. Integrity in the self cannot be separated from integration of the self into community. In her study of individuals involved in crises over racial justice Eleanor Haney observed: "It seems that it is necessary for the self to be able to identify with a community that finally is sustaining and valid for him [or her]. One of the outstanding characteristics of those who found it so agonizing to remain consistent was their sense of being absolutely alone. Although personal integrity is not simply a microcosm of one's ethos, it does not seem possible apart from a close relationship with an ethos."[24]

Christian Identity
and Human Identity

It is not surprising that in much contemporary theology and ethics the question, What does it mean to be a Christian? is eclipsed by the question, What does it mean to be a human being?[25] In part the eclipse is a healthy reaction to false Christian imperialism and exclusiveness. In part the shift simply reflects a growing sense of urgency to find viable means for meaningful survival on planet earth. However, it is an error—psychologically, sociologically, theologically—to think we can come into an unmediated identification with the human community. Some are arguing "that becoming human is, for Christians, a prior matter to becoming Christians."[26] In terms of *valuational* priority this is altogether true. But in terms of the *process* by which humanization occurs it is simply false.

Identity is always a relational matter. It always involves two questions: To whom am I related? How am I so related? As such, identity is always a social question, necessarily involving the mediation of the communities in which we exist and which exist in us. We have looked at a good bit of evidence in this regard, and I find its testimony unmistakable. The question then is this: Is there a community that promises the mediation of God's intended humanity for us?

To argue that the Christian church offers such community is not to claim that the only path to humanization is the Christian one. The grace of the God of Jesus Christ is no monopoly of Christians, and any such arrogance effectively becomes an enormous barrier to recognizing and experiencing that grace. But Christians are people, and people are social beings for whom both the medium and goal of existence is community. We confess that it is in Christian community, not somewhere else, that we have decisively met the personal-universal One. Others may and do truly meet God elsewhere. But we confess that it is here we find the criteria—the symbols, the traditions, the history of a people, the decisive revelatory event of Jesus Christ—that in spite of all our churchly distortions and unfaithfulness still offer us our best hope of participating in God's intended humanity.

Nor does this argument claim that the Christian experience of humanization is less partial or less distorted than that experienced by those who find other communities of mediation. Such a claim, too, flies in the face of much evidence we have examined and much of the church's history that we have not here named. Moreover, the claim is insufferably self-righteous. Our affirmation is at once more modest and more daring. It is that in spite of the fragmentary and misshapen humanity we experience, in Christian community we have discovered, can discover, and are discovering the relationship given by the One who binds us to the universal realm and who binds us to it in faithfulness, hope, and love. Such is the experience in community that is called to be both *koinonia* and expression of the realm of God.

All of this is fragmentary in our experience. Its fullness exists in the reality of God's being and intention. Its fullness, then, we know in faith—not "only in faith" but "truly in faith." But such an affirmation is not merely a wishful homily with which to conclude this study. It finds foundation both in faith's affirmation and in empirical investigation. We have seen striking research evidence that—even in a liberal denomination where many suspect the "devotional" orientation to faith as socially conservative and religiously restrictive—the "inner-worldly ascetic," the one who consciously acknowledges, practices, and expresses the personal relation to God, actually is more apt rather than less likely to have genuine concern for the fuller realization of the universal reign of justice and love.[27]

Though he contended for "a Christian society" in ways that I cannot accept, surely T. S. Eliot in "Choruses from 'The Rock'"captures the heart of the issue with which we have been wrestling:

> What life have you if you have not life together?
> There is no life that is not in community,
> And no community not lived in praise of GOD.[28]

The first line of his verse seems to express the hungry, yearning, sometimes desperate realization of people in a mass society. Social scientists have affirmed the second line in myriad and suggestive ways. Even when it does not insist on the Christian form of praise as the only form, Christian theology insists on the utter necessity and reality of that which is conveyed in the third line.

The poet's words say much about both the assumptions and the conclusions of this study. We have seen, if in a rudimentary manner, how the human wisdom of the social sciences must be combined with our theological reflection if we are to understand the intimate interdependence of identity, moral ethos, and community—both Christian and human. Many who might accept this methodology may, on the other hand, be reluctant to accept some of the conclusions of this book, conclusions that highlight the critical importance of the church as moral community. Indeed, there are understandable grounds for pessimism about today's church.

But if there is no life without life together, and if life together in the community of being does not come without mediation, then the potential significance of the church as moral community is inescapable. That such potential is realized, even if fragmentarily, is possible only when—but always when—there is faithful response to the One in our midst who is both Christ-in-God and God-in-Christ.

Notes

Introduction to the
Twenty-fifth Anniversary Edition

1. See Carol Gilligan, *In a Different Voice* (Harvard University Press, 1982).
2. See Beverly Wildung Harrison, *Making the Connections* (Beacon Press, 1985); Carter Heyward, *Touching Our Strength* (Harper & Row, 1989); and Carol S. Robb, *Equal Value* (Beacon Press, 1996).
3. *The Harvard Theological Review*, Vol. LVIII, No. 2 (April 1965).
4. See William K. Frankena, *Ethics*, 2nd ed. (Prentice-Hall, 1973).
5. Stanley Hauerwas, "Virtue and Character," in Warren Thomas Reich, ed., *Encyclopedia of Bioethics*, rev. ed., Vol. 5 (Simon & Schuster Macmillan, 1995), p. 2526. Compare his *Character and the Christian Life*, 2d ed. (University of Notre Dame Press, 1985); and Alasdair MacIntyre, *After Virtue: A Study in Moral Theology*, 2d ed. (University of Notre Dame Press, 1984).
6. See Richard Bondi, "Character Ethics and Pastoral Care," in Rodney J. Hunter (ed.), *Dictionary of Pastoral Care and Counseling* (Abingdon Press, 1990), p. 137. Bondi's description here and his article "Character" in James F. Childress and John Macquarrie, eds., *The Westminster Dictionary of Christian*

Ethics (Westminster Press, 1986), pp. 82ff., provide an excellent overview of the subject.

7. Op. cit., *The Westminster Dictionary of Christian Ethics*, p. 83.
8. See Kathryn Montgomery Hunter, "Narrative," in *Encyclopedia of Bioethics*, rev. ed., Vol. 4, pp. 1789–93.
9. See Stanley Hauerwas, *The Peaceable Kingdom* (University of Notre Dame, 1983), p. 35.
10. See Bondi, "Character," in Childress and Macquarrie, eds., *The Westminster Dictionary of Christian Ethics*, p. 83.
11. Ibid.
12. Ronald Preston, "Conscience," in *The Westminster Dictionary of Christian Ethics*, pp. 116f.
13. See "Faith Development," in David J. Atkinson and David H. Field, eds., *New Dictionary of Christian Ethics and Pastoral Theology* (InterVarsity Press, 1995), p. 371.

Chapter 1. Becoming More Conscious of Some "Unconscious Influences"

1. Horace Bushnell, "Unconscious Influence," in his *Sermons for the New Life* (Charles Scribner's Sons, 1907), p. 186.
2. Ibid., p. 187.
3. Ibid. Compare Horace Bushnell, *Christian Nurture* (Charles Scribner's Sons, 1916), pp. 21f., and *Sermons on Living Subjects* (Charles Scribner's Sons, 1892), pp. 108f.
4. Compare Robert A. Nisbet, *Community and Power* (Oxford University Press, 1962), p. 49.
5. James M. Gustafson, *Christ and the Moral Life* (Harper & Row, 1968), p. 4. See the entirety of chap. 1 for an illuminating discussion of these issues, around which he organizes the structure of his book.
6. John Fry, in *The Immobilized Christian* (Westminster Press, 1963), argues this point by a presentation of phenomenological images that dominate the privacies of the mind.
7. Henry David Aiken, "The New Morals," *Harper's Magazine*, Feb. 1968.
8. Compare James M. Gustafson's analysis of the relation between actions, convictions, and intentions in his *The Church as Moral Decision-Maker* (Pilgrim Press, 1970), pp. 97ff.
9. Both H. Richard Niebuhr and James Gustafson have clarified

these methodological issues. See Gustafson's "Christian Ethics and Social Policy," in Paul Ramsey, ed., *Faith and Ethics: The Theology of H. Richard Niebuhr* (Harper & Brothers, 1958), pp. 124ff., and his description of Niebuhr's method in the introduction to the latter's *The Responsible Self* (Harper & Row, 1963), pp. 12ff.

10. Gustafson, in Ramsey, ed., *Faith and Ethics*, p. 124.
11. Gerhard Lenski "Religion's Impact on Secular Institutions," in Joan Brothers, ed., *Readings in the Sociology of Religion* (Oxford: Pergamon Press, 1967), pp. 218f.
12. Gibson Winter, *Elements for a Social Ethic* (Macmillan Company, 1966), p. 280.
13. Two ethicists who are particularly helpful in expressing this understanding are James Sellers, *Theological Ethics* (Macmillan Company, 1966), chap. 8; and Max L. Stackhouse, "Technical Data and Ethical Norms: Some Theoretical Considerations," *Journal for the Scientific Study of Religion*, Vol. V, No. 2 (Spring 1966).
14. See Robert K. Merton, *Social Theory and Social Structure*, rev. and enlarged ed. (Free Press of Glencoe, 1957), p. 281.
15. See Peter Berger, *Invitation to Sociology: A Humanistic Perspective* (Doubleday & Co., 1963), ch. 2.
16. See Scott G. McNall, *The Sociological Experience* (Little, Brown & Co., 1969), ch. 2.
17. Waldo Beach, *Christian Community and American Society* (Westminster Press, 1969), outlines this approach. See pp. 69ff.
18. See Winter, *Elements for a Social Ethic*, esp. chaps. 2 and 6. Compare McNall, *The Sociological Experience*, pp. 9f. and 35, for a description of major models of sociology and their principal assumptions.
19. Paul Tillich, *Systematic Theology* (University of Chicago Press, 1951), Vol. I, pp. 9ff.

Chapter 2.
Clues from Relational Christian Ethics

1. There is a question whether relationalism is a sufficiently coherent perspective to be labeled as such. James M. Gustafson points to both diversity and commonality within contextual-

ism in his "Context versus Principles: A Misplaced Debate in Christian Ethics," *Harvard Theological Review*, Vol. LVIII, No. 2 (April 1965), esp. pp. 175ff. and 185. Edward L. Long, Jr., treats relationalism as a coherent theme in his *A Survey of Christian Ethics* (Oxford University Press, 1967), chaps. 8, 9, and 10.

2. Gustafson provides an excellent summary of this approach to Christian ethics in "Christian Ethics and Social Policy," in Ramsey, ed., *Faith and Ethics*. Compare Gustafson, "Christian Ethics," in Paul Ramsey (ed.), *Religion* (Prentice-Hall, 1965).

3. Paul L. Lehmann, "The Foundation and Pattern of Christian Behavior," in John Hutchison, ed., *Christian Faith and Social Action* (Charles Scribner's Sons, 1953), p. 107.

4. See Gustafson, "Christian Ethics and Social Policy," in Ramsey, ed., *Faith and Ethics*, p. 127.

5. H. Richard Niebuhr, "The Center of Value," in Ruth Nanda Anshen, ed., *Moral Principles of Action* (Harper & Brothers, 1952). This essay, slightly revised, also appears in H. Richard Niebuhr, *Radical Monotheism and Western Culture* (Harper & Brothers, 1960). Waldo Beach makes similar use of Niebuhr's theory in his *Christian Community and American Society*, pp. 80–84. For critical reflection on Niebuhr's value theory, see Ramsey, ed., *Faith and Ethics*, especially the essays by George Schrader and Paul Ramsey.

6. Niebuhr, *Radical Monotheism*, p. 107.

7. For an especially helpful discussion of this multidimensionality of value, see H. Richard Niebuhr, *Christ and Culture* (Harper & Brothers, 1951), pp. 237ff.

8. See Niebuhr, *Radical Monotheism*, p. 112.

9. Alexander Miller, *The Man in the Mirror: Studies in the Christian Understanding of Selfhood* (Doubleday & Co., 1958), p. 97.

10. See H. Richard Niebuhr, "Evangelical and Protestant Ethics," in Elmer J. F. Arndt, ed., *The Heritage of the Reformation* (Richard R. Smith, 1950), p. 222.

11. See Alexander Miller, *The Renewal of Man* (London: Victor Gollancz, 1956), p. 48.

12. C. Freeman Sleeper, *Black Power and Christian Responsibility* (Abingdon Press, 1969), p. 57.

13. Paul L. Lehmann, *Ethics in a Christian Context* (Harper & Row, 1963), pp. 78 and 99.

14. James M. Gustafson, "A Theology of Christian Community?" in Egbert de Vries, ed., *Man in Community* (Association Press, 1966), pp. 178f.
15. Lehmann, "The Foundation and Pattern of Christian Behavior," in Hutchison, ed., *Christian Faith and Social Action*, p. 101.
16. Ibid., p. 104.
17. Gordon Kaufman's exploration of the church's role in regard to the intended universal community of God is especially helpful. See his *Systematic Theology: A Historicist Perspective* (Charles Scribner's Sons, 1968), chap. 31.
18. I have treated some of these same issues in a more popular manner in my *The Responsible Christian* (United Church Press, 1969), esp. chaps. 1 and 5.
19. Niebuhr, "Evangelical and Protestant Ethics," in Arndt, ed., *The Heritage of the Reformation*, pp. 222f. Compare Waldo Beach, *The Christian Life* (Covenant Life Curriculum Press, 1966), p. 40.
20. Kaufman, *Systematic Theology*, p. 21.
21. See Sellers, *Theological Ethics*, pp. 53ff.
22. Daniel Day Williams, *The Spirit and the Forms of Love* (Harper & Row, 1968), p. 146.
23. Ibid., p. 5. Theologians are, it appears, increasingly aware of new forms of religiosity in a secular culture. See Martin E. Marty, "The American Situation in 1969," in Donald R. Cutler, ed., *The Religious Situation 1969* (Beacon Press, 1969).
24. See esp. Martin Buber, *I and Thou*, trans. Ronald Gregor Smith (Edinburgh: T. & T. Clark, 1937), and *Between Man and Man*, trans. Ronald Gregor Smith (Macmillan Co., 1948).
25. The most formative for ethics among the symbolic interactionists were George Herbert Mead, Charles Horton Cooley, William James, and John Dewey. Compare Albert T. Rasmussen, "The Implications of the Theory of Symbolic Interaction for the Establishment of Ethical Principles," doctoral dissertation (University of Chicago, 1943).
26. Compare Miller, *The Man in the Mirror*, p. 37, and Joseph Haroutunian, *God with Us* (Westminster Press, 1965), p. 17. Note that the title of Miller's book is reminiscent of Cooley's famous phrase, "the looking-glass self."

27. John Macmurray, *Persons in Relation* (London: Faber & Faber, 1961), p. 48.
28. H. Richard Niebuhr, "The Ego-Alter Dialectic and the Conscience," *Journal of Philosophy*, 42 (1945), pp. 353f. Compare Niebuhr, *The Responsible Self*, pp. 71ff.
29. Niebuhr, *The Responsible Self*, p. 56.
30. James M. Gustafson, *Treasure in Earthen Vessels* (Harper & Row, 1961), p. 27.
31. H. Richard Niebuhr, *The Meaning of Revelation* (Macmillan Co., 1941), p. 48.
32. Kaufman, *Systematic Theology*, p. 335.
33. Niebuhr, *The Meaning of Revelation*, p. 77.
34. Ibid., p. 78. See also Niebuhr, *Radical Monotheism*, chap. 2.
35. Niebuhr, "The Ego-Alter Dialectic and the Conscience," p. 357.
36. Ibid.
37. Ibid., p. 356.
38. See D. D. Williams, *The Spirit and the Forms of Love*, p. 202.
39. Lehmann, "The Foundation and Pattern of Christian Behavior," in Hutchison (ed.), *Christian Faith and Social Action*, p. 107. Compare Lehmann, *Ethics in a Christian Context*, p. 45.
40. Joseph Fletcher, *Situation Ethics* (Westminster Press, 1966), p. 53.
41. See Niebuhr, *Christ and Culture*, p. 238.
42. Two recent studies of conscience are particularly helpful at this point. Eleanor Humes Haney, "A Study of Conscience as It Is Experienced in Race Relations," doctoral dissertation (Yale University, 1965), provides an illuminating and comprehensive analysis of the dimensions of conscience, to which I am indebted in this section. Likewise, Eric Mount, Jr., *Conscience and Responsibility* (John Knox Press, 1969), gives a helpful survey of contemporary relational ethics as it bears upon conscience and selfhood. Both authors draw heavily upon the same ethical sources that I have, and their books are suggestive treatments in greater detail of what I have dealt with more briefly here.
43. See Lehmann, *Ethics in a Christian Context*, pp. 358, 366.
44. See Gustafson, *Christ and the Moral Life*, pp. 257 f., and Haney, "A Study of Conscience," pp. 339f.

45. Niebuhr, *The Responsible Self*, p. 75.
46. Ibid., p. 76.
47. See, e.g., Julian Hartt's criticism of Niebuhr's relational self, "The Situation of the Believer," pp. 225–44, in Ramsey, ed., *Faith and Ethics.*
48. Kaufman, *Systematic Theology*, pp. 336f. Compare p. 440.
49. G. K. Chesterton, *Orthodoxy* (Dodd, Mead & Co., 1952), p. 85, as quoted by Miller in *The Man in the Mirror*, p. 54.

Chapter 3. The Church and the Moral Self: Avenues for Inquiry

1. Gustafson, *Christ and the Moral Life*, chap. 7.
2. Ibid., pp. 248 and 256.
3. Niebuhr, *The Responsible Self*, p. 126.
4. Dietrich Bonhoeffer, *Ethics*, ed. Eberhard Bethge (London: SCM Press, 1955), pp. 17 ff.
5. Ibid., p. 18.
6. See Gustafson, *Treasure in Earthen Vessels.*
7. H. Richard Niebuhr, *The Purpose of the Church and Its Ministry* (Harper & Brothers, 1956), chap. 1.
8. Niebuhr, *Radical Monotheism*, p. 58.
9. Bonhoeffer, *Ethics*, pp. 20f. Compare his *The Communion of Saints* (Harper & Row, 1963).
10. Miller, *The Man in the Mirror*, p. 133.
11. Kaufman, *Systematic Theology*, p. 501.
12. D. D. Williams, *The Spirit and the Forms of Love*, p. 147.
13. Haroutunian, *God with Us*, p. 121.
14. James N. Lapsley, "Motives and Motivation," in John Macquarrie, ed., *Dictionary of Christian Ethics* (Westminster Press, 1967), p. 220.
15. D. D. Williams, *The Spirit and the Forms of Love*, p. 205.
16. Compare Miller, *The Renewal of Man*, p. 89.
17. Lehmann, *Ethics in a Christian Context*, p. 131.
18. Miller, *The Renewal of Man*, p. 94.
19. See Niebuhr, *The Responsible Self.*
20. See Niebuhr's "Concluding Unscientific Postscript," in *Christ and Culture* (Harper & Brothers, 1951).
21. Gustafson, *Treasure in Earthen Vessels*, p. 110. Compare Gus-

tafson, "A Theology of Christian Community?" in de Vries, ed., *Man in Community*.

22. See John Wilson, Norman Williams, and Barry Sugarman, *Introduction to Moral Education* (Harmondsworth, Middlesex: Penguin Books, 1967), pp. 192f.

23. Lehmann, *Ethics in a Christian Context*, p. 153.

24. Miller, *The Renewal of Man*, p. 97.

25. Ibid., pp. 97f.

26. See Sellers, *Theological Ethics*, pp. 133f.

Chapter 4. Socialization, Moral Development, and Reference Groups

1. See McNall, *The Sociological Experience*, pp. 73f., and W. J. H. Sprott, *Human Groups* (Harmondsworth, Middlesex: Penguin Books, 1958), pp. 27f.

2. George Herbert Mead, *Mind, Self and Society* (University of Chicago Press, 1934).

3. Ibid., p. 151.

4. Ibid., p. 175.

5. Sprott, *Human Groups*, p. 28.

6. See Winter, *Elements for a Social Ethic*, pp. 27 and 32.

7. Herbert Blumer, "Sociological Implications of the Thought of George Herbert Mead," in Walter L. Wallace, ed., *Sociological Theory* (Aldine Publishing Co., 1969), p. 235.

8. See esp. Erik Erikson's essay "Growth and Crises of the Healthy Personality," in Clyde Kluckhohn and Henry Murray, eds., *Personality in Nature, Society and Culture*, rev. ed. (Alfred A. Knopf, 1955). See also Erik Erikson, *Childhood and Society* (W. W. Norton & Co., Inc., 1950); *Identity and the Life Cycle, Psychological Issues* (International Universities Press, 1959), Vol. 1, No. 1; and *Identity, Youth and Crisis* (W. W. Norton & Co., Inc., 1968).

9. Erikson, "Growth and Crises," in Kluckhohn and Murray, eds., *Personality*, p. 195.

10. Erikson, *Identity, Youth and Crisis*, p. 103.

11. Erikson, "Growth and Crises," in Kluckhohn and Murray, eds., *Personality*, p. 199.

12. Ibid., p. 204.

13. Ibid., p. 216.
14. Erikson's emphasis upon trust, dignity, and self-worth in parents ought to be distinguished from the so-called love-oriented socialization that appears to have been employed increasingly by American middle-class parents over the past quarter century. See Urie Bronfenbrenner, "The Changing American Child," in Edwin P. Hollander and Raymond G. Hunt, eds., *Current Perspectives in Social Psychology* (Oxford University Press, 1967).
15. William J. Goode, "Norm Commitment and Conformity to Role-Status Obligations," *American Journal of Sociology*, Vol. LXVI, No. 3 (Nov. 1960), p. 252.
16. See Peter L. Berger and Thomas Luckmann, *The Social Construction of Reality* (Doubleday & Co., 1967), pp. 136f.
17. See ibid., pp. 144 ff.
18. See McNall, *The Sociological Experience*, pp. 78f.
19. Berger, *Invitation to Sociology*, p. 111.
20. Berger and Luckmann, *Social Construction*, p. 141.
21. See ibid., p. 143.
22. See Peter L. Berger, *The Precarious Vision* (Doubleday & Co., 1961), pp. 54f.
23. See Hilde T. Himmelweit, "Socio-economic Background and Personality," in Hollander and Hunt, eds., *Current Perspectives in Social Psychology*, p. 114; Urie Bronfenbrenner, "The Changing American Child," in ibid., pp. 120ff.; and Robert D. Hess and Judith V. Torney, *The Development of Political Attitudes in Children* (Doubleday & Co., 1968), pp. 256f.
24. See Jean Piaget, *The Moral Judgment of the Child* (London: Routledge & Kegan Paul, 1932). The well-known Hartshorne and May Character Education Inquiry, which predated Piaget's publication, emphasized the specificity of moral behavior and cast doubt upon the possibility of systematic understandings of moral development. See Hugh Hartshorne and M. A. May, et al., *Studies in the Nature of Character* (Macmillan Co., 1930). However, without denying that specific situations have much to do with particular behaviors, most researchers since have agreed upon the presence of developmental patterns in moral judgment. For surveys and interpretations of this research, see William Kay, *Moral Devel-*

opment (London: George Allen & Unwin, 1968), Norman J. Bull, *Moral Education* (London: Routledge & Kegan Paul, 1969), and the summaries by Norman Williams in John Wilson et al., *Introduction to Moral Education*, pp. 237ff., and in "Children's Moral Thought, Part I: Categories of Moral Thought," *Moral Education*, Vol. I, No. 1 (May 1969). I have limited the discussion of stages primarily to those that Piaget described, although others (e.g., Lawrence Kohlberg, R. F. Peck, and R. J. Havighurst, Bull and Williams) propose more elaborate schemes. This limitation seems legitimate both because Piaget's word has been so formative and because his major conclusions have been affirmed by these others in spite of their different terms and categories.

25. See Bull, *Moral Education*, p. 4.
26. Kay, *Moral Development*, pp. 152f.
27. See ibid., pp. 179ff., for a summary of this research. The cultural relativity of Piaget's conclusions has been long debated. It does appear that, for example, the weighting of his small sample toward the lower socioeconomic group (which was characterized by rigid and rather authoritarian patterns of parental discipline) led Piaget to react with blanket condemnation of the heteronomous stage and prevented him from seeing the necessity of a nonfixated heteronomy as part of moral development. Nevertheless, his major conclusions have stood the test of subsequent research, and Lawrence Kohlberg's impressive cross-cultural studies add weight to this conclusion. See Kohlberg, "Moral and Religious Education and the Public Schools: A Developmental View," in Theodore R. Sizer, ed., *Religion and Public Education* (Houghton Mifflin Co., 1967).
28. See Henry W. Maier, *Three Theories of Child Development*, rev. ed. (Harper & Row, 1969), esp. p. 204; also Bull, *Moral Education*, pp. 77ff.
29. Cf. Muzafer Sherif and Carolyn W. Sherif, *Social Psychology* (Harper & Row, 1969), pp. 133 and 406.
30. The illustration is adopted, with modifications, from Bull, *Moral Education*, p. 3.
31. Norman Williams, "Children's Moral Thought," *Moral Education*, Vol. I, No. 2 (Sept. 1969), p. 4.

32. Kay, *Moral Development*, p. 235. This coexistence of moral stages may help to explain the Hartshorne and May findings on the specificity of moral judgments.

33. Kohlberg, "Moral and Religious Education," in Sizer, ed., *Religion and Public Education*, p. 173.

34. Charles Horton Cooley, *Social Organization* (Charles Scribner's Sons, 1909), p. 23.

35. Ellsworth Faris, *The Nature of Human Nature* (McGraw-Hill Book Co., 1937), p. 42. Compare Faris, "The Primary Group: Essence and Accident," *American Journal of Sociology*, Vol. XXXVIII (July 1932), pp. 41–50.

36. See Leonard Broom and Philip Selznick, *Sociology* (Row, Peterson & Co., 1955), pp. 124–27, and Kingsley Davis, *Human Society* (Macmillan Co., 1948), pp. 294–98.

37. William F. Whyte, *Street Corner Society* (University of Chicago Press, 1943), esp. pp. 3–25 and 255–68.

38. Elton Mayo, *The Social Problem of an Industrial Civilization* (Andover Press, 1945), p. 82.

39. Broom and Selznick, *Sociology*, p. 152.

40. See the summary of the study by Edward A. Shils and Morris Janowitz in Broom and Selznick, *Sociology*, p. 147.

41. See Samuel A. Stouffer et al., *Studies in Social Psychology in World War II* (Princeton University Press, 1949), Vol. II, pp. 130–44.

42. For a description of this interpenetration, especially pertaining to the family, see Talcott Parsons and Robert F. Bales, *Family, Socialization and Interaction Process* (Free Press of Glencoe, 1955).

43. See Talcott Parsons, "General Theory in Sociology," in Robert K. Merton, Leonard Broom, and Leonard S. Cottrell, Jr., eds., *Sociology Today* (Basic Books, 1959).

44. A useful and brief account of the development of reference-group theory may be found in Herve Carrier, "The Role of Reference Groups in the Integration of Religious Attitudes," in Brothers, ed., *Readings in the Sociology of Religion*.

45. See Sherif and Sherif, *Social Psychology*, pp. 144f.

46. Merton, *Social Theory and Social Structure*, p. 307. For a minority viewpoint on this issue, see Eugene L. Hartley and Ruth E. Hartley, *Fundamentals of Social Psychology* (Alfred A. Knopf, 1952), p. 480.

47. See Harold H. Kelley, "Two Functions of Reference Groups," in Guy E. Swanson, Theodore M. Newcomb, and Eugene L. Hartley, *Readings in Social Psychology*, rev. ed. (Henry Holt & Co., 1952), pp. 410–14.

48. This listing is based upon that of Merton, *Social Theology and Social Structure*, pp. 310–26, with certain additions. There is some consensus in the discipline about these characteristics.

49. See W. W. Charters, Jr., and Theodore M. Newcomb, "Some Attitudinal Effects of Experimentally Increased Salience of a Membership Group," in Swanson, Newcomb, and Hartley, *Readings in Social Psychology*, p. 415.

50. Sherif and Sherif, *Social Psychology*, p. 187.

51. James E. Dittes, "Attractiveness of Group as Function of Self-Esteem and Acceptance by Group," *Journal of Abnormal Psychology*, Vol. LIX (1959), p. 77.

52. See Harold H. Kelley and Martin M. Shapiro, "An Experiment on Conformity to Group Norms Where Conformity Is Detrimental to Group Achievement," *American Sociological Review*, Vol. XIX (1954), pp. 667–77.

53. See Merton, *Social Theory and Social Structure*, pp. 326f.

54. Ralph H. Turner, "Reference Groups of Future-oriented Men," *Social Forces*, Vol. XXXIV (1955), p. 135.

55. Ibid.

56. Lewis M. Killian, "The Significance of Multiple-Group Membership in Disaster," *American Journal of Sociology*, Vol. LVII (1952), p. 310.

57. See the summary of Newcomb's studies in Sherif and Sherif, *Social Psychology*, p. 476.

Chapter 5.
Roles and Identity

1. For descriptions of the relation of role theory to drama, see Berger, *The Precarious Vision*, chap. 3, and Roger Brown, *Social Psychology* (Free Press, 1965), pp. 152ff.

2. Dorothy Emmet's *Rules, Roles and Relationships* (London: Macmillan & Co., 1966) is one of the few exceptions.

3. Neal Gross, Ward S. Mason, and Alexander W. McEachern, *Explorations in Role Analysis* (John Wiley & Sons, 1958), p. 319.

4. See Hartley and Hartley, *Fundamentals of Social Psychology*, pp. 487ff.

5. Berger and Luckmann, *Social Construction of Reality*, p. 74.

6. See Seymour Lieberman, "The Effects of Changes in Roles on the Attitudes of Role Occupants," *Human Relations*, Vol. IX (1956), pp. 385–402.

7. See Gross et al., *Explorations*, chap. 3; and Talcott Parsons, *The Social System* (Free Press of Glencoe, 1951), p. 39.

8. See Michael Argyle, *Social Interaction* (London: Methuen & Co., 1969), pp. 281f.

9. See Brown, *Social Psychology*, p. 154.

10. Parsons, "General Theory in Sociology," in Merton et al., *Sociology Today*, p. 35.

11. Merton, *Social Theory and Social Structure*, pp. 195–206.

12. Raymond G. Hunt, "Role and Role Conflict," in Hollander and Hunt, eds., *Current Perspectives in Social Psychology*, p. 262. Erving Goffman has explored the notion of "role distance." Such an intentional separation between the individual and the role can be a method for handling situations in which the person does not want to be identified with that role. Just as frequently, however, the separation seems to be a pretense of detachment in order that the person might actually perform the role better, which underscores the seriousness with which we take major roles even in the moments we intentionally separate ourselves from them. See the discussion of Goffman's work in Maurice Natanson, "Alienation and Social Role," *Social Research*, Vol. XXXIII, No. 3 (Fall 1966), esp. pp. 385f.; and Rose Lamb Coser, "Role Distance, Sociological Ambivalence, and Transitional Status Systems," *American Journal of Sociology*, Vol. LXXII (1966–1967), esp. p. 173. Compare Erving Goffman, *The Presentation of Self in Everyday Life* (Doubleday & Co., 1959).

13. See Theodore M. Newcomb, *Social Psychology* (Dryden Press, 1950), pp. 549–54.

14. Different ways of describing the possible types of role conflict may be seen, e.g., in Argyle, *Social Interaction*, pp. 282ff.; Brown, *Social Psychology*, pp. 156ff.; and Hunt, "Role and Role Conflict," in Hollander and Hunt, eds., *Current Perspectives in Social Psychology*, pp. 263f.

15. See Waldo Burchard, "Role Conflicts of Military Chaplains," *American Sociological Review*, Vol. XIX, No. 5 (Oct. 1954).

16. Ibid., p. 535 (italics mine).

17. J. W. Getzels and E. G. Guba, "Role Conflict and Effectiveness: An Empirical Study," *American Sociological Review*, Vol. XIX (1954), p. 174.

18. See Gross et al., *Explorations in Role Analysis*, pp. 285ff.

19. See Jackson Toby, "Some Variables in Role Conflict Analysis," *Social Forces*, Vol. XXX (1951–52), p. 327.

20. See Burchard, "Role Conflicts of Military Chaplains," p. 535.

21. Lieberman, "The Effects of Changes in Roles on the Attitudes of Role Occupants."

22. A more extended discussion of the self-consistency hypothesis may be found in Leon Festinger, *A Theology of Cognitive Dissonance* (Row, Peterson & Co., 1957), esp. pp. 274f.

23. Newcomb, *Social Psychology*, p. 635.

24. See ibid., pp. 555ff.

25. Quoted in Arthur Beckhard, *Albert Einstein* (Avon Books, 1959), p. 60.

26. Tomatsu Shibutani, "The Structure of Personal Identity," in E. E. Sampson, ed., *Approaches, Contexts, and Problems of Social Psychology* (Prentice-Hall, 1964), p. 231.

27. See Nelson Foote, "Identification as the Basis for a Theory of Motivation," *American Sociological Review*, Vol. XVI (1951), p. 18.

28. Compare the use of "person" by Hans Gerth and C. Wright Mills, *Character and Social Structure* (Harcourt, Brace & Co., 1953), p. 22.

29. Berger, *Invitation to Sociology*, p. 98.

30. Erikson, *Identity, Youth and Crisis*, p. 19.

31. Sherif and Sherif, *Social Psychology*, p. 386.

32. Kenneth Soddy, ed., *Identity, Mental Health and Value Systems* (London: Tavistock Publications, 1961), p. 4.

33. Gerth and Mills, *Character and Social Structure*, p. 81.

34. Berger and Luckmann, *Social Construction of Reality*, p. 38.

35. Anselm Strauss, *Mirrors and Masks: The Search for Identity* (Free Press of Glencoe, 1959), p. 21.

36. See Gerth and Mills, *Character and Social Structure*, p. 90.

37. Strauss, *Mirrors and Masks*, p. 164.

38. See Berger and Luckmann, *Social Construction of Reality*, pp. 95ff.
39. Ibid., p. 150.
40. Erik H. Erikson, "The Problem of Ego-Identity," *Psychological Issues*, Vol. I, No. 1, p. 113. Compare Robert Coles, *Erik H. Erikson: The Growth of His Work* (Little, Brown and Co., 1970), esp. pp. 165ff.
41. Ibid., p. 118. Compare Strauss, *Mirrors and Masks*, p. 33.
42. Ibid., p. 219. Compare Erikson, *Identity, Youth and Crisis*, p. 87.
43. See Erikson, ibid., p. 89.
44. See ibid., p. 157. Compare Argyle, *Social Interaction*, p. 361, and Maurice Stein, *The Eclipse of Community* (Princeton University Press, 1960), pp. 264ff.
45. See Prescott Lecky, *Self-Consistency: A Theory of Personality* (Island Press, 1951), esp. pp. 152f.
46. Strauss, *Mirrors and Masks*, p. 24.
47. Foote, "Identification as the Basis for a Theory of Motivation," p. 18.
48. Ibid., p. 19.
49. Ibid., p. 20.
50. Ibid., p. 16.
51. See Max Weber, *The Theory of Social and Economic Organization*, trans. A. M. Henderson and Talcott Parsons (Oxford University Press, 1947), chap. 1; cf. Gerth and Mills, *Character and Social Structure*, p. 116.
52. Gerth and Mills, *Character and Social Structure*, p. 120.
53. Strauss, *Mirrors and Masks*, p. 41.

Chapter 6. Dialogue on
Community, Identity, and Morality

1. John Wilson et al., *Introduction to Moral Education*, chap. 4. Compare John Wilson, *Approach to Moral Education* (Oxford: Farmington Trust, 1967), pp. 4ff.
2. Bull, *Moral Education*, p. 23.
3. Ibid., p. 34. Compare David Holbrook, "The Wizard and the Critical Flame," *Moral Education*, Vol. I, No. 1, pp. 25ff.
4. Holbrook, ibid., p. 26.
5. Dorothy Emmet is particularly sensitive to some of these

questions about human groups. See her *Rules, Roles and Relationships*, pp. 204ff.

6. Gustafson, in Ramsey (ed.), *Faith and Ethics*, p. 133.
7. Niebuhr, *Radical Monotheism*, p. 61 (italics mine).
8. Michael S. Olmsted, *The Small Group* (Random House, 1959), p. 49.
9. See T. W. Adorno et al., *The Authoritarian Personality* (Harper & Brothers, 1950), pp. 971ff., and Gordon W. Allport, *The Nature of Prejudice* (Addison-Wesley Publishing Co., 1954) (Doubleday Anchor edition), pp. 374ff.
10. Niebuhr, *The Responsible Self*, p. 122.
11. Berger, *The Precarious Vision*, chap. 5. Compare Berger and Luckmann, *Social Construction of Reality*, pp. 91f.; and Emmet, *Rules, Roles and Relationships*, pp. 152f.
12. Emmet, *Rules, Roles and Relationships*, p. 41.
13. See John Benson, "The Concept of Community," in Laurence Bright and Simon Clements, eds., *The Committed Church* (London: Darton, Longmann, & Todd, 1966), pp. 32ff.
14. Ibid., p. 34.
15. See Emile Durkheim, *Suicide*, trans. John A. Spaulding and George Simpson (Free Press of Glencoe, 1951), esp. Book II.
16. Quoted by Reinhard Bendix, *Max Weber: An Intellectual Portrait* (Doubleday & Co., 1960), p. 397 (italics mine).
17. See Merton, *Social Theory and Social Structure*, p. 378.
18. Compare my article "Contextualism and the Ethical Triad," *McCormick Quarterly*, Vol. XX, No. 2 (Jan. 1967), reprinted in Harvey Cox, ed., *The Situation Ethics Debate* (Westminster Press, 1968).

Chapter 7. Moral Nexus: The Personal and the Universal

1. Robert A. Nisbet, *The Sociological Tradition* (Basic Books, 1966), p. 261.
2. Bryan R. Wilson, *Religion in a Secular Society* (Harmondsworth, Middlesex: Penguin Books, 1969), p. 16.
3. Berger, *The Precarious Vision*, p. 151.
4. See Thomas Luckmann, *The Invisible Religion: The Problem of Religion in Modern Society* (Macmillan Co., 1967).

5. John B. Cobb, Jr., *God and the World* (Westminster Press, 1969), p. 116.
6. Roger L. Shinn, *Man: The New Humanism* (Westminster Press, 1968), p. 144.
7. Macmurray, *Persons in Relation*, p. 25.
8. See ibid., pp. 34ff.
9. See ibid., pp. 157ff.
10. Ibid., p. 159.
11. H. Richard Niebuhr, "The Responsibility of the Church for Society," in Kenneth Scott Latourette, ed., *The Gospel, the Church, and the World* (Harper & Brothers, 1946), p. 117.
12. The organic-covenantal tension is explored thoroughly by F. W. Dillistone, *The Structure of the Divine Society* (Westminster Press, 1951). We shall consider it in greater detail in a later chapter.
13. Erikson, *Identity, Youth and Crisis*, p. 90.

Chapter 8. Groups, Values, and Persons in Contemporary Society

1. Ferdinand Tönnies, *Community and Society (Gemeinschaft and Gesellschaft)* (Harper & Row, 1963). For interpretive surveys of the varied uses of this polarity, see Howard Becker and Harry Elmer Barnes, *Social Thought from Lore to Science*, Vol. II (D. C. Heath & Co., 1938), and Nisbet, *The Sociological Tradition.*
2. Tönnies, *Community and Society*, p. 65.
3. Compare Nisbet, *The Sociological Tradition*, pp. 47f. and 76f.
4. See, e.g., Nisbet, *Community and Power*; Stein, *The Eclipse of Community*; Kenneth Boulding, *The Organizational Revolution* (Harper & Brothers, 1953); Robin M. Williams, Jr., *American Society: A Sociological Interpretation*, rev. ed. (Alfred A. Knopf, 1960); Alvin Toffler, *Future Shock* (Random House, 1970).
5. Compare J. D. Halloran's summary, "Community in the Urban-Industrial Society," in Bright and Clements, eds., *The Committed Church*, esp. pp. 46f.; and Toffler, *Future Shock*, esp. Pt. II.
6. See Sylvia Fleis Fava, "Suburbanism as a Way of Life," *American Sociological Review*, Vol. XXI (1956), pp. 34ff.

7. David Reisman, with Nathan Glazer and Reuel Denney, *The Lonely Crowd* (Yale University Press, 1950), p. 102. Compare William H. Whyte, Jr., *The Organization Man* (Doubleday & Co., 1957), pp. 327ff. and pp. 365ff.

8. John R. Seeley, R. Alexander Sim, and Elizabeth W. Loosley, *Crestwood Heights* (Basic Books, 1956), p. 292.

9. See Robert S. Lynd and Helen Merrell Lynd, *Middletown* (Harcourt, Brace & Co., 1929), p. 248 and pp. 273ff.; James West [Carl Withers], *Plainville, U.S.A.* (Columbia University Press, 1945), pp. 73ff. and 97ff.; W. Lloyd Warner et al., *Democracy in Jonesville* (Harper & Brothers, 1949), pp. 261f.; Arthur J. Vidich and Joseph Bensman, *Small Town in Mass Society* (Princeton University Press, 1958), esp. pp. 31ff.

10. Toffler, *Future Shock*, p. 105.

11. Max Weber's interactionist position on the relation between social structure and values is, I believe, most defensible. Though in this section I place more emphasis upon the influence of social structure upon values than vice versa, this is not incompatible with a Weberian position. See Hans Gerth and C. Wright Mills (translators and eds.), *From Max Weber* (Oxford University Press, 1946), esp. pp. 61–65. Compare J. Milton Yinger, *Religion, Society and the Individual* (Macmillan Co., 1957), chap. 11.

12. For an overview, see Donald N. Barrett, ed., *Values in America* (University of Notre Dame Press, 1961).

13. See Nisbet, *The Sociological Tradition*, pp. 42ff., and his chapter in Robert Lee and Martin E. Marty, eds., *Religion and Social Conflict* (Oxford University Press, 1964).

14. See Louis Wirth, "Urbanism as a Way of Life," *American Journal of Sociology*, Vol. XLIV, No. 1 (July 1938).

15. Ibid., p. 12.

16. Ibid., pp. 15f.

17. See Gerth and Mills, *From Max Weber*, chap. 8. For excellent discussions of Weber's analysis, see Talcott Parsons, *The Structure of Social Action* (McGraw-Hill Book Co., 1937), pp. 506ff., and Merton, *Social Theory and Social Structure*, pp. 195f.

18. See Merton, ibid., pp. 204ff. Compare James M. Campbell, "Organization Man Revisited," *Life and Work*, Vol. X, No. 5 (Summer 1968).

19. Toffler, *Future Shock*, p. 127.
20. Gerth and Mills, *Character and Social Structure*, p. 100; cf. p. 94.
21. See Hendrik M. Ruitenbeek, *The Individual and the Crowd: A Study of Identity in America* (New American Library of World Literature, 1964), chap. 2.
22. See ibid., pp. 120ff. and 178f.
23. Luckmann, *The Invisible Religion*, p. 97.
24. See David Riesman et al., *The Lonely Crowd*, pp. 37f.; C. Wright Mills, *White Collar* (Oxford University Press, 1951), pp. 182ff.; Erich Fromm, *The Sane Society* (Rinehart & Co., Inc., 1955). Compare Stein, *The Eclipse of Community*, p. 264. Stein's entire discussion of identity diffusion is most helpful.
25. Harvey Swados, "The Myth of the Happy Worker," in Maurice R. Stein, Arthur J. Vidich, and David Manning White, eds., *Identity and Anxiety* (Free Press of Glencoe, 1960), p. 199.
26. Stein, *The Eclipse of Community*, pp. 271f.
27. Vidich and Bensman, *Small Town in Mass Society*, p. 310.
28. Toffler, *Future Shock*, p. 305.
29. Everett Cherrington Hughes, *Men and Their Work* (Free Press of Glencoe, 1958), p. 7.
30. Berger, *The Precarious Vision*, p. 59.
31. See John Kenneth Galbraith, The *New Industrial State* (New American Library, 1967), p. 164.

Chapter 9.
Churches, Members, and Moral Styles

1. See Jeffrey K. Hadden, *The Gathering Storm in the Churches* (Doubleday & Co., 1969), chap. 1.
2. H. Paul Douglass, "Church and Community in the United States," in Kenneth Scott Latourette et al., *Church and Community* (London: George Allen & Unwin, 1938), pp. 227f.
3. Seeley, Sim, and Loosley, *Crestwood Heights*, p. 65.
4. See Vidich and Bensman, *Small Town in Mass Society*, p. 228.
5. See Gibson Winter, *Religious Identity* (Macmillan Co., 1968), chap. 1; and Paul Harrison, *Authority and Power in the Free Church Tradition* (Princeton University Press, 1959), esp. pp. 44ff.

6. See Will Herberg, *Protestant-Catholic-Jew* (Doubleday & Co., 1955).

7. Robert N. Bellah, "Civil Religion in America," in Donald R. Cutler, ed., *The Religious Situation: 1968* (Beacon Press, 1968), p. 336.

8. See Gerhard Lenski, *The Religious Factor* (Doubleday & Co., 1961), p. 42; also the articles by Nicholas J. Demerath III and Yoshio Fukuyama in *Review of Religious Research*, Vol. II, No. 4 (1961).

9. See Robert Lee, *The Social Sources of Church Unity* (Abingdon Press, 1960).

10. Victor Obenhaus, *The Church and Faith in Mid-America* (Westminster Press, 1963), p. 141. Compare W. Widick Schroeder and Victor Obenhaus, *Religion in American Culture* (Free Press of Glencoe, 1964), p. 117.

11. One possible exception to this diffusion argument is found in Gerhard Lenski's Detroit study, op. cit. His argument concerning the religious factor, however, has been questioned by Andrew Greeley, whose research emphasizes ethnic factors. See Greeley, *Religion and Career* (Sheed & Ward, 1963); cf. B. R. Wilson, *Religion in Secular Society*, pp. 146ff., and Roland Robertson, *The Sociological Interpretation of Religion* (Oxford: Basil Blackwell & Mott, 1970), pp. 62ff.

12. See B. R. Wilson, *Religion in Secular Society*, chap. 4; also, David O. Moberg, *The Church as a Social Institution* (Prentice-Hall, 1962), pp. 183ff.

13. Lynd and Lynd, *Middletown*, p. 339.

14. Vidich and Bensman, *Small Town in Mass Society*, p. 258.

15. See B. R. Wilson, *Religion in Secular Society*, p. 121; also his "Religion and the Churches in Contemporary America," in William G. McLoughlin and Robert N. Bellah, eds., *Religion in America* (Houghton Mifflin Co., 1968), p. 101.

16. See H. Richard Niebuhr, *The Social Sources of Denominationalism* (Henry Holt & Co., 1929), for the pioneering study.

17. See Liston Pope, "Religion and the Class Structure," *The Annals of the American Academy of Political and Social Science*, Vol. CCLVI (March 1948).

18. See Russell R. Dynes, "Church-Sect Typology and Socio-Economic Status," *American Sociological Review*, Vol. XX (1955), p. 558.

19. See Erich Goode, "Social Class and Church Participation," *American Journal of Sociology*, Vol. LXXII, No. 1 (July 1966); and Charles Y. Glock, Benjamin R. Ringer, and Earl R. Babbie, *To Comfort and to Challenge* (University of California Press, 1967), chaps. 4 and 5.

20. See Nicholas J. Demerath III, *Social Class in American Protestantism* (Rand McNally & Co., 1965).

21. See Liston Pope, *Millhands and Preachers* (Yale University Press, 1942), ch. 12.

22. Lenski, *The Religious Factor*, pp. 66f.

23. For an illuminating interpretation of the Durkheimian and Weberian emphases in current sociology of religion, see Thomas C. Campbell and Yoshio Fukuyama, *The Fragmented Layman* (Pilgrim Press, 1970), chap. 1.

24. See Joseph Fichter, *Social Relations in the Urban Parish* (University of Chicago Press, 1954), pp. 7–79.

25. See Lenski, *The Religious Factor*, chap. 1; Campbell and Fukuyama, *The Fragmented Layman*, chap. 2; and Charles Y. Glock and Rodney Stark, *Religion and Society in Tension* (Rand McNally & Co., 1965), chap. 2. Compare Robertson, *The Sociological Interpretation of Religion*, pp. 51ff.

26. See Fichter, *Social Relations in the Urban Parish*, pp. 21ff.; Glock, Ringer, and Babbie, *To Comfort and to Challenge*, p. 31.

27. See Schroeder and Obenhaus, *Religion in American Culture*, chap. 5.

28. See Charles H. Page, "Bureaucracy and the Liberal Church," *The Review of Religion*, Vol. XVI (1951–1952).

29. See Douglass, "Church and Community in the United States," in Latourette et al., *Church and Community*, p. 206; B. R. Wilson, "Religion and the Churches," in McLoughlin and Bellah, eds., *Religion in America*, p. 84.

30. Vidich and Bensman, *Small Town in Mass Society*, p. 308.

31. See Luckmann, *The Invisible Religion*, chap. 6.

32. See Glock, Ringer, and Babbie, *To Comfort and to Challenge*, p. 21; Yoshio Fukuyama, "The Major Dimensions of Church Membership," *Review of Religious Research*, Vol. II, No. 4 (Spring 1961).

33. See Page, "Bureaucracy," p. 149.

34. See Gerhard E. Lenski "Social Correlates of Religious Interest," *American Sociological Review*, Vol. XVIII, pp. 535f.; Yinger, *Religion, Society and the Individual*, p. 93.

35. Glock, Ringer, and Babbie, *To Comfort and to Challenge*, p. 65.
36. Cf. Luckmann, *The Invisible Religion*, pp. 75, 96f.
37. See Campbell and Fukuyama, *The Fragmented Layman*, p. 58, and Glock and Stark, *Religion and Society in Tension*, chap. 2, for evidence of the strong private-need orientation of members in two socially liberal denominations.
38. See Campbell and Fukuyama, *The Fragmented Layman*, esp. chaps. 11 and 12.
39. See the comments by John E. Biersdorf, *Social Action*, Vol. XXXVII, No. 6 (Feb. 1971), pp. 25f.
40. See Harrison, *Authority and Power*, pp. 44ff.; and G. Winter, *Religious Identity*, chaps. 1 and 5.
41. See Kenneth Underwood, *Protestant and Catholic* (Beacon Press, 1951), pp. 85f.
42. Robert Lee and Russell Galloway, *The Schizophrenic Church* (Westminster Press, 1969), pp. 132f.
43. Underwood, *Protestant and Catholic*, p. 303.
44. See Berger, *Invitation to Sociology*, p. 114.
45. This point is central to the argument of Ernest Q. Campbell and Thomas F. Pettigrew, *Christians in Racial Crisis* (Public Affairs Press, 1959).
46. See Schroeder and Obenhaus, *Religion in American Culture*, p. 182, and Lenski "Religion's Impact," in Brothers, ed., *Readings in the Sociology of Religion*, p. 233.
47. See Luckmann, *The Invisible Religion*, p. 75.
48. See esp. Ernst Troeltsch, *The Social Teaching of the Christian Churches*, trans. Olive Wyon (Macmillan Co., 1931), Vol. I, pp. 331ff. The reinterpretations of and additions to the typology by Niebuhr, Pope, Yon Weise, Becker, and Wilson are important and well known. For criticisms of the typology, see articles by Paul M. Gustafson, Erich Goode, Nicholas J. Demerath III, and Allan W. Eister in *Journal for the Scientific Study of Religion*, Vol. VI, No. 1 (Spring 1967), and articles by Goode and Demerath in the same journal, Vol. VI, No. 2 (Fall 1967). Though there are dangers in its use, particularly the tendency toward looseness of definition and the tendency to oppose church and sect as dichotomous constructs, the typology is still a useful tool.
49. Niebuhr, in *The Social Sources*, argued that the inevitable movement from sect to denomination is required by the religious socialization of the second generation. This argument

rightly has been modified by those who point to the persistence of certain sects for several generations (see B. R. Wilson, *Religion in a Secular Society*, chap. 12). Nor is the movement unidirectional; the Roman Catholic Church shows increasing signs of denominationalism.

50. See ibid., pp. 224f.
51. See Russell R. Dynes, "The Consequences of Sectarianism for Social Participation," *Social Forces*, Vol. V (May 1957), p. 334.
52. Troeltsch, *The Social Teaching of the Christian Churches*, p. 339.
53. See Niebuhr, *The Social Sources*, chaps. 2 and 3.
54. See W. E. Mann, *Sect, Cult, and Church in Alberta* (University of Toronto Press, 1955), esp. chaps. 1 and 2 and pp. 154ff.
55. See Underwood, *Protestant and Catholic*, p. 386.
56. See Benton Johnson, "Do Holiness Sects Socialize in Dominant Values?" *Social Forces*, Vol. XXXIX, No. 4 (May 1961), pp. 309–16.
57. B. R. Wilson, *Religion in Secular Society*, p. 211.
58. Marty, "The American Situation in 1969," in Cutler, ed., *The Religious Situation 1969*, p. 40.
59. Troeltsch, *The Social Teaching of the Christian Churches*, p. 331.
60. Underwood, *Protestant and Catholic*, p. 94.
61. See Bernard R. Berelson et al., *Voting: A Study of Opinion Formation in a Presidential Campaign* (University of Chicago Press, 1954), esp. p. 69.
62. Thomas F. O'Dea, *American Catholic Dilemma* (Sheed & Ward, 1958), pp. 160f.
63. Ibid., p. 142.
64. See Underwood, *Protestant and Catholic*, p. 94.
65. Fichter, *Social Relations in the Urban Parish*, p. 106.
66. O'Dea, *American Catholic Dilemma*, pp. 155ff.
67. See B. R. Wilson, *Religion in Secular Society*, pp. 243ff.
68. As reported by *The Christian Century*, Vol. LXVII, No. 30 (July 26, 1950), p. 896.
69. Niebuhr, *Radical Monotheism*, pp. 62f.

Chapter 10.
The Church and Moral Community

1. See Durkheim, *Suicide*, p. 389. Compare Nisbet, *The Sociological Tradition*, p. 156.

2. See, e.g., Haroutunian, *God with Us*, ch. 1; and Beach, *Christian Community and American Society*, chap. 2.
3. Buber, *I and Thou*, p. 45. Cf. Paul E. Pfuetze, *The Social Self* (Bookman Associates, 1954), chap. 4.
4. For useful summaries of Christian images of the church, see Alan Richardson, A *Theological Word Book of the Bible* (Macmillan Co., 1951), pp. 81f.; Paul S. Minear, *Images of the Church in the New Testament* (Westminster Press, 1960), esp. chap. 5; Clyde Holbrook, *Faith and Community* (Harper & Brothers, 1959), pp. 111ff.; and E. Clinton Gardner, *The Church as a Prophetic Community* (Westminster Press, 1967), P. 2.
5. J. Robert Nelson, *The Realm of Redemption* (London: Epworth Press, 1951) pp. 57f.
6. Harvey H. McArthur, "Kingdom of God," *The Westminster Dictionary of Christian Ethics*, p. 189.
7. Paul Tillich, *Systematic Theology* (University of Chicago Press, 1963), Vol. III, p. 359.
8. George W. Webber, *The Congregation in Mission* (Abingdon Press, 1964), p. 123.
9. Tillich, *Systematic Theology*, Vol. III, p. 165.
10. See Dillistone, *The Structure of the Divine Society*, for the definitive work on this polarity.
11. See John C. Bennett, "The Church and the Secular," *Christianity and Crisis*, Vol. XXVI, No. 22 (Dec. 26, 1967).
12. See Emil Brunner, *The Christian Doctrine of the Church, Faith and Consummation* (Dogmatics, Volume III) (Westminster Press, 1962), esp. pp. 19–37.
13. Beach, *Christian Community and American Society*, p. 41. See chaps. 2 and 3 for helpful discussions of other polarities.
14. Reinhold Niebuhr has particularly illuminated this problem. See esp. *The Children of Light and the Children of Darkness* (Charles Scribner's Sons, 1944).
15. See Robert O. Johann, "Authority and Fellowship," in Cutler, ed., *The Religions Situation 1969*, pp. 667ff.
16. See, e.g., Tillich's polarities, *Systematic Theology*, Vol. III, pp. 182ff.
17. See Edward Farley's argument in C. Ellis Nelson, *Where Faith Begins* (John Knox Press, 1967), pp. 208f.
18. See Lenski, *The Religious Factor*, chap. 2 and p. 296.
19. Erikson, *Identity, Youth and Crisis*, p. 106.
20. See James E. Dittes, *The Church in the Way* (Charles Scribner's

Sons, 1967), esp. chap. 3. The larger issue Dittes is arguing is that the resistance that appears to thwart the church's ministry may at times be the best occasion for that ministry.

21. Ibid., p. 124.

22. Ibid., p. 114.

23. See Paul Tillich, *Morality and Beyond* (Harper & Row, 1963), chap. 3.

24. See Karl Barth, *Church Dogmatics*, Vol. II, Part 2 (Edinburgh: T. & T. Clark, 1957), chap. 8.

25. See Gustafson, *The Church as Moral Decision-Maker*, pp. 109ff.

26. See ibid., pp. 83ff.

27. Compare Frederick Denison Maurice, *Theological Essays*, 3rd ed. (London: Macmillan Co., 1891), p. 343; and J.A.T. Robinson, *On Being the Church in the World* (Westminster Press, 1960), pp. 14ff. In regard to sociological heterogeneity and race in America, the new black pluralism must be respected and taken seriously not as reverse racism but as the attempt to get at the difficult problem of black identity in a society permeated by white racism. Yet the racially integrated church can and should continue to be a Christian hope and goal. See Joseph C. Hough, Jr., *Black Power and White Protestants* (Oxford University Press, 1968), esp. p. 144.

28. See Evon Z. Vogt and Thomas F. O'Dea, "A Comparative Study of the Role of Values in Social Action in Two Southwestern Communities," in Yinger, *Religion, Society and the Individual*, p. 568.

29. See Gustafson's perceptive treatment of language in *Treasure in Earthen Vessels*, chap. 4.

30. See Brian Wicker, "The Church: A Radical Concept of Community," in Bright and Clements, *The Committed Church*, pp. 260ff.

31. Sybil Marshall, untitled article, *Moral Education*, Vol. I, No. 1 (May 1969), p. 21.

32. See Muzafer Sherif and Carolyn W. Sherif, *Intergroup Conflict and Cooperation: The Robbers Cave Experiment* (Institute of Group Relations, 1961), esp. chap. 8.

33. Allport, *The Nature of Prejudice*, p. 44.

34. This distinction is well expressed by Macmurray, *Persons in Relation*, pp. 174f.

35. E. R. Wickham, *Church and People in an Industrial City* (Lon-

don: Lutterworth Press, 1957), pp. 229f. F. D. Maurice and Horace Bushnell earlier gave similar formulations to the role of the church.

Chapter 11.
The Church and the Moral Ethos

1. Emile Durkheim, *Moral Education: A Study in the Theory and Application of the Sociology of Education*, trans. Everett K. Wilson and Herman Schnurer (Free Press of Glencoe, 1961), p. 87.
2. See, e.g., the essays by Frederick S. Carney and James M. Gustafson in Gene H. Outka and Paul Ramsey, eds., *Norm and Context in Christian Ethics* (Charles Scribner's Sons, 1968).
3. Shinn, *Man: The New Humanism*, p. 170.
4. Niebuhr, *Radical Monotheism*, p. 37.
5. Rubem A. Alves, *A Theology of Human Hope* (Corpus Instrumentorum, 1969), p. 98.
6. See, e.g., Gene H. Outka, "The New Morality: Recent Discussion within Protestantism," in Richard McCormick, S. J., et al., *The Future of Ethics and Moral Theology* (Argus Communications Co., 1968), pp. 70ff. This is a helpful discussion of rules, though it does not deal with their community context.
7. While there is much in Joseph Fletcher's position with which I agree, his concept of rules is subject to this criticism. His neglect of community means also a neglect of the social and historical nature of the self. See *Situation Ethics*, esp. chaps. 2–4.
8. See Paul Ramsey, *Who Speaks for the Church?* (Abingdon Press, 1967). Compare Hadden, *The Gathering Storm in the Churches*, pp. 234f.
9. See R. M. Williams, *American Society*, pp. 30ff., and Marion J. Levy, Jr., *The Structure of Society* (Princeton University Press, 1952), pp. 102ff.
10. Huntington Cairns, "The Community as the Legal Order," in Carl J. Friedrich, ed., *Community* (Liberal Arts Press, 1959), p. 29.
11. See Frederick Denison Maurice, *Social Morality* (London: Macmillan Co., 1886), chap. 1.
12. For a suggestive discussion of this in legal theory, see John Ladd, in Friedrich, ed., *Community*, esp. pp. 288f.

13. Josiah Royce, *The Problem of Christianity* (Macmillan Co., 1913), Vol. I, pp. 192f.

14. F. D. Maurice expressed this in his notion of the human-divine society. See *Social Morality*, chap. 8.

15. Bushnell, *Christian Nurture*, p. 71.

16. Ibid., p. 22.

17. Goode, "Norm Commitment and Conformity to Role Status Obligations," p. 252.

18. Ibid.

19. Sellers, *Theological Ethics*, p. 145.

20. Niebuhr, *The Purpose of the Church and Its Ministry*, p. 35.

21. Bonhoeffer, *Ethics*, p. 67.

22. See Mount, *Conscience and Responsibility*, p. 163, for a helpful summary of the relational perspective on this. On the functional prerequisites of society, cf. Miller, *The Renewal of Man*, pp. 97f. and supra, chap. 2. Out of this perspective I have interpreted Lawrence Kohlberg's cross-cultural research results in a way different from that of Kohlberg himself, supra, chap. 6.

23. Roland H. Bainton, *Christian Attitudes toward War and Peace* (Abingdon Press, 1960), pp. 209f.

24. Ibid., p. 221.

25. See James S. Coleman, *Community Conflict* (Free Press of Glencoe, 1957).

26. Alec R. Vidler, *The Church in an Age of Revolution* (Wm. B. Eerdmans Publishing Co., 1961), p. 264.

Chapter 12.
The Church and Moral Identity

1. Toffler, *Future Shock*, p. 88.

2. Wilhelm Herrmann, *The Communion of a Christian with God*, trans. J. Sandys Stanyon (G. P. Putnam's Sons, 1913), p. 118.

3. See David Granskou, "The Concept of Selfhood in the New Testament and Modern Ethics," *Religion in Life*, Vol. XXX, No. 1 (Winter 1960–1961), pp. 92–104.

4. See J. Wilson et al., *Introduction to Moral Education*, pp. 192ff.

5. Marie Jahoda's definition is discussed by Erik Erikson, in *Identity, Youth and Crisis*, p. 92.

6. See Gordon W. Allport, *The Individual and His Religion* (Macmillan Co., 1951), chap. 3.

7. See David C. Duncombe, *The Shape of the Christian Life* (Abingdon Press, 1969), esp. the summary on p. 23.
8. See Gustafson, *Christ and the Moral Life*, chap. 7; cf. his chapter in Outka and Ramsey, eds., *Norm and Context in Christian Education*, esp. pp. 26ff.
9. See Dennis H. Wrong, "The Oversocialized Conception of Man in Modern Sociology," *American Sociological Review*, Vol. XXVI, No. 2 (April 1961), pp. 183–93.
10. Schleiermacher makes these distinctions in his *Christliche Sitte* (Berlin: Reimer, 1843); see also Robert Munro, *Schleiermacher* (Paisley, Scotland: A. Gardner, 1903), pp. 253ff.
11. See Royce, *The Problem of Christianity*, Vol. I, pp. 140–59.
12. I am indebted to Peter Berger, *Invitation to Sociology*, chap. 6, for his helpful description of freedom in sociology. Elsewhere (cf. *The Precarious Vision*, chaps. 5 and 10), however, he sometimes uses language that suggests the impact on the self of immediate social involvements can be largely escaped (see his arguments on "bad faith"). This would suggest role transcendence rather than the kind of role transformation that I shall argue.
13. See Gustafson's judicious treatment of both the strengths and serious limitations of the moral pattern approach to Christ, *Christ and the Moral Life*, chap. 5. Cf. Mount, *Conscience and Responsibility*, chap. 6.
14. Niebuhr, *The Responsible Self*, pp. 144f.
15. See William J. Goode, "A Theory of Role Strain," *American Sociological Review*, Vol. XXV, No. 4 (Aug. 1960), pp. 483–86.
16. Ibid., p. 493.
17. Dittes, *The Church in the Way*, p. 109.
18. This treatment of the relation of church roles to nonchurch roles is informed by Niebuhr's typology in *Christ and Culture*.
19. See Leonard Reissman, "Role Conceptions in Bureaucracy," in Karl de Schweinitz and Kenneth W. Thompson, eds., *Man and Modern Society* (Henry Holt & Co., 1963), pp. 528–36.
20. Compare Wickham, *Church and People in an Industrial City*, pp. 253f., Hendrik Kraemer, *A Theology of the Laity* (Westminster Press, 1958), p. 173; and Robinson, *On Being the Church in the World*, p. 18.
21. Kyle Haselden, *The Racial Problem in Christian Perspective* (Harper & Brothers, 1959), p. 194.

22. Paul Ramsey, *Christian Ethics and the Sit-In* (Association Press, 1961), p. 59.
23. For insightful psychiatric interpretations of the problems in black identity, see William H. Grier and Price M. Cobbs, *Black Rage* (Basic Books, 1968).
24. Haney, "A Study of Conscience," p. 330.
25. See, e.g., Michael Novak, *A Theology for Radical Politics* (Herder & Herder, 1969), chap. 7.
26. Ibid., p. 114.
27. See Campbell and Fukuyama, *The Fragmented Layman*, pp. 222ff.
28. T. S. Eliot, *Collected Poems, 1909–1962* (Harcourt, Brace & World, 1963), p. 101.

Index of Names and Subjects